The Way
Is a River of Stars

by Helen Burns

© Copyright 2021 by Helen Burns

All rights reserved. No part of this book may be reproduced in any form or by any electronic or mechanical means, including information storage and retrieval systems, without permission in writing from the publisher, except by reviewers who may quote brief passages in a review.

Photographs by Author and fellow pilgrims

ISBN: 978 0 9874644 0 8 (Paperback Edition)
Printed and bound in Australia

Published by
Sentient Books
www.sentientbooks.com

Second Edition
First published 2013

Santiago Cathedral

Santiago
Arca
Melide
Eirexe
Portomarin
Sarria
Triacastela
Ocebreiro
Ruitelan
Cacbelos
Molinaseca
Rabanal de Camino
Astorga

Leon

Carion de los Condes

Hontanas
Hornillos de Camino
Burgos

San Juan de Ortega

Granon
Azofra
Ventosa

Viana
Los Arcos
Estella
Puenta de la Reina
Cizur Menor
Pamplona
Larrasoana
Roncesvalles

St. James the Greater

Camino de Santiago Route Map
741km

Contents

1. Wild Monkeys, Wild Blackberries and a Tortoise
   Roncesvalles to Larrasoana   1

2. Walking a Prayer
   Larrasoana to Pamplona   17

3. Death and the Wedding
   Pamplona to Cizur Menor   33

4. House of One Hundred Doors
   Cizur Menor to Puente la Reina   43

5. Mermaid in a Viper's Nest
   Puente la Reina to Estella   57

6. The Succour of Stars
   Estella   73

7. Gifts
   Estella to Los Arcos   87

8. Alice Through the Laundry
   Los Arcos to Viana   101

9. Heaven has a Price
   Viana to Ventosa   113

10. The Falcon and the Dove
   Ventosa to Azofra   131

11. View from the Bell Tower
   Azofra to Granon   139

12. Crossing the Mountains of the Goose
   Granon to San Juan de Ortega   151

13. The Path to Your Door
   San Juan de Ortega to Burgos   173

14. Shorn Sheep
   Burgos to Hornillos de Camino   195

15. Seven Ingredients
   Hornillos de Camino to Leon   207

16. Water Pouring into Water
   Leon to Astorga   229

17. The Bright Blessed Day, the Dark Sacred Night
   Astorga to Rabanal de Camino   243

18. The Tower and the Rainbow
   Rabanal de Camino to Molinaseca   255

19. *Tathata*
   Molinaseca to Cacabelos   267

20. The Donkey and the Laughing Man
   Cacabelos to Ruitelan   281

21. Music
   Ruitelan to Triacastela   293

22. Angels and Bridges, Lanterns and Brooms
Triacastela to Portomarin   309

23. Room at the Inn
Portomarin to A Rua   321

24. Silver Bells and Cockle Shells
Santiago de Compostela   335

Select Bibliography   359

About the Author   361

An unimaginable sweet yearning drove me to walk in the fields ...

             Goethe, *Faust*

Cual si en suelo extranjero me hallase,
timida y hosca, contemplo
desde lejos los bosques y alturas
y los floridos senderos
donde en cada Rincon me aguardaba
la esperanza sonriendo.

What if you find me in a foreign land,
timid and sad, considering
far from those forests and mountains
and those flowery footpaths
where in each corner
hope is waiting for me smiling.

       verse from *On the Banks of the Sar*
         Rosalia de Castro 1837-1885

Another day, another winding path.

I take off my boots and hand them to the customs officer. Dirt is packed into the balding tread of their soles and he passes them to quarantine. I sit to the side and stretch out my toes. 'What's this?' he asks as he tugs at the chipped weather beaten shell tied to my pack. 'Just a shell, a scallop shell. It means…' my voice trails off into the commotion of a tourist group pushing their way toward the exit doors. '…it means I've been to the end of the world and come back again.'

Some say the real Camino begins at home and as I stride out into the eucalypt air of Brisbane in my sanitized shoes I feel pared down, whole, uncomplicated. I've walked a month of mountains and *mesetas*, watched springs turn into rivers and grapes into wine. I've laughed and cried for no reason and good reason, made friends in an instant, fallen on my face and lived to walk the next day, held stubbornly to the idea of a destination until the road wove its own way into my heart.

1

Wild Monkeys, Wild Blackberries and a Tortoise

Roncesvalles to Larrasoana

Desire sometimes defies explanation. You sit down on a Sunday morning, tea and toast, weekend paper, no complaints. You reach the travel section and there on a double spread stretches a map of Northern Spain, eight hundred kilometres of road winding across its length. The tea goes cold as you read and reread every word.

Two years, five months and eight days later, here I am crammed into a bus old as the days of Franco, chugging up into the Pyrenees. I crave every detail in this mist-soaked landscape, a dream dreamt again and again, now as real as the boots on my feet. Red-checked curtains pulled across windows of farm houses ready for the night and a profusion of dahlias and chrysanthemums in each narrow front yard. Church steeples with moss covered shingles; a paddock of milked cows filing out from a crooked tin shed. There are deep etched lines on the face of the old woman beside me. The basket on her lap is full of bread, tomatoes and beans.

One by one locals alight at village stops until all that remain are pilgrims, a few loners like me and the rest couples. We fall silent as night descends, winding higher and higher into country that tomorrow we will walk. The driver turns on the radio and a scratched voice blares over the engine. I hear a word sounding like *lluvia* and a torrent of numbers. *Lluvia* means rain – that much I remember from my taped set, Spanish in Ten Easy Lessons. For a moment I panic thinking perhaps I had forgotten to pack a raincoat. A ridiculous thought given the agonizing time it had taken to arrive here – the meticulous lists, the packing and unpacking, and my downright determination.

With a splutter of exhaust the bus lurches to a halt at a cluster of buildings dwarfed by a backdrop of dense beech forest. We are herded across to the monastery office, given a pilgrim's passport, our *Credencial del Peregrino,* then pointed in the direction of a medieval stone granary.

Since the twelfth century the Roncesvalles monks have sheltered pilgrims and the tradition continues. I open a thick door of gleaming glass and enter a cavernous dormitory with a vaulted ceiling high as a cathedral. A *hospitalero* sits at the entrance greeting each expectant face. She is from the Netherlands and, after walking the Camino, has returned as a volunteer to offer pilgrims practical and moral support.

'At six o'clock there is a blessing for pilgrims in the church.'

Taped to the wall behind her is a verse from an old Latin hymn: Our doors are open to the sick and well, to Catholics as well as pagans, Jews, heretics, beggars and the indigent, and it embraces all like brothers. Sisters too, I whisper to myself, and Buddhists.

At the church entrance two angels kneel either side of a seated Madonna and child. The stone carving above the door is so finely chiseled I can count the feathers on their outspread wings. Inside candles offer the only light, fitting for an early Gothic church. Five priests in white habits stand at the front; the oldest, stifling yawns between prayers, seems oblivious to our presence while the Virgin of Roncesvalles watches on. We are fortunate to have her company. For more than five centuries she was hidden from view; revealed to pilgrims only after elaborate ritual. Today her silver encased wooden body is dressed in a white tunic of brocade and lace. In medieval times she stood under a silk canopy but above her now is an ornate roof of shining, hand beaten silver. The priests' balding heads reflect its glow.

After mass pilgrims are called to the front of the church. We are a scruffy bunch, in shorts and boots, red noses and windbreakers. The priests sing a centuries old blessing for our safe journey. 'Dear Lord Jesus Christ …

be for them a guide at the crossroads, their shade in the heat, their light in the darkness, their comfort in weariness...' The deep resonant harmony of their five voices brings tears to my eyes. Why this sudden welling of emotion? As the last notes are sung I look up again to the figure of Mary. The candles have burned low, the last flames flickering high into the darkness, bouncing light across her radiant face.

I am a choir girl again. In the dark sacristy there is a secret staircase leading to the bell tower. I slip a taffeta robe over my head. Its crisp ironed pleats move with a grand rustle as I walk into the pew behind the altar. Our cue to sing was the sound of the organ and with a different hymn each week we, the choir, marked the beginning of ceremonies. And I remember afterwards treading across a mauve flowered carpet of jacaranda flowers left each summer by the one tree in the grounds of St Andrews. A long time ago.

My plans to walk the Camino, a Catholic pilgrimage across Spain, raised a few eyebrows among Buddhist friends and more brow furrowing when I explained that at the end of the pilgrim road, in Santiago de Compostela, lie the holy relics of Saint James, also known as the Great Moor Slayer. I preferred the image of him as a barefoot pilgrim, leaning into his hazelnut staff in a wide brim felt hat pinned with a scallop shell and following a path marked by the stars of the Milky Way.

My mother was the one person to share my conviction, though I am sure it was not for the same reasons. She is Catholic, or at least used to be, and my father was an agnostic. As a compromise they married in the Church of England and we were dutifully bundled off to Sunday School for a weekly dose of parable and prayer. It was the minimal prescription for a middle class child growing up in the sixties and left me fundamentally ignorant of what lies at the heart of Christianity. Yet here I was about to walk a path back into the spiritual roots of my childhood. Or to be more specific, my mother's childhood.

Under a waxing moon we walk up from the monastery to Casa Sabina for a pilgrims' *menu del dia*, menu of the day, Navaresse style. The room is full and I take the last chair at a table with three men. Red wine, white bread, asparagus soup, fresh trout, chips and caramel yoghurt are brought out in succession and plonked on our table. With an equal lack of ceremony we eat. A father and his teenage son sit either side of me. They are cycling to Santiago. How long it will take? '*Dos semanas*, umm, two weeks,' he breaks into English. Opposite sits a *peregrino* with a shock of grey hair and a few days worth of stubble. This is his third Camino, he tells us in cryptic bursts of gravelly Spanish. He eats and drinks with gusto and between mouthfuls insists on scribbling down the name of the best restaurant in Santiago.

'Casa Manolo, very good, cheap, near the cathedral.'

It may as well be in heaven, I think, with thirty solid days of walking between me and a platter of their famous scallops. He pours more wine then puts his fingers to his lips in an exuberant kiss and I have no idea whether it is for the wine, the restaurant or me. I am intrigued by the thick, hardback volume of Don Quixote lying beside his plate. Fine paper, small print. It must weigh a kilo. 'Are you carrying this?' I ask incredulously. He picks it up, holds it to his chest and with a beam of pleasure replies, '*Si, si!*' There's something of Quexana's whimsical madness in his eyes as he flicks through the pages. Quexana, the fantastical stepson of Miguel Cervantes, who at the tender age of nearly fifty, and after eight days of deliberation, takes upon himself the title, Don Quixote de la Mancha. Valiant knight and chaste lover. His quest? Adventure. Four hundred years later, I feel as if I sit beside someone on a similar pursuit. As our plates are cleared and flagons of wine emptied I look around the room crammed with round tables full of flushed happy faces. Maybe we all carry a secret Quixotic dream on this first night of our journey.

In the company of a hundred men and women I wriggle into the cocoon of my sleeping bag feeling suddenly alone; no curl of another body around mine, no warm breath against the back of my neck. I drift into a fitful sleep.

My preparations for the Camino had demanded a ruthless

stripping of possessions – no luxuries, no ornaments – but as I picked up my pack ready to leave home, flustered by the insistence of a car horn, I turned and saw the glint of a silver pendant and chain in the morning sunlight streaming through our bedroom window – Tara, the one who leads across. She lay on a hand stitched pouch, a gift from a Buddhist teacher. He had folded a prayer written to Tara and slipped it inside. In the tilt of her head and the gesture of each hand were all the nuances I had come to know of a *bodhisattva* who vowed to be reborn only as a woman until the world was emptied of suffering. Tara, the Mother of all Buddhas, most loved as the compassionate, sometimes mischievous, saviouress. I picked her up and touched her to my forehead. She was coming too.

Her silver body against my skin felt cool as water on a summer day. There had been moments when my plans to walk the Camino seemed more like a frustrating list of things to do. David had initially said he would come but, 'Next year would be better.' In the last ten of our twenty five years together we had not traveled out of Australia. We were overdue. Next year comes and it's, 'What about the following spring? It will be a holy year.' Another postponement and again I would deflate. Meanwhile, accumulating in a corner of our bedroom was an assortment of quick-dry clothes, special trekking socks, inner socks, a hands-free torch, an ultra-light sleeping bag, maps, guidebooks, snore-proof earplugs and a large day pack. I am not a messy person but I refused to move them. I was going and here was the proof.

Finally I said, 'Let's go in August! I cannot wait any longer.' To which David replied, 'I think you better just go on your own. Get it out of your system.' It? I remember wondering what that meant. Then he added, 'The thought of a marathon walk is not my idea of a holiday.'

Holiday? Was this what I was doing? Pilgrimage? I was unsure of that too. But at least I could pack my waiting bag. A delicious relief flooded my body as I swallowed back the hint of fear and regret rising in my throat. In that moment I saw clearly the game I had been playing with myself all this time. On one hand wanting us to travel together because, well, that's what you do in a relationship. And on the other, harboring the desire to walk alone. David's decision to stay, as long as it was in coming, had exempted me from having the courage to speak. My gratitude was bittersweet. I knew he didn't want me to go. I knew I had to.

In a fine mist my first day begins. I am tentative and impatient all at once and take long strides down a path that yesterday was just a line on a map. Under the canopy of an oak forest I peel out of my raincoat; one less layer between me and this soft moss-bedded world. I touch the small silver Tara against my skin remembering a description of her face – radiant as the rising sun, or a full moon, enough to illuminate the trees.

A small pyramid of stones sits on top of a Camino waymarker; each stone and shard of slate representing a prayer like those on Tibetan pilgrimage routes. I find a pebble. What do I pray? Where do I begin? I nudge my stone into a sliver of space and whisper thank you. For now gratitude is enough.

A blue tin sign with a stylized yellow scallop shell like the rays of a rising sun tipped sideways points back into the forest. These are the Camino's arrows. Purists might argue that with the morning sun on your back all you need do is follow your shadow, or better still the Milky Way – a fine theory for night owls – and in the ninth century these may well have been the only options. I breathe in air dense with the scent of wet lichen and crushed acorns. The clunk of hidden cowbells, my footsteps and the rhythmic creaking of my backpack are the only sounds breaking the early morning silence. I pinch myself and whoop out loud for joy. The mist lifts, the forest clears and soon the path changes from dirt to the cobbled streets of the village Burguette.

Typical of medieval pilgrim towns Burguette has one main street wide enough for a horse and cart. Geraniums spill from boxes under each red shuttered window of the whitewashed houses either side. In the Middle Ages the town's main livelihood came from pilgrim trade; barbers and cobblers in particular. Ernest Hemingway described the view from his inn here on one of his visits in the 1920s – the goats, the mountains and the cracked wooden roof of an old diligence. Each day with a supply of worm bait in tobacco tins, flies and tackle, a bottle or two of wine, boiled eggs and bread for lunch, he trekked through beech forests and across open fields of yellow gorse to the Irati River to fish for trout. I slow down and sense how easy it must have been for him to leave the world behind.

In Spain the only people awake at this hour are pilgrims, farmers and bakers. Sure enough, hidden away down an alley is a *panaderia* open for business. Off with my pack and into the tiny shop, so warm, all the windows have misted over. '*Uno café con leche, por favor y madeleine.*' Good strong coffee with a lemon cup cake. I listen to the sounds of Basque conversation around me, inhaling between sips thick swirls of acrid cigarette smoke. Spain and smoking are synonymous and there's no point in holding my breath. I toy with the idea of spending a day and night here to seek out some of Hemingway's haunts then catch myself calculating how many days lie ahead before Santiago de Compostela. I've only been walking a couple of hours – have I turned into one of those destination focused pilgrims greedy for the finish line? I swirl the coffee grounds at the bottom of my cup. No, I want to savor every minute.

Moving, the act of placing one foot in front of the other, is a simple thing but today I am exhilarated by it. Walking new land somehow equates to new mind and I feel propelled forward as effortlessly as each flush of fresh blood coursing through my veins. Nothing is better than not knowing what is around the corner, over the next hill. On long car trips as a child I hardly closed my eyes for fear of missing something. Then later in Buddhist meditation retreats, with a bare wall in front of me or with eyes closed, it was the practice of internal inquiry that, at least on good days, spurred me on.

Retreats began with a vow of silence. It was a silence that extended beyond tongue waggling to no eye contact, reading or writing. Ten days with no worldly distractions felt like a seismic shift and in this rarefied environment I experienced for the first time the vagaries of my frolicking mind; how it leapt from one boulder to the next. Many times, no matter how great my intention for mindfulness at the beginning of a meditation, all manner of past memories, fantasies, fears, sleepiness and restlessness would tumble in at random derailing any hopes for equanimity. Instead, I was rattled from the inside out. 'Like wild monkey,' a Zen teacher laughed at the end of one exasperating interview.

Moss covered boulders line the banks of a stream and each time it crosses my path I am soothed by the whoosh of its water song. Reeds and river stones play with its flow like fine-tuned instruments. To my right the silent dark blue ridges of the Pyrenees are cloaked in mist. On the edge of each village are vegetable gardens with beans dripping from handmade trellises, tomatoes, roses and dahlias. Beyond and into the fields I am overjoyed to find wild white yarrow and brambles full of ripe blackberries. Berry picking in cow paddocks at home meant the occasional find of a native raspberry, exotic looking red orbs, all juice but no taste. These burst sweet and sour into my mouth.

With a sprig of yarrow in my hair and blackberry

seeds between my teeth I begin the first climb into a forest of pine trees dropping away either side into verdant gorges. At the top is a small wooden cross engraved with the name of a Japanese pilgrim. There are beads from a broken necklace and handwritten prayers on paper wedged into the stones at the foot of the cross. How many days had he been walking until here, his last day? Was it his first day like mine? And then I am struck by the thought – as much as I take pleasure in each step, I still take it for granted that I will finish.

Further along, the ruins of an old building house a family of cows. I breathe in the scent of fermenting hay and wet manure. One cow moves closer to inspect me, the bell around her neck clanging. The dark and empty top floor is now a dilapidated gallery for ETA slogans and the graffiti of cartoon gun-toting supermen. But it was once the Venta del Puerto, an inn offering pilgrims shelter on this isolated pass. On winter nights cows would have served a dual purpose, fresh milk for supper, the rising heat from their bodies keeping the pilgrims warm on their beds of hay.

The path descends then meanders through pasture. Yellow arrows point the way through villages: El Espinal, Mezkiritz, Biscarret and Lintzoan. Wild herbs line the trail and I greet them like old friends, Comfrey, Dock, Self Heal and Applemint. I was a herbalist in the days before herbal lore bowed to the powers of science, burying itself in licenses and legalese, in a world where everyone needs to be insured against everything. It was a lost cause trying to keep up with the latest double blind studies and chemical compounds. I pick a comfrey leaf still wet with dew and brazenly chew its bitter juice. Suggesting a patient do this for a broken bone or a stomach ulcer would qualify me for a modern version of witch lynching. I pick another one for later, imagining a village wise woman at the back of Venta del Puerto pounding leaves to make a poultice for bruised feet and sprained ankles. Brewing a thick green tea of mullein and comfrey root in mid-winter for frostbitten pilgrims.

From a high ridge I ponder the lush green expanse of Basque country to the west, its mountains and valleys stretching beyond the horizon. The reality of an eight hundred kilometre walk, the hint of an ache across my shoulders, feet beginning to feel hot and the foreign sensation of cantankerous pelvic bones under my well padded hips temper my elation – and this on day one. Helen, do you realise what you are doing? A small wooden sign reads Larrasoana, six kilometres.

Halfway there, in the village of Esquirotz, two young Spanish boys and a girl bathe their feet in the trough of cool water spilling from a fountain. I notice brand new boots at the side of one boy whose eyes are squeezed shut in pain. In my preparations I had read long dissertations on foot care by past pilgrims. All the do's and don'ts. Wear your shoes in. Well I had two years to do that. Some aficionados suggest stopping every two hours to let the feet breathe and, for good measure, a change of socks. Then there are the intricacies of how to treat a blister.

The ultimate panacea is a stop at each village fountain or stream for the ritual bathing of toes. Today I am too impatient.

The Puente de los Bandidos, a fourteenth century three-span bridge, leads across to the village of Larrasoana. The *refugio*, once the town's public hall, sits prominently in a small plaza ablaze with pink and white petunias. Santiago Zubiri Elizalde, doubling as mayor and *hospitalero*, stands at the door. With a big four front teeth smile he ushers me in, talking all the while in Spanish, before calling his daughter. She points me to the last bed in a room of six bunks. I look around and count eleven men. Big, burly men. There must be some kind of mistake. For a second I am stunned then remember the words spelled out at Roncesvalles, *el peregrino no exije, agradece*. Pilgrims don't make demands, they are grateful. I take a deep breath and unroll my sleeping bag. No one is talking. Everyone looks exhausted.

At Larrasoana's one bar the nightly task feeding road-weary pilgrims begins early by Spanish standards. I sit at a table with four Frenchmen and choose a Basque white bean soup and chicken served with the ubiquitous chips. Red wine flows and a lively conversation in French begins, sometimes all talking at the same time, interjected with attempts at translation. Typically, the subject is food. The superlatives of *foie gras* washed down with a glass of sauterne from Bordeaux. Then there's a lot of lip-smacking talk about *maice* and *canard cassoulet*. I nod in approval but wonder at what point did French cuisine degenerate to the eating of mice with duck. We move from course to course until the subject of *maice* comes up again. I feel impelled to investigate and, a tad too loosened by wine, venture into the realm of charades, squeaking and wiggling my nose. The four men look at me in consternation. '*Maice*? There is stunned silence then an eruption of laughter, 'N*on, non, maizzze*!'

Daniel, a retired policeman, sits opposite in a bright red shirt. I am sure my face is the same colour. This is his second Camino after recovering from a heart operation. He takes his pills with wine and reminisces about his Algerian grandfather helping build the Eiffel Tower. Around his neck he wears a crucifix on a gold map of Africa. Leaning against the wall behind him is a walking stick, a tortoise intricately carved at its pommel, his companion for a slow and steady pilgrimage to Santiago.

Warmed by wine, food, convivial company and aching muscles I collapse into bed. I remember the earplugs. '*La Musica Peregrinos,*' our big-hearted Larroasana mayor had chuckled in an earlier conversation about the inevitable snoring. I was in for quite a concert.

2

Walking a Prayer

Larrasoana to Pamplona

Remembering present company, I wiggle out from my sleeping bag whilst demurely tying a sarong – in my quest for minimalism pajamas did not make the packing list. A nose-blasting scent of menthol assaults me and I look across the room to see a man smothering his feet in Vicks Vaporub. Innovative. I wonder if the penetration of camphor and eucalyptus makes for a sprightlier step? The serious business of preparation before a day's walk plunges everyone into a private world and I decide this is not the best time to ask questions. Instead I enjoy the odd sensation of rubbing paw paw ointment between my toes, another handy hint from the feet fetish people, as a precaution against blisters. My socks slide on and I double knot the laces of my boots.

The Rio Arga splashes and gurgles transparent over a

stony bed as we wind together through forest. At a clearing the reflection of trees and sky in water is so perfect it reminds me of that Zen parable comparing meditation to cleaning dust from a mirror. A few paces further, almost hidden from view, the riverbank is littered with tissue paper. I scrunch my nose up in disgust at what appears to be a public toilet. Daniel arrives behind me with a hearty, *'Bon jour.'* He looks over in the same direction and waves his stick in the air, pointing to the toilet, 'Ah civilization,' and to the river, 'Ah meditation!' and continues along his way leaving me standing in the midst of two worlds.

After a steep climb in the company of three Spanish pilgrims, who share their packet of chocolate biscuits and a bawdy sounding song, I follow a ridge with views back to the Pyrenees. It's hard to believe I have walked for only a day and a half, they seem so far away. Low clouds cover the highest peaks, sending tributaries of mist into each ravine. Below, the Arga is a churning rapid crashing over boulders and consuming the air with its mist. Her source, the mountains, is also my beginning point. We are traveling the same direction and her white water music adds to my euphoria. The destination of the pilgrimage may well be Santiago but here is truly enough.

The Basilica de Arre, a monastery and hospice, stands on the banks of the lazy flowing Ulzama. It once belonged to the Monastery of Roncevalles and is the most complete medieval complex surviving in Navarra. Simple accommodation for twenty pilgrims is offered and though it is too early to throw my pack down I am curious to see what lies behind the quiet solidity of its stone arches. Through an alcove in the dim light of a tiny room an old priest silently hunches over his desk while opposite him a young pilgrim girl in tears, talks with a demanding tone. Another time perhaps. I tip-toe back into the bright sunlight.

Pamplona has spilled over her old walls and spreads out across the plains below. After two days immersed in green I feel as though I am being swallowed by the jowls of industry. Cars, bitumen roads, apartment blocks, shops and throngs of people. A phone box! My heart races at the thought of calling home. Hearing David's voice I am instantly suspended in a capsule holding just the two of us as the world rushes by. I gurgle on about the first two days of walking and soak up the sound of his slow drawling voice echoing down the line. Gone is his usual economy of words.

'How's the weight of your pack, not too heavy? No rain here yet. I've been watering the garden every day but most of your winter herbs are turning to seed. Morning break at main beach yesterday was perfect... only a couple of us out there. Had some great rides.' Small reassuring details. We say our goodbyes and I walk on in a dream. It seems like a contradiction to feel so happy to be alone yet so elated to have had a conversation with him.

I still feel the thrill of twenty years ago when I look at David – those clear blue eyes, that unwaveringly steady demeanor – and the same dread if ever we argue or disagree. The intensity of these feelings maintains a passion and dynamism in my relationship with him but somewhere along the way *I* had gone missing. The compensation was a relatively comfortable life neatly packaged in each day's routine. Despite a library of Buddhist books on my shelves and annual retreats teaching the same message over and over – hidden in each ordinary moment are the seeds of enlightenment – I yearned for something more. At the age of almost fifty my life was either half over or half beginning. I needed time alone. I needed to be thrown out into the world to find my feet again.

A crossroads with no signpost snaps me back into the present. The tearful girl I had seen in the convent office joins me and together we spot a minuscule arrow pointing right. Elana's long brown hair is half knotted, half plaited and her dark eyes look directly into mine. She shoulders a faded canvas pack that looks ancient as the civil war. But she is young, a new bohemian, born in Barcelona, and I am old enough to be her mother. Elana's tears have transformed into an infectious optimism.

'A lot of pilgrims, they walk too fast. They miss things,' she says. I agree, as I make a concentrated effort to slow down. Elana shares a wealth of legend about the Camino. 'There is a bridge that comes later. If you take off your shoes and walk across it, you feel all the pilgrims who have gone before you.' We swap stories of our journey so far. I tell her about my sleeping companions last night. 'One woman and eleven men!' she exclaims.

'That's very auspicious.' I feel like I've passed some kind of initiation and slow my pace even more.

As we cross the floodplain to the base of the old city Elana babbles along like a river about the Camino. She wanted to stay for free at the last *refugio*. 'The church owns it and we are pilgrims. We shouldn't have to pay,' she says, raising her hands into the air willing God to hear her. I had heard some *refugios* operate by donation, especially when church affiliated, but with so many pilgrims nowadays this might not be sustainable. And anyway, whether they are run by the church, as at Roncesvalles, or by village councils or private individuals, the cost is rarely more than seven euros, sometimes as little as three.

I remember a discussion among friends at home, when organizing a meditation retreat, about what to charge. Some argued that we should offer everything by donation. The concept of karma was spouted, 'If we give of our own free will, we will be rewarded in our next life.' An idea, I think, not so different from the basic Christian belief, if I am good now, I will go to heaven later. In Burma benefactors are praised, their names engraved on temple plaques. So popular is the tradition that people must wait their turn to give. Whole families came to the monastery I once stayed at on the day of their meal offering to the yogis. We ate in silence while outside the dining room our donors noisily celebrated, feasting on sweets and ice-cream. It's a convoluted topic but for today at least I prefer to keep silent. We fall into a quiet rhythm together crossing the Bridge Magdalena and through the parkland circling the old city walls.

Pamplona sits regally on a bluff, the perfect choice for early Roman settlements, commanding views across the lowlands and providing a vantage point for control of entry into Spain from France. There used to be a hospital for pilgrims outside its fortress walls for those arriving after dark when the city gates had closed, barricading the city from thieves and foreigners. We cross the wooden bridge that spans the moat and enter Pamplona though the Portal de Francia. Yellow arrows point the way down a cobbled Calle del Carmen to a plaza surrounded by ramshackle houses. Groups of teenagers mill around a fountain where moss covered fish squirt water. Two street smart boys play guitar on the steps of a derelict shopfront oblivious to the rock music and techno beats vying for airspace from the windows above. Elana stops to ask about places to stay. A long conversation ensues. My guess is we are standing in the middle of a squat district. Perfect for Elana. Part of me is torn to stay; join her precarious gypsy quest for a free ride across Spain. But I crave solitude and quiet and slip quietly around the corner, wondering if I will see her again.

Had I been on such a street in the Middle Ages a merchant dealing in black-market Compostela certificates might well have accosted me. Businessmen who plied their trade back and forth to Santiago accumulated a new Compostela each time which they could then sell for a handsome sum. Clients were usually petty criminals who had been given the choice of walking the Camino or a five year jail sentence. After a carefully timed and pleasant hiatus in town he could return home and present the judge his certificate – proof indeed he had walked as a pilgrim across Spain, at that time an untamed land of wolves, rabid dogs and bandits.

At the end of a steep street is a stone walled complex run by the Sisters of the Holy Spirit. At one o'clock, on the dot, a black-frocked priest scuffles past with a key. Inside, up two grand flights of stairs are a labyrinth of dormitories and bunk beds. Rooms with a view to the east of fields and mountains, and to the west across the plaza and the red terracotta tiles of a church roof with a delicate wind vane spinning on its dome. I choose a bell tower view from a room with only four beds. Luxury. With my boots airing on the windowsill I settle back on a top bunk to daydream and, before long, make that easy Spanish slip into siesta.

In a slowed down post-nap mid-afternoon mood, I follow my instincts through the old city and arrive at its heart, the Plaza de Castillo. Except for an old couple in the bandstand and a scattering of tourists wandering its perimeters the large square is deserted. Café Iruna, over a hundred years old, with its marble tables and wicker chairs spilling into the shade of the arcade, sits like the grand *senora* of cafes. This was Hemingway's watering hole for coffee, wine and absinthe whenever he stayed in Pamplona. It was an institution for writers and artists and a focal point for his novel *The Sun Also Rises*. His descriptions of languid hours between bullfights and country excursions, in the clipped English and laconic drone of an American expat biding time, were an engaging departure from *The Old Man and the Sea* I had studied at school. Here I am, finally, swinging through the same doors. The scene transforms into a rococo wonderland. Golden columns, chandeliers hanging from an ornately paneled ceiling and huge mirrors behind the bar that multiply the spectacle to the size of a ballroom. There are three menu prices: one for the bar, the next for tables inside and the most expensive reserved for outside. I choose the bar and perch on a tall stool, order wine, and watch the first of the day's tapas arrive. Sultry jazz counterbalances the banter between two waiters, both dressed in immaculate white shirts, black vests and trousers. A mountain of lemon gelati reflects more gold into the mirrors and piles of black olives glisten with oil. A few sips of house red are all that's needed to fuel my imagination.

Iruna's stucco walls reverberate with the festivities of San Fermin. Bullfights, concerts, Basque dances, the procession of religious relics, fireworks, copious quantities of alcohol and all night reveling. San Fermin, the patron saint of bullfighters. What must this saint think of the drunken young men throwing themselves into the path of running bulls? Since 1591, every year for nine glorious days, they abandon the mundanities of life for wild and wonderfully reckless celebrations. The ghost of Hemingway sits at a table behind me, oblivious, musing a toreador's victory while savouring yesterday's catch.

Restored by the cool and the wine I leave my fantasies behind and float through the doors into a softening late afternoon light. The streets are coming to life: couples promenade, children race about on scooters and skates and the elderly gather in groups on park benches to chat. Around the plaza, like a frame, the colours of each building dapple with shadow as the sun falls behind them. Pale green, terracotta and white; each of their five storeys with filigree iron balconies and always geraniums. I hear the sound of hymns and see, through the green shuttered doors of a top floor room, the silhouette of a choir rehearsing.

The cathedral will be open now. It stands at the end of a long narrow street on the edge of the city, more fortress than church. Maria, a curvaceous twelve ton bell, is suspended in the North tower. Spain' largest bell and still ringing. Like many European churches the Cathedral of Pamplona stands over the site of Roman ruins. This one dates to 74 BC and includes the remains of houses, a forum, markets and baths. A convergence of pre-Christian sites with a church is never a coincidence. There are places that naturally engender a sense of the sacred, of wonder, or power. Whether it is a hill commanding a view, a spring where water has rejuvenative qualities or simply a place where one instinctively feels in harmony with the elements, these earthly treasures will always be sought for prayer and communion. Inevitably these are also the places most plundered. History shows time and again how one religion's foundation becomes the bricks and mortar of another.

I bypass the main entrance, a severe neo-classical façade, and enter into the hush of the cathedral through the huge twin doors of the Portada de San Jose carved with an intricate geometric design by fifteenth century artisans. An old woman is saying her rosary near the front and I choose a pew near her; just the two of us. The Virgen del Sagrario looks over us from her shrine behind the main altar. The scent of oiled timber and candle wax, the subdued light and unearthly quiet sink into my bones. I stay for a while because there is no place else to go, until the women, it is always the women, come to clean, add fresh water to the flowers and shake incense ash from lace altar cloths.

Through the Puerta del Amparo, the Door of Succour, lies an otherworldly place, one of the most elegant Gothic cloisters in Europe, where sunlight and delicate shadows play. The vaults above are incomparably graceful. In eight centuries how many bowed heads, how many sandalled feet have walked between these colonnades? It's as if the pad of all those footsteps still resonate in the stone. Here in this microcosm is an example of how the Camino might show me the way.

Each step taken in a pilgrimage has purpose, in and of itself. Some pilgrims speak of Santiago as the sole reason for their journey but in Christianity there is also the practice of walking a prayer: letting the recitation of a prayer infuse into the rhythm of breath and body as you walk. The prayer may drop away leaving you with a sense of reverence each time your foot touches the earth. In Buddhism there are walking meditations too. During retreats, periods of sitting alternate with walking. Not aimlessly but slowly, back and forth on a chosen path, mindful of every movement. Each foot lifting, moving forward, then touching the ground. Once I slow down and settle into the practice I begin to notice sensations in my feet – a tingling in a toe, pressure as I touch the ground or lightness when I lift a foot. And each time my mind is distracted by a thought, an ant crossing my path or the song of a bird, I gently bring it back to physical sensation, to what is real in each present moment.

An hour of walking meditation often felt more difficult than an hour of sitting. But the more I practiced the more I realized the universe of flux within my body – and it was happening in spite of myself. Each step held potential for insight into the phenomena of constant change and when mindfulness penetrates the body, mysteriously, it also begins to penetrate the world. Eventually it was the walking that helped me most, to extend mindfulness into everyday life. It was like a bridge between the sequestered world of a retreat and the busyness outside. In the most essential of all Buddhist sutras, the Four Noble Truths, it is said that life is a continual play between moments of neutrality, light / desire and shadow / aversion. Here in this ancient cloister, step by step I tread a literal path from shadow to light, light to shadow and on.

A door leads to the quadrangular kitchen where, until the seventeenth century, food was still being prepared for pilgrims. Now an empty room it has a twenty seven metre chimney at its centre. I stretch back and gaze up into its dark smoke-stained void, let out an audible breath and it comes back to me. Then the sound 'hooo' and it reverberates, a sonorous, magical echo. I'm all alone and it's safe to sing. I chant, *'Om tare tuttare ture soha,'* over and over. The words ripple and overlap carrying me buoyant around the room. I laugh and then laugh again as it tumbles back to me.

Om tare tuttare ture soha, is my rosary and prayer for the way. It is a mantra asking for the blessing of White Tara, her protection and her compassion. Sometimes, if my mind is consuming itself with unintelligible chatter, singing this mantra helps to wash the clutter away. In my notebook I had copied a verse from an old Tibetan prayer and I read it again: With brightness of face of a hundred autumn moons, her pleasing complexion emits the shining lustre of thousands of stars, dispelling the darkness of ignorance – on her let us meditate.

Here I am in autumn on the eastern edge of the Camino – the Way of Stars, the Milky Way – singing her syllables into a blackened vortex. She is warm against my heart. Each fine detail on my tiny silver pendant is a reminder of all that Tara embodies. Sitting on a moon disc, her hands dance a mudra. Her right hand open in a gesture of generosity offering enlightenment while the fingers of her left symbolize the natural union between compassionate action and the realization of emptiness. Her seven eyes see all suffering and recognize the way of liberation from suffering. The three in her head represent purity of body, speech and mind. The eyes in the palms of her hands and soles of her feet symbolize compassion, loving kindness, sympathetic joy and equanimity towards all beings.

With outstretched arms I turn a full circle. The air tastes sweet and rare, my feet tingle on the smooth stone floor. Through the doorway I catch a glimpse of a Romanesque Madonna and, at the corners of her mouth, the dimples of a smile. Caught unawares by her luminous gaze I realize her message is not so different. Those compassionate eyes calling me in and at the same time letting me be, leaving me to dance my way.

Outside stars appear one by one. It is Friday night and it seems the whole city is taking a walk. Incredibly, the maze of rooms back at the *alburque* have filled. Not a bed to spare. I hear English voices and join a group of pilgrims intent on the culling of backpack contents. Spread over the floor are piles of clothing, a walkman, a couple of guidebooks and various cosmetics. Ron, a tall wiry Dutchman with ginger hair and eyebrows, clips in, 'However heavy you are, take ten percent and that's the best weight to carry.' Gillian keeps moving things from one pile to another. Attachment to the barest luxury is being tested. 'I can poste-restante. That way I can have them in Santiago,' she says in a broad country accent that reminds me of home. 'The *hospitalero* says the post office have boxes you can buy and, would you believe, even special stamps and stickers for *peregrinos*. They must be doing a booming trade with us.'

Fiona, also from Australia, sits on the floor with a bandaged knee. She had walked the difficult extra day from France over the Pyrenees with a fifteen kilo pack. Coming into Pamplona her knee decided: enough! She pulls two weeks supply of anti-inflammatory medicine from a carton. 'The doctor who prescribed this didn't exactly hesitate. How am I going to carry this, it's the size of a big bible!' Beside her sits Unkangles, from Spain, married to an Irishman and walking the Camino for the second time. 'He knew you wouldn't want to stop. Pilgrims don't. Those drugs are nasty but at least you'll be able to walk.'

In my fine tuned preparations, bordering on obsessive, I weighed everything. I mean everything. Sleeping bag seven hundred and fifty grams, soap one hundred grams, socks sixty, shirt one hundred and fifty, bra fifty and so on down the list. I even ripped my guidebook into three sending the two latter sections on to Burgos and Leon, one third and two thirds of the way to Santiago. With a mix of sacrilege and mischief I tore the pages from their binding. But today I carry no regret. My pack is comfortable and so far I lack for nothing. Living with one change of clothes is a relief. How much time and mental energy we expend in making choices: what to wear, which brand of toothpaste to buy, which seat on the bus to take, what to cook, when to come, when to go. Life is fraught with choice. Everything except breathing. The nature of the Camino is physically demanding but with material needs stripped to the minimum, at least my mind is allowed some reprieve.

The floorboards eventually reappear as possessions are divided into neat piles of essential and superfluous. It is almost nine; dinner in Spain is now being served. Statuesque Sylvia takes the lead into town. She is Spanish but has lived much of her life in England. For a year she was a student in Pamplona so we follow her through a series of secret alleyways to the street famous for the running of the bulls. Every second shop window is crammed with Basque dolls dressed in red and white, wine gourds hanging from rafters and endless variations of bull and toreador printed onto t-shirts, tablecloths and tea towels. In her soft brogue Sylvia explains how the running of the bulls is, 'much more than this tourist trap.' For centuries, with prayers to San Fermin, young men and their fathers would make an annual pilgrimage to Pamplona from surrounding farms and villages to run with the bulls. 'It's a rite of passage. Once a boy has out run a bull he becomes a man.'

We stop at the door of a bar. 'This is a famous place,' Sylvia shouts as we squeeze inside. An overwhelming number of hams hang from the ceiling and underneath a crush of hungry customers clamour to order at the long bar spilling over with layer upon layer of tapas. We crouch on low stools to feast on flavours of anchovy, pepper, cheese, frittata and mushroom. As the wine flows and our stomachs fill we dissolve into peals of laughter until Ron notices the time. Five minutes to curfew. At ten o'clock most *refugios* lock their doors. In Spain this is a challenge.

We limp, reel and skip our way back arriving breathless at the door just as it is closing. The priest, with a twinkle in his eye, lets us tumble in.

3

Death and the Wedding

Pamplona to Cizur Menor

Last night's feast percolates in my belly. While everyone else heads out the door and joins the road I make a rush for the bathroom. This can't be happening, it's only day three. Perfect, a little voice rings inside my head.

Refugios ask that you be on your way by eight o'clock but I am unsure about walking. Fiona's knee is still swollen and she is too. We ask if we can leave our packs in the office. Through the empty streets we go; Fiona limping and me taking cautious steps between stomach cramps. Every curtain is closed, every door locked. It seems all of Pamplona sleeps after last night's revelry. In a small plaza, a circle of people are gathered around two paramedics kneeling over an old man. A pilgrim? But I notice his shoes, soft leather brogues. We stand at the edge like frozen voyeurs. The paramedics methodically pound the pale skin of his chest. I feel powerless, remembering.

I was eighteen and returning home. An ambulance was parked in our driveway and my Dad was lying on the grass of our front lawn, still and very white. I watched as two men returned with a stretcher in warp-like slow motion. The doctor looked up at me from my father's side, his stethoscope loose around his neck, his hand dropped away from my father's pulse.

'Go inside Helen, your mother needs you.' He was a family friend and couldn't look me in the eye. His words ring in my head as real and final as they sounded that day and every emotion I experienced then, I feel returning now.

The paramedics keep pounding. I am shaking and want to cry. The paramedics just keep pounding. How much longer can they continue? 'Please just let him go,' I whisper. Time disappears: we stand holding our breath, as if this might suspend the passage from life to death. All my lofty ideas of a pilgrimage, of anything, vanish.

Pamplona wakes oblivious, street cleaners with their trucks and hoses begin to wash down the plazas and alleyways. I feel out of sync, an intruder. I cannot speak their language and I am walking away as the medics, still, refuse defeat. I am alive when someone is dying.

The waves of stomach cramps continue and I welcome the pain. In the euphoria of being here I have forgotten humility. When life goes well, or simply chugs along at a comfortable pace, a sense of invincibility creeps in. I forget how precious life is. Each moment.

In the main plaza shutters are opening and shop owners sweep leaves from their doorways. A flower seller brings buckets of roses into the square and brown paper bags full of baguettes are delivered to cafes. Fiona decides to stay another day and rest her knee. I choose to continue, mailing a parcel for her and buying some medicine on my way out of town.

Then, at my feet, there is a bouquet of crimson chrysanthemums. In the disorienting labyrinth of city streets I have returned to the place where the old man was. I close my eyes remembering him. Around the corner photographers are scrambling for position at the entrance to the Church of San Cernin. Women in strapless satin gowns and embroidered shawls with long fringes brushing precariously close to their stiletto heels cluster about the stairs as a bride steps from a limousine to take her father's arm. It is a vision perfect: the contained pride and joy in a father's face as he watches the women arrange his daughter's long veil. More people arrive and I am jostled against the wall on the other side of the street, caught up in the celebration. There is death and there are weddings.

Consuela, a pilgrim from Madrid, joins me at the edge of the old city. We need no polite preliminaries, we chat like old friends. I am ever grateful to her for pointing out the correct Spanish translation for years, *ano*. I had previously, on several occasions I am sorry to say, asked the unfortunate question, 'How many *anyo*, are you?' The translation for *anyo* being, ass hole! The sound of her laughter, worthy of an operatic singer, dilutes my horror. So much for my Spanish in Ten Easy Lessons!

We leave the Basque mountains behind, the canopies of forests and the bustle of Pamplona. Fields of dry wheat coloured grasses and a hot blue sky stretch ahead and above us. Thistle seeds at loose on the midday wind fill the air. I catch one, 'He loves me, he loves me not, he loves me …' I catch another one and make a wish.

It was in this valley, Llanura de la Taconera, that the famous battle between Charlemagne and the Muslim leader Aigoland took place over twelve hundred years ago. The road we walk is the same that separated the two armies. More than a thousand men fought. Christian against Muslim. Muslim against Christian. The slaughtering continued until Aigoland finally conceded defeat and converted, along with his surviving troops, to Christianity. On the hot breath of wind buffeting us it is easy to imagine the wrench of voices, clashes of steel on steel and the whinny of frightened horses. Does anything ever change?

I harbor doubts about the depiction of St James riding a wild-eyed, white stallion, and wielding a sword over the decapitated heads at his feet. Perhaps the slain bodies can be seen symbolically as my own demons but the consensus that he was indeed the great Moor Slayer sits uneasily in my relationship to him. Am I an unsuspecting pawn walking in the shadow of a man who killed in the name of a God?

The medicine begins to slow my stomach cramps. Cizur Menor, a short five kilometres is enough walking for today. Consuela continues with a '*Buen camino,*' good journey, the universal salute between pilgrims. Locals too often wave us on with these words, sometimes adding for good measure, 'Pray for us when you reach Santiago.'

Cizur Menor has two *refugios*, the first attached to a Knights' Templar church at the entrance to town and the second, beside the home of Mariabella. I had heard glowing reports of her hospitality and walk an extra few streets. On a tall wooden gate half hidden among an oasis of trees is an iron bell. Mariabella appears. '*Hola*. You have come to stay? Speak English? Welcome.' She has effervescent eyes and stands as high as my shoulders in a floral dress and apron.

'Maybe it is possible today I put all women in this room,' she says opening the door to a simple, spotless dormitory with twelve bunks. The odds of snoring bedfellows are instantly, immeasurably reduced and I thank all the merciful saints and Mariabella in particular.

'Do you have any blisters?' She takes me to a chair in the garden and inspects a red patch of skin swelling on my big toe. After piercing it and putting on a bandage for the night she hands me a small syringe and some plaster. 'Keep this in case you need it, or maybe for another *peregrino*.' Later I see her attending a pilgrim whose feet are a mass of weeping welts and I feel guilty about taking her time. For my cramps, Mariabella's advice is flat coca cola. Not exactly a herbalist's first choice but the sugar and caffeine rush their drugged path straight to my tired head and, miraculously, calm the tapas calamity in my belly.

I wash my clothes in an old laundry tub under the sprawling branches of a fig tree at the bottom of the garden and Mariabella returns to her table spread with a huge, intricate jigsaw puzzle of the world. 'That looks so difficult. Won't it take forever?' She chuckles and says, 'I have my whole life.' The bell rings and she leaves a half finished South America to open the gate.

The fortress tower of the Church of St Miguel looks back across the plain to Pamplona. Tiled roofs and church steeples stipple the horizon. Hot wind whips and churns off the plain and whistles relentlessly through the turrets of the tower – a sound of loneliness. This centuries-old weather pattern has sculpted the flutes of columns and the bricks of the east facing walls smooth. With my back braced against the church I face the wind and let it blow through me.

Sheltered on the western side is a heavy wooden door with a half moon shaped tympanum above. Here a stonemason once strived for perfection, chiseling into it a crismon. Shaped like a rosette, elegant and hieroglyphic, its design incorporates a cross with the Greek syllable chi-rho, the first letter of Christus, and the signs for alpha and omega symbolizing Christ's omnipotence throughout time. I step underneath and inside to a pervasive and deep silence magnified by the thick walls. The insistent pounding of wind on stone outside turns to a muffle.

One candle flame burning on the altar joins with the muted light of an afternoon sun filtering through narrow alabaster windows.

As I sit to the side and close my eyes unexpected tears come but they are not from sadness or homesickness. My weakened body perhaps? I feel raw, as exposed to the churning wind as the stones outside. Or is it the memory of the old man in Pamplona, the touch of Mariabella's hands still warm on my feet? There is nowhere to go and no need to wipe these tears away. Two pilgrims with the *hospitalero* from the adjoining *refugio* arrive. They listen to the guide as she points here and there with a running commentary. One of them turns to ask if they are disturbing me and I shake my head. I am reassured by their presence. I remember that quality of awareness where mind and heart rest together, supple and at ease. A place of allowing where there is no judgment one way or another, where the habitual barriers between self and other are dissolved. How can intrusion exist in such a place?

Back in Mariabella's garden washed clothes flap from every inch of line. South America is finished and she looks up from feeding her pet turtle to recommend Cizur Menor's one restaurant. The old wooden inn's décor is understated and expensive, the kitchen, ultra modern. I hesitate but notice there is a *menu del dia* and a long table already filled with pilgrims, first customers for the night. We dine like knights and ladies, in fact probably a lot better. France outnumbers Spain, England and Australia, and our conversation soon reverts to the finer points of gastronomy. The fish baked with lemon thyme and leeks is perfection, the Basque bean soup, too much oil. 'Pass the salt, the cook forgot the salt.' I wrap dessert in a napkin for tomorrow, sadly this sliver of dark chocolate tart is too dense and sherry-sweet for my stomach tonight.

One of our group, Tony, is a Benedictine priest. Coming from an Anglican background, and hoping not to appear too ignorant, I ask him, 'Why in mass, the congregation receives bread, but only the priest the wine?' His answer is long and complicated. This recent church ruling harks back to medieval times and has caused some conflict. With a spark of irreverence Tony says, 'I did not entirely agree with the change.' Then in a more serious vein he explains, 'But my vows ask that any opinion I have be surrendered to God.' His willingness to give up personal preference could be misconstrued as cowardice but as I listen to him I understand the courage and humility it takes. Boundaries exist in any discipline, at least in the beginning. I think back to the strict, often grueling timetable of my first silent meditation retreat in the seventies. It felt like a contradiction to the peace slogans and freedoms being espoused at the time. The strict schedule was like a corral; with no worldly distractions my wildhorse mind kicked into overdrive. 'Keep the reins on your horse not too loose, not too tight,' was my teacher's encouragement. 'Patience and perseverance.' Within these perimeters thoughts begin to loosen their grip and slowly the mind is able to settle.

We walk back under a full moon. Tony is traveling with two older French women. They began their pilgrimage in France three years ago taking a ten day break each year to rejoin where they left off. I like the gentle, clear nature of Tony and the fact that he prefers his vocation to remain unknown. At Mariabella's gates we view a golden moon and talk about the parallels and differences between Buddhism and Christianity. Tony had once attended a conference chaired by the Dalai Lama and recalled his simple message of kindness and compassion toward all beings as the common foundation for all religions.

A pilgrimage is essentially an inner journey, nonetheless this evening's meeting feels like a quenching glass of pure water. We may never see each other again but tonight we gather together a little footsore, sharing our stories and ideas in a strange land on a road walked by pilgrims for aeons. Our common denominator spins irrevocably on its axis wrapped in prayers for peace and an enduring spirit of hope and community. I climb the three stairs to my top bunk and fall asleep to the sound of women softly breathing.

4

House of One Hundred Doors
Cizur Menor to Puente la Reina

I leave before sunrise, full of energy, my body light as I swing on my pack. At the edge of the village a passing car slows and honks its horn. The driver shouts something unintelligible and points the other way. Oops. In my elation to be walking well again, I had forgotten the arrows and assumed there was only one road. There is never only one road! An English pilgrim joins me and we recross the dark streets, our torch lights bobbing ahead of us. We spot one golden arrow pointing down a small lane and walk together into the daylight, a hint of silver sky between the mountains on the horizon and a cathedral of tumbling clouds. I slow down and fall behind to be alone.

Fields of dark wheat stubble radiate as far as the eye can see. With the sun my shadow appears, my new walking companion – appropriate I think, as a symbol for a pilgrimage. At the beginning of the day it's a long, thin stick figure stretching ahead and as morning progresses I watch it shrink until eventually I step into it. Do I join my shadow or does my shadow disappear?

Silhouetted on the mountain ridge ahead are lines of tall white windmills. I hear the sound of a beat in rhythm with their turning, a surreal accompaniment to the dawn, and add Tara's manta to the mix, her words soft on my tongue. At a thicket of blackberries I pick handfuls of dark ripe fruit until the presence of a shaggy black dog silences me. We stare at each other until he decides to saunter away. Around the next corner two pilgrims, more like cowboys in their knee high boots and leather holsters, are breaking camp and saddling their horses, one dappled, one white. The air is a fertile mix of wood smoke, cigarettes and horse dung. The dog paces impatiently between them. '*Buenas,*' is all we say.

Further along I discover the real origin of that beat pervading the air. From a deserted villa on a distant hill, thundering across the wheat fields, comes the heavy bass of techno music – not windmills at all. I feel a fool, a bit like Don Quixote setting eyes upon windmills and taking them for giants, except I have no lance, or steed to carry me forth into battle against this soundbeast I am hearing. *Om Tara tuttare...* will have to do. A safer weapon, I think, for my duped mind, as I begin the climb to Sierra del Perdon and its silent white wind beacons.

A row of sculpted steel pilgrims, a dog, a donkey and a horse, all of them braced against the icy wind, are the silent welcoming committee at the top. Beside them a plaque reads: Where the Way of the Stars and the Way of the Wind Meet. From here I can see roadworks stretching from Pamplona, a scar through the valley, looking as though it has every intention of tunneling right through the mountain I am standing on to get to the other side. I sit for a while listening to the sound of the wind, the real turning of windmills, the crunch of day old bread breaking in my hands.

To the west stretches a vast landscape of brown, edged with a haze of mountain, and at my feet a scree scattered trail plummeting through a forest of gnarled oak and boxwood. For the first time I am thankful to have trekking poles. A group of pilgrims on mountain bikes career past at breakneck speed. Decked out in skin-hugging lycra they have an air of seriousness tantamount to a Tour de France. 'Viva La Tour de Santiago,' I whisper as I step aside from another cloud of dust. '*Buen Camino*,' we shout in unison. Shades of fluorescent green and yellow, racing car red and black, blur past my eyes. I don't envy their speed.

Wheatfields give way to orchards of almond trees and vineyards. Navarra, renowned for its red wine, is gearing up for harvest. Grey gnarled branches twine around waist-high trellises heavy with plump, purple grapes. At the village of Muruzabal I decide to detour but again, no signposts. A woman walks toward me with clear blue eyes and a smear of white flour across her forehead. '*Buen Camino*,' she smiles wiping her hands on a pinafore apron. In my primitive Spanish I ask, '*Como se va a Eunate?*' She takes me by the hand through side streets to the edge of town and points the way.

I hear trickling water as I head down the hill and the voice of a foot fetishist quips in my head. Take off your shoes, bathe your feet! I backtrack to find a fountain pouring into a long trough. A moment's consideration of the fourteen kilometres already walked is all I need. Lying on the ground I swing my legs up and over so they can soak in the ice-cold water. Hidden from the road by a thicket of blackberry, I let my eyes bathe in a cloudless sky and listen to the chitter of birds and the lazy mooing of cows. My feet tingle back to life. It is as if I am being lapped by the natural world. A sensation all the more delicious each time I hear footsteps and the chink of pilgrims' walking sticks as they pass by, oblivious to my private spa.

I could skip down the road but decorum prevails until another crossroad with no signpost, just three hundred and sixty degrees of vineyard. With arms outstretched I turn full circle, face toward the sun. 'Empty mind,' a Zen teacher used to say. So this is what it feels like. No care, no idea and no need to know.

Someone heads my way. Spanish, which is a good start, and a pilgrim, but he doesn't know the way either. We discuss the possibilities until a tractor rumbles along and the farmer points to the right. Only then do we recognize each other, from the church at Cizur Menor. It was José who had asked if their talking was a disturbance.

He looks different. In the subdued light of the church I had seen the wizened profile of a working man but here was someone young with soft searching eyes lighting up the contours of an angular face. José begins our conversation with the pilgrim icebreaker, 'Why you do the Camino?'

I stumble for words having no neatly packaged answer. 'I am actually Buddhist,' hoping he won't be offended, 'I need time to be alone, to be challenged, physically.' Big pause, 'and spiritually.' It seems an inane reply. I want to find myself, see black Madonnas, walk across an entire country, meditate, meet people. All of these felt real but didn't make it onto my tongue. 'And you?' José resigned from his job in Madrid to be here. 'I have no idea about the future. I am hoping for answers,' he says. 'All I know is I couldn't sit in that office one more day.' I feel a sense of relief. There is no right answer.

There are two kinds of Spanish men. The machismo cowboy-come-toreador and the sensitive romantic knight. José is definitely the latter. I feel myself melting in the intensity of his gaze and even though I am probably old enough to be his mother I allow myself a brief moment of pleasure. He is enamored with the idea of Australia and when I tell him I sell tickets in a cinema once a week, this seems paramount to paradise. 'Do you like Clint Eastwood?' he asks. 'Yes, but what about Pedro Almodovar?' I counter. We swap movies, books and dreams until the bell tower of Eunate appears in the distance.

Eunate – octagonal church of possible Templar origin.

It sits like a solitary note in a field of sunflowers. The flowers have gone to seed and their dark heads are bowed. A hint of yellow petal and green leaf remain but essentially it is a sea of rustling ochre and umber. An artist would use these same colours on his brush to paint the arched walls of the church; they are as natural as the landscape itself, justly deserving the name Eunate, from the Latin *eu nato*, well born. Built in 1170 no one knows exactly why it is here. After the discovery of several graves containing scallop shells some say it served as a burial chapel for dead pilgrims. Others believe it was built by the Knights Templar, members of the Benedictine order who, since the twelfth century, had the dual role of protecting pilgrims while waging war against Muslim invaders. Eunate's octagonal design harks back to the Knights' first temple in Jerusalem, the Church of the Holy Sepulchre. As an archetypal symbol, the octagon has a history pre-dating Christianity. Its eight sides are said to represent the transition of a square to a circle; from the imperfections of a material world to transcendence. Like a jewel, this small church sits at the confluence of two roads originating in Le Puy and Toulouse, both traditional departure points for the Camino.

Leaving our packs at the gate we walk across the arched colonnade to the outside of the apse, a single story half-octagon attached to the main building. Carved into the corbels beneath the eaves are enormous faces with African features and Moorish style turbans. Stone monsters and musicians with over-sized heads and fiddles look down from the capitals of each arch as we enter the church.

Tony stands in front of the altar in a plain white robe, his hiking boots peeping out from underneath, offering French mass to a small pilgrim gathering. The phantom weight of my pack and all the kilometres behind me are instantly tempered as he begins a Gregorian chant that resonates in my heart and between the graceful repetition of arched stone circling us. There are two levels. On the second, narrow alabaster windows are framed by columns decorated with ornate leaf patterns and curious faces with beards twisted into the shape of snail shells. Above, the vault is suspended by eight ribs meeting at the centre without the support of a master key stone, a Mozarabic method skillfully blending Islamic and Christian design. The angles within each of the ribs are different and as my eyes travel down their length I see how it translates into each of the eight walls of the church also being different.

Shafts of light pour in narrow streams from the skylights centred between each rib of the dome above. I find myself becoming aware of the space between my ribs as they expand and contract with each breath. An uncomplicated, connected moment.

Behind Tony, on a stone pedestal, sits a Romanesque Virgin, her soft, steadfast gaze reminiscent of the one in Pamplona. Two beeswax candles burn either side flickering pools of light across her golden tunic and red skirt. She holds a sheaf of wheat in her right hand and fresh red roses in her left. On her lap sits the man-child, Christ, his right hand held up in a blessing. I listen to Tony chanting the last prayer in Latin and am spellbound by this intimate convergence of past and present.

Tony folds the altar cloth and leaves one candle burning. Someone comes to sit beside me – Fiona! We hug like long lost friends and walk out into the glare of a midday sun, Fiona still limping but steady as a tortoise. We linger against the walls of this ancient church, in its solitude and sunflowers. Before leaving I make one last circumambulation, weaving through flowers higher than me, listening to the crunch of fallen petals and leaves underfoot, captivated as a child in a fantastical forest. Eunate. Its Basque name translates as House of One Hundred Doors, an apt metaphor for life. Behind each door awaits a different manifestation of oneself. But there are walls between them and openings and closings. These are my thoughts as I make one pilgrim footprint after another, moving from one encounter to the next.

I learn the art of walking again – slowly. Fiona winces with pain each time she puts pressure on her knee but is determined to continue. In Obanos we find the whole village congregated in an oak-lined plaza around a group of dancers and musicians. Everyone is dressed in white with the traditional Basque red bandanas and waist sashes. This is the last day of a festival held each August commemorating two saints, Guillermo and his sister Felicia, who made the pilgrimage to Compostela from the French court of Aquitane. On their return Felicia decided to live the rest of her life as a hermit in Navarra. Guillermo fell into a rage and tried to drag her home but in his fury, killed her. Realizing the enormity of his sin he returned again to Compostela to pray for forgiveness. For the second time he stopped in Obanos, and here he remained, weeping for his sister until he died. Guillermo's residency continues, his silver encased skull taking pride of place in the local church of San Juan Bautista.

Today there is only celebration. Villagers sit under the shade of trees watching a dance troupe twirl to the music of a five piece band playing tunes on two accordions, a flute, a violin and a drum. The women are dressed in long sleeved white blouses with blue vests and ankle length blue skirts that billow out as they swing in circles with their partners. The men wear white with blue braces and red pill shaped hats tied with a ribbon. A little boy speeds past me on a bicycle decorated with bull's horns and red streamers and brakes at a stall selling teddy bears and pink elephants. The dancers finish to whistles and applause and, slowly, families take their leave, no doubt for a feast at home and then siesta. I watch them wistfully as they disappear down narrow streets and behind doors. We shoulder our packs for one more hour of walking.

The last kilometre follows a bitumen road and we are buffeted by exhaust fumed wind each time a car zooms past. I look to the fields for respite and spot a stork, perched on a nest splayed over the edge of a high solitary brick chimney. Storks are now protected in Spain and if a nest is found on a chimney such as this, farmers are not allowed to demolish them. So the tilling of fields goes on under the watchful eyes of a family's heritage home. Storks mate for life and each year, after wintering in Africa, they return to the same nest to lay their eggs.

There are several options for our nesting tonight. We decide on the *refugio* run by the Padres Reparadores, an order originating in Germany and find adjoining top bunks above two burly Spanish men who look like potential sources of some serious snoring. In the next bed is an older woman from Argentina. She seems to have adopted them, repeatedly calling out to her two *ninos*. Her boys.

I wash my clothes and take them to the back garden where dozens of long lines stretch under clear fiberglass. It's a hothouse, next best thing to a spin drier. (A tell tale sign of a pilgrim is half dry washing pinned to the back of their pack – socks, bras and underpants all a flutter.)

Our room overlooks a plaza and an archway leading to the old town. To the left is the site of a twelfth century hospice for pilgrims. Under oath the Knights Templar offered lodging here for free but were allowed to profit from their guests through sales of bread and wine. In its place stands the eighteenth century monastery of the Padres Reparadores, now a school, and opposite, the Church of the Crucifix with a sea of ornate scallop shells chiseled into its stone porch. We follow the same narrow street pilgrims in the Middle Ages would have walked, lined today with souvenir shops and bars. Gone are the tinkers and tailors, barbers and traders of religious trinkets, bread, meat and ale.

Puenta la Reina grew up and not out. The ground floor of many houses is built from solid stone dating to the fourteenth and fifteenth century. Above, two or three more levels, in very different styles of brick and stone date from the sixteenth to eighteenth century. I look up to the highest story, often used for grain storage, and see under the eaves, long decorative sculptures, each house with a different design. They remind me, strangely, of delicate timber carvings found half a world away in the traditional houses and temples of Nepal.

Spanning the width of the River Arga, now wide and deep, are the six graceful Romanesque arches of the town's namesake, the Bridge of the Queen. This was the bridge Elana talked about. We walk over its curve, on stones polished to a shine by centuries of footsteps, and look back across the river to town. In this late afternoon light the houses are the shade of earth and wheat, bleached like the hills that surround them and as natural to the landscape as clouds to sky. I feel at home in a tired body and as familiar to the elements as the town is.

A cool breeze blows from the west. Fiona and I sit on the riverbank and watch a young girl sketching the faces of an old couple. Narrow houses behind us lean together at a precarious angle with a tangle of grape vine and pink flowering creepers clinging to their stone and timber walls, their tendrils curling around shuttered windows and winding up as far as the shingled roofs. The gnarled trunk of one grapevine looks as old as the stone foundation it has split into two, a symbiosis in time as assuring as the presence of the old married couple. Across the bridge's path, in a small garden, a goat tugs at the branches of a tree over a neighbour's fence and a coop of chickens scavenge among scraps of food. Time for dinner.

Menu del dia, seven euros. Inside vacuous pop music competes with soccer on a television hanging from the wall. A table of old men sipping from brandy glasses scrutinize us as we walk through to the restaurant. The barman grunts a greeting. Behind him two rows of bottles stretch the length of the room, a shelf of Spain. Tantalizing sketches and paintings on each label – amarillo lemons, plump maroon plums, sprigs of elderflower, charging bulls, flamenco dancers and a faded line drawing of a villa peeling from the last bottle. Sherries, wines and spirits. I ask for a nip from the lemon bottle. We sit at a lime green tabletop under the whirl of a ceiling fan and choose Navarran asparagus to begin, their white gold. Thick white stalks splayed on a plate, dressed with a simple vinaigrette. The juiciest, tenderest asparagus I have ever tasted. Fresh, grilled mountain trout with chips. Water or wine? Silly question. Little prepacked crème caramels finish us completely and we glide back to the *refugio* by lantern light.

In the plaza a group of pilgrims gather to drink in the stars as the 'mother' of the two boys sings an Argentinean song in her husky voice, a perfect accompaniment for her lone tango about the square.

5

Mermaid in a Viper's Nest
Puente la Reina to Estella

It is a mystery, the exodus of a hundred or more pilgrims each morning. We wake, pack our belongings, splash our faces with water. We venture into the half light, into the chaos of backpacks and walking poles against the *refugio* walls. Small groups mill about, stretching, chatting and making last minute adjustments before setting off into deserted streets. We all walk the same road but it never seems crowded. Everyone has a rhythm as varied as their reason for embarking on the journey. Our weaving in and out of villages, through vineyards and over open roads threads us like a string of beads, never too tight or too loose.

I had set out intending to walk alone with a kind of missionary zeal but slowly this is falling away. There are welcome periods where I join another lone walker or group for an hour or two till one of us strides ahead. Inevitably, with some goodbyes, there is the expectation of meeting again. I think of Daniel all the way back in Larrasoana wearing his Algerian cross. How is it possible our paths have not crossed since then? I sometimes catch myself hoping to see him at the next *refugio*, red wine in one hand and tortoise walking stick in the other, extolling the beauty of an imperfect world. But here lies one of the Camino's lessons: seize the moment. Sometimes one encounter, one opportunity, is all I will be given.

Fiona takes her first dose of anti-inflammatory pills with bread, a sort of communion for the body, and we begin the day together. The water flowing under Puenta la Reina looks as dark and quiet as the morning. The path turns to fresh bulldozed dirt and a steep winding ascent up the side of a gouged and scarred mountain. We are in the midst of major road works and the morning shift is just beginning, assaulting us with dust clouds, the rumble of dozers and steamrollers. Perhaps this is an extension of the highway forging its way from Pamplona but this time I am not looking down on it from the safe height of a windswept ridge. Troops of helmeted men riding steel beasts pay no attention to us. Here it feels as if, in our slow motion journey across Spain, we are nothing but ghosts.

The first recorded pilgrimage to Santiago was in 950. It followed much of the road built by Romans two centuries earlier, in their relentless conquering of Europe. By the eleventh and twelfth centuries, at the pinnacle of the Camino's popularity, an estimated half a million pilgrims walked each year polishing the hand laid stone with their feet. History it seems is repeating itself. As the Camino experiences a renaissance so too does the road. Forces of economics and engineering are transforming the straight efficiency of Roman roads into four lane highways. Pilgrims can choose to walk alongside these blurs of tar, holding fast to their staffs as they are buffeted by speeding traffic. The real pilgrim, I am told, takes the fastest way to salvation. She is not interested in scenic distraction or worldly pleasure. She is intent on the miraculous Saint James and the rewards of heaven. She might be walking for someone who cannot walk or for the cure of a sick relative or the absolution of a deceased parent. For better or worse I am none of these and will always take the alternative footpath away from time driven routes. But today we are caught between the two. The route to Estella crisscrosses roadworks and detours many times adding dust suffocating kilometres to our journey.

The village of Maneru offers respite. She sits on an embankment circled with flower and vegetable plots, unharried by change. Pilgrims rest in her plaza on red park benches beneath Poinciana trees. The two *ninos* are here slicing a sausage into pieces for everyone. I chew my piece like gum enjoying its juices of smoke and pepper washed down with cool fountain water.

Near the end of yet another detour, a bank of low grey cloud blows over us, and our shadows disappear.

Cirauqui, Basque for nest of vipers, appears in the distance crowning a rocky hilltop. It's the kind of name that shoots foreboding into your shoes but all I see is postcard perfect: a layering of red and brown terracotta tiled roofs etched in a half moon across the skyline; a church bell tower at the pinnacle reaching up like a finger pointing to heaven. Dirt turns to cement and we begin a steep climb into the medieval heart of town.

Pausing at Ciraqui on my way to the stone mermaid.

In search of the church I leave Fiona and walk through a low Gothic arch in the old city wall, cross a small plaza then up a flight of steps to San Roman.

Cirauqui's twelve centuries of history begins here. San Roman was rebuilt first in the twelfth and then again in the seventeenth century. Today it is closed. I take off my pack and wander around fortress-like walls to a Mudejar style portal at its entrance. From a fusion of Gothic and Islamic design a mermaid, running fingers through her flowing stone hair, fixes me in her gaze. What is she doing here?

I stand before her with child's eyes. Every girl loves a mermaid: dream-like, whimsical creatures free to glide through the deep. A fairy tale; not to be mistaken for the sirens of Greek mythology who lured helpless men to their deaths – this was the church's preferred take. Her voluptuous curves provided a potent symbol for a medieval and patriarchal tradition: a dire warning against temptations of the flesh. But tracing back to her pagan roots she is one of the oldest and most persistent symbols of female energy; her part-fish body representing the fertility of women. I think of each full moon when the ocean tides peak just as the cycle of my body comes full circle. Mermaids have also been worshiped as a symbol of transcendence; encompassing two worlds they are capable of rescuing souls wandering through a sea of delusion. I run fingers through the knots of my uncombed hair and give San Roman's door one more push before turning away.

The scent of fresh baked bread wafts through Ciraqui's streets. Fiona rests against the white picket fence of a cottage near the end of the village, a tourist *pension* offering a simple breakfast to passing pilgrims. Inside is a sumptuous garden of chrysanthemums, lavender and roses. The charge for stewed coffee and bread rolls with tomato is exorbitant but we are ravenous. We eat from fine china set on a lace tablecloth. Around us are all the comforts of home: gingham curtains over the kitchen windows, a wood stove, plump floral sofas and a rocking chair. I settle back into padded cushions and inhale the fusion of flowers and warm bread, happy to pay the price.

The vipers in Cirauqui's nest must still be sleeping. I've seen not a single snake and leave enamored and surfeit with a tinge of sadness to be departing just as it is waking. Old people appear at the doors of their houses. One woman sweeps and another clips dying geranium flowers from her windowbox while three men in black berets take up their places on a bench to survey another day's passing parade.

Gnarled cypress trees line a wavelike section of worn paving stones. It is as if the earth has tremored and the road ripples and winds over its contours refusing to give way. Such is the tenacity of Roman roads. We cross the ruins of a bridge and zigzag up a hill. A two thousand year old path leads us to what is now acridly familiar – tar and the sound of jackhammers splitting open another mountain. I stare down my frustration and shift the weight of my pack. Oh for a leafy cobbled path, the babble of a stream, ripe apples falling from a forgotten tree. But there is nothing to do but step one foot in front of the other. The morning coffee, dishwater tasting as it was, gives me a surge of energy.

'Meet you at the next village,' I wave to Fiona and head off into the grit of gravel dust and jangle of metal on rock. An hour or so later wild grasses feather my ankles and the sky turns blue. The spectacle of ripe wheat sweeping as far as the horizon animates me more than a shot of caffeine ever could. Fiona's company, her down to earth chatter-boxing and dry Australian humour has been a welcome change but walking alone fills me with a different kind of happiness. It is as though, this time, my choice to go ahead comes from a place of ease rather than anxiety.

I was a shy one growing up, and still am if I look truthfully, preferring a lone ride on my horse or a roller skate around an empty rink while everyone congregated at a rugby match. Somewhere along the way I demonized this into fear. Later, choosing a Buddhist meditation retreat took preference over a seaside holiday. In those long hours of sitting came the first hints of what it means to step out of the labels I had plastered onto myself. Practicing each day's teaching felt medicinal for my self-inflicted wounds. But even the best dressed bandage kept in place for too long will fester what lies beneath. Sunlight and fresh air are needed; the bandage has to go. It was interesting to observe how removing a label requires a leap of faith and to understand also that any anticipation of pain, before removing a band aid, only exacerbates the pain. I found myself in unexplored territory, a place untarnished by judgment. I could let go.

So here I am arms and legs in full swing on another unconventional holiday. I breathe in for a count of three steps and out for ten. At the end of each cycle all that is left is a primal urge to breathe in again. Maybe this long walk to the end of the earth will give me the courage and the time to peel away a few more layers, let my fears loose on the wind, tread away my doubting mind till not one doubt is left. Maybe a month of the rising sun warming my back, of breathing in the air of wheat fields and wild grasses, will give the raw places inside me the chance to surface for air.

A sea of horsetail, a herb for healthy hair and bones, clings to the banks of a ditch. Each bright green stalk, like a jointed needle, has a delicate spike for a flower. Two hundred million years ago it grew as a giant fern like tree. I bend down and brush my hand across their resilient stems. It's a soft tickling sensation that belies their ancient use as a scouring pad. A bunch of dried leaves can polish metal clear as a mirror and as a final sanding leaves wood smooth as new skin. A little like meditation I think, polishing the mind clean. Seeing the moment afresh, as it is, without barnacles of judgment.

Small cultivated fields of Navarran asparagus appear either side of the path, their shoots peeking out from mounds of soil. Each day offers another feast of blackberries and grapes, of comfrey and applemint. Little wings have sprouted on my feet. It is not that I have a destination to reach over six hundred kilometres away, it's not even that I want to reach the next village. My sprint to the next rise is joy enough.

From the safe height of a Gothic bridge I look down to a trail of willow leaves rippling the Rio Salado. The water looks harmless enough but, pilgrims beware, the twelfth century *Codex Calixtinus* warns: deceit lurks in the dark green shadows of its banks. In the Camino's first written guide its authors describe being duped by locals into thinking the Salado's water was healthy and drinkable. Watched by the impious Navarrese sharpening their knives on river stones the guide's authors said: We watered our horses in the stream, and had no sooner done so, than two of them died and these men skinned them on the spot.

I take off my pack, peel out of clammy socks, wiggle dry my toes and chew stalks of horsetail until Fiona arrives. In the midday heat it is easy matching my pace to hers. Although her pills mask the acute pain, walking is still a struggle and I admire the way she chatters on. We talk about relationships and, as the road loosens our tongues, divulge intimate secrets. Two middle-aging women sharing disappointments and conquests, laughing and fearless.

Figs, the fruit of love, hang profusely from an old tree. They are green and hard but my mouth still waters. I will have to slow right down if I am to include their purple season in my roadside foraging. Reaching Santiago pales in comparison to the possibility of picking soft figs for breakfast. A couple of crates lean against its wizened trunk and we take a seat. Footsteps and the familiar rhythm of walking sticks announce company. An older man with the lope of a bear comes puffing towards us, red faced and somewhat dazed – the weight of his pack, the heat, the hills and finding himself miles from anywhere in particular. We make space for him. His name is Ivano and he comes from Italy. That's about the extent of our conversation as he knows not a word of English and we, nothing of Italian. Nevertheless it's a pleasant interlude, sipping warm fountain water together under fig leaves. Ivano doesn't stay long and as he half dances, half lollops into the distance I am aghast at the way his huge backpack shakes and wobbles precariously to the right.

The village of Lorca takes its name from the Arabic word for battle in commemoration of a Muslim conquest in 920. Today it clings to the edge of a main road like one of those barely noticeable highway stops. Walking in the relentless haze of an August afternoon with what was supposed to be twelve kilometres turning into sixteen or twenty, a brick veneer shop on the outskirts of town appears like an earthly paradise. Pilgrims rest against its walls downing coca cola. I order a *bocadillo* with *jamon* and cheese, standard fare at most bars, but what comes is a crusty roll as long as my forearm. I share half with a Japanese American. He has that, have a nice day air about him, just too nice to be true. But who am I to talk, walking on air and feeling so happy?

Inside, at the end of a long room, the grandmother is stirring a simmering pan of meatballs in tomato stew while her daughter slices down the middle of another baguette, rubbing into it the juices from a halved tomato. Just as I soaked in the floral cushions and rocking chair at Ciraqui I suddenly ache to sit down at their table and breathe in everything that makes domesticity as comforting as it is – an apron dusted with flour, a sink of dishes, even the Spanish drone of soap on the television in the corner. For a moment I wonder what I am doing walking the length of a country on the other side of the world when at home the routine of my days had been so reassured. Perhaps predictable is a better word, I think to myself, and the moment passes.

Only nine kilometres to go. Five to Villatuerta then another four to Estella. Fiona and I wind around hills and through country where tenth and eleventh century hermits once lived. If it had been morning I would be tempted to take a detour from the detours in the hope of finding a long lost cave but instead am propelled on by the thought of two more hours, maybe more if the roadwork continues, and an unaccustomed ache percolating around my hips.

It is easy to imagine how, eight centuries ago, a haggard pilgrim felt arriving at the miracle site of the Church of Santo Sepulcro. Long ago a scorned Jew threw a crucifix into the River Ega. It came to rest at the river's edge and refused to move. In celebration of an all-knowing all-seeing God a church was built at the entrance to Estella. We stand back to take in an arena of intricately carved biblical figures. Across the centre is the familiar tableau of the Last Supper. The more we look the more we see. The Crucifixion, Mary, and two figures dressed in traditional pilgrim garb: cloak, staff and hat. After traveling through Navarra where the reception was, according to the *Codex Calixtinus*, often barbarous and well informed of all vices and iniquities, a pilgrim, seeing his like glorified in stone, must have felt relief to have arrived at Estella's gates, a place where, the Codex continues: Bread is good, wine excellent, meat and fish are abundant in a town overflowing with delights. Each Gothic face carries a different expression and the folds of their robes fall like real velvet and homespun linen. To the left is a farmer leading a fat pig and to the right, a curious congregation of monsters and beasts.

Centuries ago only the church owned libraries – lantern lit cavernous rooms full of tomes and manuscripts painstakingly written and illustrated by hand. Villagers, having no access to these and no reading skills, were conveniently kept in the dark – ever in need of redemption by an almighty church. Traveling minstrels and puppet shows were their only source of entertainment along with occasional plays, usually with biblical themes, hellfire and damnation providing excellent opportunity for maximum drama. I try to imagine the implication of this; how the weird and wonderful displays of ordinary life and the myths and fables before me might have satisfied a yearning for meaning.

But philosophizing pales at the thought of a bath and bed and we join the line of pilgrims spilling out the front door of Estella's *alburque*. Our shelter for tonight is a rambling room with sixty bunk beds on a wooden floor that creaks under every step. There are two quaint but clean showers for the room and I am grateful to be one of the first as the drainage is faltering already. We handwash our clothes in a courtyard under the psychedelic eyes of Buddha, Jesus and Siva painted over its old brick walls.

Half-shaven men in black berets scrutinize us flicking our fresh shampooed hair dry as we walk across a modern replica of Estella's Romanesque bridge. We, the Camino itinerant, must provide an endless source of entertainment for the locals. But we also carry their prayers. A man tips his hat and another calls out to us in a torrent of Spanish. Santiago, is the only word I recognize but as I watch him make the sign of the cross over his heart I can hazard a guess. That's one more prayer I'll be saying to St James.

In a slow mix of enchantment and aching bones we wander down cobbled streets. The main plaza lies quiet as if waiting for its patrons to roll from their siesta beds. We find a café, order ice cream and pay the extra price to sit outside and watch the mellowed light of afternoon dance about the square. I stretch my legs and lean back content with the knowledge I have traveled, really traveled, the distance from one town to another. We may be strangers to the locals but nevertheless I feel at home in Estella. I've not stepped off a plane or out of a car with my camera and guidebook, I have walked every inch of the way, chewed on grasses, drunk from village fountains, inhaled dust from bulldozed roads and the chlorophyll air of oak forests, to arrive here.

Church bells signal evening mass and we follow their deep clangs to a flight of steep winding steps up to the Iglesia de San Pedro de la Rua. I catch a flicker of deflation on Fiona's face as she considers the ascent. We take them slowly, one by one, and are greeted with an eerie mix of nature, myth and symbol carved into the twelfth century doorway. At its crown is a relief of St James riding a boat of stars and from the ocean a giant hand surfaces, raised towards him in a blessing. Below, among a tangle of ornate flowers, is a lamb, the lamb of God, and to the right a centaur standing guard. I then come face to face with the haunting gaze of another mermaid only this time she has two tails. If her message is indeed a warning against carnal pleasure, I take no heed. My body is satiated enough from the day's walk and I enter, vindicated, into the dark cool of this watched house.

I had expected the soft murmuring of rosary chants from the women who gather before mass but instead there is music. A quintet sits at the entrance to the central apse fine-tuning their instruments: two mandolins, a mandola, a guitar and a double bass. Behind them rise three tiers of stained glass windows above three stone niches. A Virgin, a crucifixion and a saint waver in candlelight between a column of writhing snakes and another of human figures caught in a tangle of vines.

We join a shuffle of elegant bodies, men in dark tailored suits and women draped in long fringed shawls slipping so casually off their strapless shoulders. Seated just in time we are relieved to notice in their midst a few pilgrims looking as disheveled as us. The quintet is from Luxembourg. Two women dressed in black chiffon and velvet hold the mandolins while three men in black suits and silver blue ties sit to their left. A hush descends, even the flicker of candle light steadies as the woman who leads raises her torso and, with a staccato breath and shake of her head, begins. My heart practically bounces from note to passionate note of an Allegro by Vivaldi.

Often I find the surrounds of a church sobering. Its peace I appreciate but the dire warnings to sinners and graphic depictions of suffering alienate me. This is when the serene face of the Buddha shines. By his example one can sit and watch the mind cavort in all directions with no threat of damnation, like watching a play of light on water. Physical pain and the torment of thoughts move slowly from emotional response to an awareness that allows me to see without the hindrance of judgment. I can begin to observe whatever is present impassively and, eventually, compassionately.

Tonight however there is no need to shield my eyes from judgment. Instead I am lifted into *allegria*. The concert continues with a Zen like composition, then three Spanish pieces and ending in a sensual fandango by Enrique de Ulierte.

Fiona nudges me and points to her watch: five to ten. Again! I feel a bit like Cinderella, minus glass slippers, racing down Estella's lantern-lit streets. After such a concert we may have heavenly wings attached to our dusty boots but will the *hospitalero* be sympathetic?

6

The Succour of Stars
Estella

Fiona's knee has swollen beyond recognition and although *refugios* limit stays to one night the *hospitalero* says she can rest here for as long as it takes. Without too much deliberation I decide to keep her company, at least for a day.

It's strange to be walking without the weight of a pack and even stranger to have no destination beyond breakfast. After only a week the routine has worn indelible tracks into my psyche and I feel a mix of guilt and liberation at not having to go anywhere. As we move into the morning routines of Estella another world opens: the inky smell of newsprint from a pile of today's papers, crates of ice and bulbous-eyed fish delivered to the fishmonger, children racing ahead of their mothers on the way to school, suited businessmen disappearing into banks, a barber sharpening his razor and two nuns carrying baskets of baguettes. They turn the corner ahead of us and, lifting the white hems of their habits an inch, ascend a flight of stone stairs like a pair of silent doves. I follow them with my eyes up to the church beyond a steep rise of shingled roofs.

We drink coffee from Betty Blue mugs and crunch into chocolate croissants. I am restless to explore and arrange to meet Fiona after her appointment with the local shaman, recommended by the *hospitalero*. We are, after all, on a religious pilgrimage – miracles can happen. I return to the stairs where the nuns disappeared. The church at the top, dedicated to San Miguel, is more like a rambling fortress which makes sense given his archangel duty to lead heaven's troops against the devil's. A gathering of saints and sinners grace the stone entrance but I am impatient to walk further up the hill to the Church of Le Puy. And anyway, this door is locked with an iron arm.

Medieval streets wind steep and dark between drab high rise apartments smothered in graffiti. The transition is a surprise and for a moment I hesitate. Heavy shadows fall between buildings and the few figures I pass seem insular, hands in pockets, eyes downcast. A mix of fearlessness, instinct and naivety take up the challenge in spite of the little voice inside my head saying, Go back. Just like the time I wandered out of Bombay's Victoria railway terminal after arriving on a midnight train. Go back!

All the station's retiring rooms were occupied and the platforms a patchwork of ragged bodies sprawled from one end to the other. Every hotel was either locked or full so I kept walking, further and further into the bowels of the city until a man befriended me and invited me to his home. I have no choice, I remember thinking as I followed him through alleyways and over open drains. We climbed eight flights of stairs to be ushered into a tiny, two room flat by Raj's mother. She prepared a basin of water for me to wash and spread a mat and blanket on the floor for a bed. Just as I lay down, exhausted and grateful, there was a rough banging at the door. Two policemen entered, batons swinging from their waists, and insisted I leave with them. I was incredulous and pleaded to stay but to no avail. Someone had complained there was a white woman in the middle of Bombay's red light district. For the few night hours remaining I slept fitfully on a hard bug infested bed at their station.

Here in Estella I feel as though I am walking through convoluted layers of time. Towering above the seam of apartment blocks are the ruins of the church of San Pedro de Lizarra. To Basques, Estella will always be known as Lizarra, with its literal translation of either ash tree or star. Neither seem apparent here, only an eerie Romanesque shell for cobwebs and bats. Past the keep out signs and wire barricades I watch how sunbeams stream through holes in the roof, illuminating a flurry of airborne dust all the way down to the church's splintered floor. I climb further into a sanctuary of tall conifers and detour from the concrete path so I can walk the last leg across a soft bed of pine needles. If green has a perfume this is it.

In front of the Iglesia de El Puy reigns a statue in memory of a thief who once tried to steal silver and jewels from the Virgin inside. After stripping her bare he began to make his way down the mountain, or so he thought. Instead, thanks to the marvelous powers of our Lady, he merely paced around the church all night dragging his bounty behind him. In the morning he woke at her feet surrounded by the local authorities. As punishment his hands were chopped off and nailed to a wooden pillar outside the church. Eventually these were replaced by hands of stone and now, in times more benevolent, a triumphant Virgin stands on top of a stone pillar.

I can't believe my luck when I push the front door. It opens. Inside is an expanse of light as wide as it is long and the reason behind the old Basque name of Lizarra is revealed. The church is shaped like a star. It is, after all, built to mark the place where shepherds watched more than nine hundred years ago the nightly shower of falling stars. Following their silver trail they discovered a cave hidden behind a bramble of thorns and inside an image of the Virgin. Despite all efforts to move her down to the Church of San Pedro she, like the crucifix in Estella's river, refused to budge and so her star strewn cave became a shrine. Today this Virgin's home is a monument to the 1940s: all concrete, steel and neo-modern stained glass.

The main altar is circular with a sparkling set of cup and chalice and a silver Madonna. I circumambulate her stage brightly lit by the expanse of cubist stained glass and we are washed in rainbows of morning sunlight.

There are two Madonnas. The other, in a small nave, looks almost identical and it is to her I go. In a plastic yoghurt container at her feet is a small posy of rosebuds. On her lap sits the tiny body of Jesus, his right hand raised in a blessing and his left holding a red apple. Their wooden bodies are dressed in robes of pure silver and their throne sits above a silver crescent moon. I had anticipated she would have black skin like her namesake in Le Puy but she is the colour of alabaster. For a moment I am disappointed but this soon vanishes under the delicate spell of her gaze. Her mouth turns upwards in a gentle smile and her eyes emanate kindness beneath whimsically raised eyebrows. Both her hands are over sized; her right holding a filigree of silver lilies, a symbol of purity, and her left resting softly at the side of her son.

Estella's El Puy Madonna riding a crescent moon.

I close my eyes and see a swirling of stars until eventually they disappear and I am left in the folds of a velvet darkness. Like a jigsaw puzzle, pieces start falling into place. The Camino is a journey to the shrine of St James. Little is said about the Virgin Mary but it is more often to her image, not his, that I am drawn. My hand reaches for the silver body of Tara rising and falling against my chest. I give you permission, she seems to be saying like a medium for reconciliation, one woman to another.

I see my mother's face, her eyes blue pools of longing, and begin to understand her deep connection with

Catholicism, even now, so many years after leaving it behind. Her Anglican marriage to a non-believing son of Seventh Day Adventist missionaries launched a relationship fraught with angst and underlying resentment. At least that is how it appeared to me, the young, disenfranchised daughter. But the older I become the more difficult it is to place blame. For my mother I am sure there was a fundamental lack of nourishment and ritual in her new church: no rosary or confessional, no High Mass and billow of frankincense. Every few weeks she made a clandestine visit to the Carmelite monastery near our house to spend an afternoon pouring out her heart to its Mother Superior. In the middle of their conversations, my mother once reminisced, Mother Aimee would break into a therapeutic laugh then ring the little bell on her table, calling for a tray of tea and Iced Vo Vo biscuits.

I begin to have an inkling about my early departure from the church. I remember questioning my mother about the improbability of a God who allows so much suffering. But how can someone adrift in their own despair, answer? I was a child moving between parallel worlds: one of make-believe and the other of simple truths, distillations of black and white, yes and no. Then came the shades of grey, the abyss between concepts of right and wrong and slowly the milk teeth of innocence eroded. Over time I became disillusioned with the productions of Sunday church and the interminably long hour of weekly religious classes at school. Turn the other cheek, seemed an impossibly radical departure from the dog eat dog code of the playground. And I remember the day of my white dress and veil and my mother taking me by the hand to confirmation in a place she could not call home.

My eyes stay closed and in a strange confluence I see Mary's eyes merge with Tara's. Might their joined gaze burn deeper into a place more primal than my learned beliefs? I remember my last day in Madrid before beginning the Camino. In a room of the El Prado museum a painting by Rubens stopped me in my tracks. At first I mistook his portrait of Juno with child for Mary. Under a halo of light her face shone with the serene love of a mother but there was nothing demure about the swathe of transparent red silk draping her voluptuous body. From her left breast she, together with her baby, squeezed a stream of milk into the night sky where it became a river of stars.

Juno was a Roman fertility goddess whose pagan origins stretch back thousands of years. Like Mary she was called the Queen of Heaven and it was believed whole galaxies sprouted from her breast milk. Many of her qualities were assimilated into the persona of Mary. They share the lily and the Milky Way as symbols. Wherever drops of Juno's milk fell, lilies grew, symbolizing the self-fertilizing power of the feminine. I wonder was Mary's immaculate conception an extension of this myth? How apt, I think, on a journey following the Milky Way I've come to a star shaped church on a hill where showers of stars once fell. I can almost smell the perfume of the lilies in Mary's hand. Now that would be a miracle.

An old woman shuffles in the door and sits at the

back of the church. I say a prayer to Tara, visualizing her riding a thousand stars, 'Set me free from the darkness of ignorance.' And to Mary, 'Please remember my mother.'

The day outside is as clear as can be and the mountains circling the town are tinged with purple. I take the shortest route back feeling like a mountain lamb on the loose, free from the shepherd's crook.

Fiona still limps but is bubbling over with enthusiasm for the hour spent in the hands of Estella's shaman, a glorious man of indeterminate age with long silver hair and dressed in an ankle-length white robe. 'I feel like every inch of me has been rocked and pummeled but in the end,' she says, with resignation, 'he says I have to rest.'

I wonder if we will see each other again after tomorrow. 'Fiona, I think the fact we have at least walked a day and a half together deserves a celebratory lunch,' and she agrees. We step into a black and white tiled lift and stop-start up two floors to a recommended restaurant. The clientele are dressed to the nines – coiffed hair and pearls, twin sets and high heels, silk ties and business suits all wrapped in a hint of cigar smoke. A waitress sweeps us to a table, past lattice panels and annexed walls each painted with a *trompe l'oeil* underneath a cloud painted ceiling hung with artificial vines. We are seated beneath a plump bunch of plastic grapes, poured a glass of red and handed menus, large menus. And all in Spanish. Resorting to my mini-dictionary we begin a journey into Spanish gastronomical vocabulary – *pollo* for chicken, *pescados* for fish – but in the end are clueless about the preparation of anything. We collapse into a pool of wine-fueled giggles.

A low, amorously accented, voice comes from behind, 'May I help you?' Seated at the table next to us he appears amused by the predicament of two shabbily dressed damsels. He on the other hand is casually attired in perfectly ironed trousers, linen shirt and loosened tie. We are briefed from the first parchment page of fish beginning with *cocochas*, cheek of hake grilled with parsley and garlic to *truchas con jamon*, trout stuffed with ham then journey onward to page two, *caracoles con tomate al tomillo*, succulent snails cooked in a thyme tomato sauce, *conejo con pochas al verduras*, rabbit in a dish of haricot beans and vegetables and lamb chops, sounding much more interesting as *chuletas de cordero a la navarra*. We graciously avail ourselves the pleasure of his recital, one that finishes with a flourish of *fruta, pastel de queso* and *crema* caramel.

'Are you walking the Camino?'

We laugh. 'How did you guess?' With a gentlemanly twinkle our knight wishes us a safe journey, culinary and otherwise. We place our orders then settle back for a long lunch washed down by the finest house red. I am tempted to sample the snails but memories surface of my last encounter with these culinary treasures on a very different continent.

I had wandered away from the main town of Bassam, up the beach to a fishing village on the Ivory Coast, and was hailed into a palm-roof shack. It was the middle of a hot day and the sand burned through my sandals. Inside two women stirred enormous pots of stew. They pointed to a wooden bench and table covered in sleeping flies, all of whom woke with a deafening buzz. A deep bowl filled to the brim with the house specialty soon arrived. To an audience of laughing children I proceeded, as adequately as a white faced woman flushed by hormones and African heat can, to delicately tackle crab legs between my teeth alternating with gingered mouthfuls of snail, a combination of rubber and grit. It was only the oily consistency of the stew that made swallowing possible. I ate as much as I politely could before retreating into the sun, crisscrossing sand dunes in a hasty shortcut home, uncertain about the low and lower rumblings beginning in my belly.

Our meals arrive. I touch the cheek of hake with my fork and it breaks into buttery melt in the mouth pieces. Fiona's choice of humble lamb chops comes arranged in an arc on a large white plate drizzled with anchovy and lemon sauce. Ever attentive to the level of wine in our glasses the waitress returns, this time with the dessert menu. I've walked almost a hundred kilometres and have not one qualm about eating cheesecake. It comes crowned with rose petals on a pool of raspberry syrup.

In a blur of contentment and urgent comprehension of the absolute wisdom of siesta we wind our way home. A shop dedicated to chocolate however, delays our return. Inside we find an astonishing array of every imaginable flavour in choices of dark, milk and white. We choose three: *negro con pimienta, con pacharan* and *con limon*. Like bars of gold we divide them into halves before collapsing into bed.

I watch a silver disc of moon rise from the tiny balcony of our dormitory then stroll down the street to a leafy plaza by the river before reaching the steps of San Pedro. Just as the street lanterns begin to flicker on, a hand takes mine. She is old and hunchbacked, dressed in black with a crocheted shawl wrapped around her shoulders. The wrinkles on her face multiply as she smiles. I can understand one or two words she says but have no idea where we are going as she hobbles further down the road – me taking one step for every three of hers. We come to a stone archway and a dark flight of stairs. She points up to them and with a squeeze lets go my hand, '*Gracias,*' I say, though not sure what I am thanking her for, and climb to the top.

At first all I find is a busy road and a kerbside of weeds but to my left over the ramparts of an old stone wall I look down onto a manicured square of grass surrounded by rose trellises. On two sides in half-shadow stand the cloisters of San Pedro. The rush of cars behind my back disappears. It is as if each set of twin columns holds at bay the distraction of the world. In the final remnants of light I watch a chiseled garden of stylized leaves and flowers, mythological beasts, a scythe and a saint, fade into the dark. There are figures that look to heaven and others that look into the eyes of their companions. I realize I am holding my breath in response to the overwhelming face of our human condition; of fear and wonder, sorrow and joy, suffering and compassion, and I whisper into the ear of night a prayer for the safe journey of everyone I love.

7

Gifts

Estella to Los Arcos

It is still dark and our bunks are so close together there is no room in the aisle for two people to dress and pack. I fumble about for a torch and clothes and peel out of my sleeping bag as I pull on my trousers. By now the ritual of departure is pleasantly familiar. I tighten the straps of my stuff bag and feel satisfied the way everything I need takes up so little space. Fiona watches sleepily from her bed and we hug each other goodbye with a promise to keep in touch.

From cobblestones to bitumen, past houses and small factories, a bakery and a petrol station to the edge of Estella and abrupt darkness on a dirt road – I am exhilarated to be walking again but it is tempered with a hint of fear being alone in an unknown place. Two torchlights bob ahead and I relax – there will always be pilgrims on the road, before and behind me.

The abbey of Irache looms ahead, a black silhouette between lines of tall conifers. As if calling up the dawn, wind whips the dust and whispers eerie songs through the trees while a lone dog barks from behind a fence infusing the surrounds with an extra dash of foreboding.

Irache was one of the wealthiest and most powerful Navarran monasteries. Here in 1052 the first hospice for pilgrims was built as an extension to the existing Benedictine monastery. By this time the order of monks, established under San Benito in Visigoth times, had deteriorated from their original vows of humility and poverty to a privileged life, rich in land and weighty in government. In the early twelfth century St Bernard of Clairvaux bemoaned his order's slide into worldly ways. He criticized the Romanesque penchant for decorating churches with elaborate depictions of monsters and sirens, centaurs and unicorns: Blasphemous and foolish decorations for a House of God and a distraction to the monks' meditation. In a challenge to the Christian link with a lingering pagan psyche St Bernard formed a breakaway group of monks and returned to a life of simplicity and honest work.

When the Benedictine University of Sahagun moved here in 1605 Irache reinvented itself again. Degrees in philosophy, medicine, canon law and theology continued to be granted until the early nineteenth century. Today Irache's claim to fame is its *bodega*. The fountain is a modern set of taps, one for wine and one for water, and reads: Pilgrim, if you want to arrive in Santiago with strength and vitality take a good sip of this great wine and drink to felicity… wine starts flowing at 10:30am. I'm disappointed, never having had the opportunity to test myself with a glass of red so early in the morning. But it's probably just as well, Los Arcos is seventeen kilometres away.

I wind up a hill to the fortress walls of Azqueta clammy and cold from the heavy morning dew. Azqueta still sleeps and I rest in a small plaza by the church. Tucked into the side pocket of my ergonomic pack is a tub of lemon yoghurt and half a baguette. I have the luxury of a twenty first century breakfast and a plastic spoon to eat it with. So absorbed am I in this repast that I fail to notice a small grey bearded man walking towards me. '*Passaporte, passaporte!*' He doesn't look official, dressed in a checked shirt open at the throat and a grubby pair of bright blue trousers but there is a quiet air of authority about him. I fumble through my belongings, find it and hand it over but he shakes his head and says, 'No, *credencial.*'

'Oh, sorry, *lo siento,*' *realizing* he means my pilgrim passport, not my Australian one. Feeling a bit ridiculous, I take it from my pocket and hand it over. He turns and walks away. I guess this means I follow. Quickly gathering together my bag I catch up with him as he turns a corner at the end of the village.

Inside a large barn sits an oil stained green tractor and from the ceiling hang hundreds of gourds. He surveys the scene then cuts one down, gives it to me then takes it back, turns me around and ties it to my pack. Many pictures of St James show a gourd or *calabaza* tied to his staff or belt. For him it was a vessel for water and for me it is a symbol of my journey to Compostela.

We cross the road and enter his home. Along each wall are shelves brimming with jars of preserves: apricots and purple plums suspended in syrup, lemons studded with peppercorns, apples with cloves, rows of chillies and capsicum glistening in the dusty light and hanging from the roof beams, long threads of wrinkled red chillies and braids of garlic.

'*Me llamo, Pablito,*' he says as I watch him stamp my *credencial* and indeed at the bottom of the stamp there is his name, Pablito Sanz. Above is the design of a cross and a staff. This all becomes clear when he takes me out to the back yard and shows me with great pride an old stone embedded in the ground. It stands at knee height and looks a bit like a headstone. An intricate Templar cross is carved inside a circle. Two more pilgrims walk into the yard, an Irish girl, Rose and Luis from Spain. He offers us all the choice of a *bordon* from a jumble of hazelnut staffs propped against the fence. These Pablito has foraged and cleaned ready for pilgrims in need of a walking stick. It is the perfect wood, both strong and flexible and another symbol of the Camino. Not only can it be used on hazardous mountain passes and as defense against rabid dogs, it is also the weapon of choice for chasing the devil away and a symbol for the wood of the crucifix. I feel a little disappointed that I have my high tech aluminium poles and for a moment covet the idea of walking with something more traditional.

Pablito and his pilgrims.

Rose and Luis choose a staff. As I stand beside Pablito admiring the stone it dawns on me that I may well be in the company of a true knight. I feel safe in his unassuming presence and sense a selfless conviction and pleasure in him as he cares for pilgrims. He has a farm to manage but this is his real vocation. In the kitchen Pablito pulls out a tattered cardboard box full of scallop shells. For me these are the most fascinating of all Camino symbols; a complex one reaching beyond this Christian pilgrimage, deep into the world of myth. Souvenir shops along the way display them in every size and kitsch medium imaginable but for some reason it never felt right to buy one. 'Choose,' Pablito commands then picks a shell for me. I turn it around in my hands feeling its slightly tattered edge and the delicately flecked pink ribs corrugating its sea-bleached back. He threads it onto a length of string and ties it around my neck. A simple gift but I am overcome.

With the tap tapping of the little gourd bouncing on my pack and the tinkle of Tara against the shell around my neck I feel light as a feather winding back through Azqueta then down to another plain of wheat fields. I wonder how Pablito came to have so many shells in a box underneath his kitchen table when they are more commonly found on Galician beaches seven hundred kilometres away.

Miraculous, verging on nonsensical, shell legends abound. Take for example the prince who falls into the treacherous waters off the Atlantic coast and is assumed dead. His body is covered in an armor of scalloped shells when St James pulls him to safety. Entering the cathedral of St James was tantamount to entry into the Milky Way, a celestial realm of forgiveness and immortality, and a scallop shell worn on the hat or lapel of a pilgrim symbolized a successful quest to Santiago. Ownership of this shell took on divine meaning. It spelled the acquisition of a star. There is another legend too: eating scallops before reaching Santiago is bad luck for a pilgrim. I suddenly wonder whether that logic extends to wearing my new shell before entering Santiago's pearly gates.

The expanse of ochre wheat ahead is a perfect canvas for my wandering mind. A shower of rose petals and Botticelli's Venus float before my eyes, her seductive pose and sweep of long blond hair as she is blown on her scallop shell boat by the breath of wind gods. Born from the sea she is a proclamation of beauty and fertility, innocent and sexual. Pagans used the seashell as a symbol for a woman's vulva and it is on this primeval metaphor that Venus rides to shore.

I rub my fingers over the ribs of my gift and notice how perfectly it fits into the palm of my hand. It feels rough where the sea has buffeted its surface into pockmarks while its white underbelly is smooth as porcelain. This potent little shell holds yet another meaning. Some say its shape is like the back of an outstretched hand and serves as a reminder to pilgrims of the good deeds they must perform. So intrinsic was its message that many tombs of pilgrims contain more mollusc shells than bones.

'Hey peregrino! Hola.' Across a gully in a jungle green plot stands a man in blue overalls. Dwarfed by tall trellises of beans he takes his hat off to reveal a shock of silver hair. He waves. Is he waving to me? Of course he is, there's not another soul in sight. I wave back and let my pack drop by the road before scrambling down. He speaks not a word of English but our communication is filled with superlative 'oohs' and 'aahs' as I am taken on a tour of his garden. Rows of shallots, cucumber vines, radish, tomatoes, lettuce and flashes of orange and red dahlias scattered in between. It is a simple and warm encounter and I think to myself, in any other circumstance I would not risk heeding the call of a man in the middle of nowhere. But I feel part Peter Rabbit lured into a field

brimming with earthly delights and part privy to a Garden of Eden where there is no question of right or wrong just a natural exchange between two human beings.

He picks me two enormous ox heart tomatoes.

'Pepinos?' he asks as we walk towards the road, and he pulls two cucumbers from a vine. I carefully squeeze them into the top of my backpack. We shake hands and continue our appointed ways; he to the planting of seeds and their harvest and me the planting of footsteps, one in front of the other. It must be midday, my shadow has almost disappeared.

A close hot haze fills the air and the buoyancy of a morning filled with unexpected gifts turns into the bare boned sensation of the extra weight on my back. Who would think a couple of tomatoes and cucumbers could make such a difference? In front of me stretches an infinity of wheat broken occasionally by golden cubes of haystacks. Reclining in the cool shadow of one is an older woman, boots tossed to the side. Her bone china skin is flushed and strings of wet grey hair cling to her perspiring face. Her name is Johanna and she walks alone too. With our backs against the down and prickle of the hay we feast on the tomatoes, wiping away the warm juices dripping down our chins as overhead clouds roll in.

The Cogoticos de la Raicilla, a series of small perfectly conical hills studded with conifer trees breaks the tedium of straight and flat. They seem an almost mythic apparition of nature but then again it might just be heat and exhaustion setting in. Are those armored knights on horseback galloping towards a band of robbers? Or just a barking dog and a flock of geese taking flight? Silence again and then the soft sound of raindrops on vine leaves. Walking alone for hours at a time has keened my senses. The rain is only light but the random patter of it is as musical as a water sonata played upon leaf instruments and a dusty road. I poke out my tongue for a taste and feel each gentle thudding note whenever I catch a drop.

The path turns and crosses into another valley where, at last, the staccato rush of a stream and a small forest break the monotony. Monotony? My mind slips from one edge to the other. What happened to walking with no thought of arrival or need of memory or fantasy to pass the time? What about simply walking?

Early meditation retreats gave me a template for this natural junction between consciousness and environment. But learning this was often a difficult process, beginning before dawn and lasting late into the night – a passage of time that sometimes took on the dimension of one hellish eternity. My mind felt like a caged and cornered animal. It would cartwheel, ache with boredom, topple in on itself with exhaustion and then suddenly, as if out of the blue, turn transparent as light, resting on the rising and falling of the breath, aware of subtle movements within the body and within the room. This place of no reaction sounds passive but is in every sense active and energizing. I might be lucky enough to ride its wave for a few moments or the better part of an hour before slipping back into my habitual messing-about-in-a-boat-mind. What I want to be able to accept is that this is not a lesser place to be. It is grist for the mill. More elusive is the experience outside the sphere of both present and distracted minds. A state (or non-state) where there is dissolution of self and other and in its place – pervading pure awareness. To will such an experience, however, only serves to drive me further into the bowels of that boat risking tighter knots between the ropes of desire and aversion. Similar, I think, to wanting Los Arcos to appear round the next corner and then being disappointed when it is not.

'First there is a mountain, then there is no mountain, then there is,' I begin chanting the lines of a long ago song as I step into the shade of tall medieval houses lining the long main street of Los Arcos. Raindrops on stone sound different, more bass. I feel as though I am walking into a deserted wild west movie set as my footsteps echo off the walls. I feel like a bit of an echo myself, vacant, insubstantial and suddenly very tired.

Pilgrims mill about outside the *refugio*, washing flaps on the lines stretched across a pebbled yard and the *hospitalero*, an elderly Belgian volunteer, sits at his desk. He takes me through a series of rooms within rooms to one at the end with a door and only two double bunks. Jackpot. A young German girl and an elderly Danish couple are my room mates for the night.

The presiding Madonna of Los Arcos, I had read, is black. But when I adjust my eyes to the church's filtered light I find she has the olive skin of a gypsy. The geometric folds of her veil and skirt are gold like the half dome above where, in contrast to her tranquil gaze, a field of cavorting cherubs tumble in their celestial gravity free zone. On either side, painted in retablos, saints make grandiose gestures while souls drowning in purgatory look up beseechingly. St James is there, as always, this time with crystals for eyes. They twinkle as if to say: Your virtuous thoughts, pilgrim, hold only as much merit as your faith. When you walk with a pure heart while sharp stones press into the soles of your feet, only then, will the doors of heaven be open to you.

I look back to the dark face of Mary, her lips softly parted. 'The doors are open,' she says.

The Baroque and Rococo columns, heavy with the twisted gold of sculpted vines and flowers, are beautiful but I suddenly feel weighed down by such opulence. Give me the tangle of beans and cucumbers and the scorch of the sun. As I turn to leave I see a barricade at the back and behind its single red velvet rope is an open coffin. I check to see if there is anyone around before ducking underneath for a closer look. What I see jolts the air out of my lungs. Lying inside on perfectly white linen sheets edged with lace and a pillowcase embroidered in a cross hatch of red is the life size figure of a crucified Christ. Spattered blood drips from the palms of his hands, his knees and feet and the crown of thorns on his head. The detail of veins and muscles beat realism into his body but his face is gaunt and yellow with closed eyes and an open mouth as if his last breath was surrendered long ago. It is a macabre sight but apparently a common one in Catholic Spain. I imagine what it must be like for a child to see such an image for the first time and how it must shock into submission any God fearing soul.

I stumble through a side door, nauseous, and thank God for roses. In the middle of a Gothic cloister a profusion of pink, apricot and crimson blooms saturate the air with sweet, intense perfume. I follow a path in the shape of a cross that divides the garden into four neat squares. Tight perfect rosebuds and the fine veined petals of opened flowers brush against my face. I bend the stem of a pure white rose to take a deeper breath and am sharply reprimanded. A thorn pierces my finger. Pleasure and pain. The world I am born into, my mind and my body, all of it constantly changing.

Returning to the *refugio* I stop at a small tobacconist and paper shop. On a shelf of religious icons and painted china plates is a tattered journal of the history of Los Arcos and inside a picture of the Santa Maria Virgin. Lo and behold she is pitch black. It is an old photo, maybe 1950's, and I take it to the counter, excited by my discovery. The shop attendant looks at me with a stern, evasive expression and says he knows nothing. I am frustrated with my lack of Spanish but receive his message strong and clear. There is no point in persisting. At least though, I have found proof of a case where a black Virgin has been painted a lighter colour. Different people have different theories. There are those who insist all Madonnas were originally white and only as a result of fire or the ravages of time did their skins blacken. Others vow on their gypsy hearts that she was conceived black. Goddess devotees swear by the dark fertile earth that she remains true to her origin, a primal procreative symbol for the universe.

The Danish couple have prepared a supper of ham, cheeses, green salad and bread. We eat at a long table in the courtyard sharing stories about the day. Irish Rose is here, a gregarious Italian man, Ilse the young German girl from our room and a strangely intense Yugoslav man who is biking the Camino. Flaps of weathered and wrinkled skin hang from his forearms and chin and under a clinging lycra ensemble his body ripples with muscle He doesn't say much but whenever anyone speaks he leans towards them so there is hardly the breadth of a nose between. Is he deaf? The thick lenses of his glasses magnify his eyes into an unnerving owl-like glare. No one seems to know him but, as is the inclusive world of pilgrims, he is welcomed and fed.

I may have the luxury of a two bunk room, but it is false security thinking that a three to one female majority grants insurance from the snore factor. No sooner are lights out when, from the bed below, the most unladylike sound effects begin, as disconcerting as a room full of elephants. Ear plugs only dull my unnerving proximity to each gutteral-wrenching breath in and hiss-whistling breath out. Oblivious of her powers she sleeps into the night and eventually sleep creeps up on me until all of us are woken by the crash of thunder, fluorescent streaks of lightning, and rain pelting into our room. Ilse, visibly frightened, jumps up to close the window. I wiggle deeper into my sleeping bag and think of monsoon storms at home. This is a storm of tropical proportions and loud enough to drown the sound of a snore. I fall back to sleep.

Sleep so deep I did not hear the ambulance siren. The old Yugoslav man had some kind of seizure. One pilgrim said he died, another said he was in hospital. No one seemed to know.

8

Alice Through the Laundry
Los Arcos to Viana

There is always a cemetery at the end of a Spanish village. Within a few minutes of leaving sure enough I come to the walls and locked gate of Los Arcos's final resting place. Through its grilles I see Templar crosses and angels with broken wings. Strands of lichen hang from dead branches like a shroud and faded plastic flowers in stained jars lean against some of the tombs. Above the gate reads an inscription: I was what you are. You will be what I am.

I linger, holding on to the rusted ironwork of the gate, peering into this quiet rectangle of hidden bones and stone. What happened to the man who shared our meal last night? Does he have a family? Has he been set free from his pilgrimage? A light mist of rain begins to fall and I am sobered by the thought of how transitory life is no matter how much we lavish ourselves with clothes, books, gadgets, lovers, experiences – ultimately we come and go alone on this journey, this life-long pilgrimage, birth to death – but pare these layers of desires and accumulations and you are free from exterior, at least, baggage. Perhaps that's why I am waking each morning of this Camino with an almost naïve optimism. At last, unfettered from work, domesticity, a mailbox full of bills and a wardrobe of clothes – I mean how many shirts do you really need? Words like ridiculous, dreamer, impractical, slash and burn their way through my pious meanderings until eventually I let go of the graveyard gates and settle into the rhythm of walking. The simple truth is: what is happening now is all there is.

But like the taunt of some mischievous God I end up as a trio, alternately being overtaken, then overtaking, a couple of Italian women who talk loudly and incessantly not only to each other but into their constantly ringing mobile phones. My high and mighty ideas of being here-now are put to the test each time auld ang syne loops its loony way into my ears and across the fields we walk.

We remain inextricably linked until the village of San Sol. I take a detour up to the church of San Zoilo hoping that an interval in God's house will put some distance between us. But it is locked and instead I sit for a while on a low stone wall facing west, listening to the sounds of a village day beginning – the sweep of a broom on cobblestones, steel on steel as shutters are pulled up from shop windows, a late rising rooster and the whistle of a farmer behind a herd of cows in the valley below.

The steep rocky footpath, damp from the seepage of a spring, winds down before ascending again into Torres del Rio. This is the spring that, according to *Codex Calixtinus*, leads into a river poisonous to man and beast, and its fish too are no less dangerous to eat. It looks harmless enough but I notice a sign on a fountain at the foot of the hill warning, *non potable,* not drinkable.

From 1109 the monastery of Irache claimed Torres del Rio as its property until two centuries later its citizens were able to raise enough funds to buy their independence. In this period the Knights of the Holy Sepulchre in Jerusalem took charge of their church, San Sol. I become breathless as I climb the steep street and at first hardly notice it. Another locked door with unadorned columns either side. An old man points me around the corner to a house with a latched gate and a small garden of knee high zinnias. I knock the brass hand of its green front door. '*Por favor, iglesia?*' I ask the lady who answers. '*Momento,*' she whistles through a gap in her front teeth and returns with a key. Smiling she takes me by the elbow and we walk back to the church.

Inside is a perfectly proportioned octagonal chapel and I am instantly drawn to the middle of the room. Reminiscent of Eunate, it is all the more enchanting because it is empty. Its frame of Islamic style arches and cupola have a symmetry that seem to defy the gravity of stone and were it not for the crucifix, austere and angular, hanging in the altar niche I could be standing in a mosque. Nowadays it is often only in the marriage of architecture that poignant reminders of true religious harmony are found. I imagine, in this unadorned space, a service where Christians and Muslims prostrate together each to their own God for this is how both religions prayed thousands of centuries ago in Byzantine Europe.

I look up to the dome, across to the unadorned arches and crucifix and down to the smooth stones under my feet. What mortar is strong enough to hold all these elements together? Could it be as simple as Mathew's message: Do unto others as you would have others do unto you. Or Shantideva's words: Give away yourself for others, holding others dear as now you do yourself.

I feel the nape of my neck lengthen as if pulled by a fine string to the dome's centre. Thoughts arise and then burst like soap bubbles in this ingenious configuration of stone and space; science and spirit. Two chattering pilgrims enter and the spell is broken. The old lady returns to her table near the entrance with a vase of fresh zinnias and taps her fingers on the donation tin. With a shaky hand she dates the Santo Sepulcro stamp in my passport and I drop three euros into her fountain.

For the rest of the day I walk with Lara from the Netherlands; our paths had already crossed in Los Arcos and in Santo Sepulcro. She is a breathless mix of vivaciousness and Dutch pragmatism and we fall into an easy rhythm through the first vineyards of Rioja. Chemical spray or not we squeeze the flesh from skins of plum-dark grapes, sweet and spiced, into our mouths. I feel so comfortable with her that, when she describes seeing me for the first time combing my 'long beautiful hair' in the *refugio*, I can't help but recount a conversation I once had over a campfire. It was a Tibetan Buddhist retreat, one where we could talk freely between teachings. Among the group was a tall, animated and undeniably charming New Zealander. He also made flattering comments about my hair and I retaliated with, 'And how would you like to find a strand in your soup.' Was this my perverse sense of humour or some kind of self sabotage, or was I still reeling from the afternoon's teaching on impermanence?

'Existence is insubstantial,' our Tibetan Rinpoche had said before guiding us through a meditation. With eyes closed we began a methodical tour of our primary attachment, visualizing each component of our body: pus, blood and bone. Nudity took on a new dimension as we imagined, with xray eyes, two skeletons making love. And finally the worms crawling through eye sockets as we rotted in our graves.

Lara takes all of this in her stride, she is, I learn after my odd confession, a practicing psychotherapist living in the south of Spain. We laugh the kilometres away and I am taught the finer points of her favourite Spanish word, *claro*. It sits well on her tongue, crisp and matter of fact and can be used in most conversations as a way of affirming agreement or an understanding – clarity. There are words in Spanish that feel more succinct than their English equivalents. *Tranquilo* is another. Relax, don't worry.

We descend towards Viana down the Barranco Mataburros, donkey killing ditch, a rough loose stoned path collapsing into potholes and no path at all as the gully erodes either side. I imagine the patience of a medieval pilgrim being tested as he hauls a cantankerous donkey behind, that is if the donkey had been lucky enough to make it this far, given the number of poisonous Navarran rivers. Though we carry the entire weight of our possessions on our backs, two feet and two poles seem a far preferable alternative to the addition of four stubborn hooves and long, laid back donkey ears.

Viana's plaza borders the Church of Santa Maria de la Asuncion, also home to a small *refugio* and *hospitaleros* Yves and Juliette, a gentle French couple reveling in their role as surrogate parents. Yves leads me up a narrow spiral of stairs to two dormitories. The smallest has only five mats on the floor, all empty bar one taken by a young girl. I choose a place by the window and hope for the best. Juliette calls from the kitchen, she is cooking and we are all invited to dinner. She hands me a colander of fresh boiled eggs. What simple pleasure it is to hold them. Their shells slip off in easy ribbons and I drop them one by perfect one, soft, dimpled and white, into a bowl.

In the plaza's café old men sit on cracked leather-upholstered stools at the bar, soccer blares on television and cigar smoke funnels around the plastered ceiling while black storm clouds build around the church spires outside. I order a pacharan on ice, now an obligatory ritual at the end of each day's walk, thanks to the inebriated regales of Hemingway in his tales of Basque bull fights and fishing. Today I raise my glass to Viana for it was here in 1816 that the first bottle of Pacharan was produced, a smooth marriage of blackthorn berries, a few coffee beans and a vanilla pod, infused in a spirit of anise. I savor each unhurried sip as I watch a rush of elegant pedestrians, umbrellas at the ready, making their way down the medieval streets. *Muy noble, muy ilustre*, very noble, very illustrious, says Viana's fifteenth century emblem. It is true.

Through a maze of narrow lanes is another church, San Pedro, once a thirteenth century Gothic glory and now no more than a skeleton. Inside its walls is a park and I imagine God taking kindly to grass for his floor and a thunder clapping sky for a dome. Nobody is here, just me, a few errant plastic bags and a deflated ball. Rain starts in heavy sparse drops and I make a hasty retreat to the *refugio*. Lofty thoughts of God and nature are of no avail when I look to the mat beside mine. Close enough to be my dearly wedded husband lies a rotund man with the flushed cheeks of a yodeler and ominously huge nostrils. He greets me with an aloof grunt and rolls over to face, on the next bed, his hiking partner, an equally portentous male. You take a gamble and you suffer the consequence. I slink back down the stairs filled with overwhelming dread at the prospect of their all night serenades.

Bells for mass begin to ring – maybe a few prayers will help. Inside thunder is replaced by the lilt of baroque music, each note traveling high as the highest nave, elevating me from despair into the realm of harp plucking angels. The fact it comes from a small cassette recorder hidden behind the altar does nothing to dampen my illusion. I tiptoe away from the main altar to a deserted transept and the figure of Saint Catherine, the audacious and beautiful one, carrying her palm leaf of martyrdom. A clap of thunder muffles its way through the stone walls and I imagine her tied to the infamous Catherine Wheel after denying Maxentius, emperor of Rome, her hand in marriage. His command for her torture on this cruel spiked wheel was rendered futile by avenging angels who threw bolts of lightening at it, shattering it to pieces. When she was eventually beheaded, milk not blood flowed from her neck. Considering this macabre legend I feel a tingle at the nape of my own neck but it's just the cool trickle falling from my rain soaked hair.

The priest calls all pilgrims and I leave my hiding place to join them in a prayer for our safe journey to Santiago. He invites us on a tour of the cathedral's inner sanctum and we walk single file past relics of old bones in dusty urns and cobwebbed displays of bishops' vestments behind grimy glass panels – thick robes of burgundy velvet embroidered with gold thread. In a room vaporous with furniture polish, priceless paintings line the walls. The Black Virgin of Guadalupe has pride of place in a gilded frame at the head of a long table lined with high backed tapestry chairs. Here we are privy to the secret realm of priests and clergy, a place where man transforms himself into a messenger of God. With a ritual prayer he will don a cassock of black linen, and with a kiss, a silken stole and a starched white collar. He is ready now for the sacrament of reconciliation behind the grilles of oak paneled booths at the back of the church.

The relics return to sleep and we bustle out the door replete with history and hungry for the spoils of Juliette's kitchen. A young priest joins us at the *refugio's* table set with bowls of hot soup, thick with beans and marbled chunks of *jamon*. Flagons of wine and slices of bread are passed with pâté and sausage followed by a platter of the eggs now halved and wobbling delectably between tomato quarters topped with sprigs of basil. A feast of home cooking a *la Espanol* with a touch of French flair. For dessert, a salad of melons, apples, oranges and syrupy prunes.

Over our meal the priest introduces himself and we follow suit around the table, like a quick world tour: Italy, Spain, Australia, Ireland, Brazil, Australia, Spain, Germany. The last introduction is from Austria, my neighbor for the night. His voice is soft but the husky undertones and constant clearing of throat alert me again to what lies ahead. I am exhausted and ache all over from today's walk and want nothing more than sleep. I make a silent pact to somehow charm my way out of that room.

As everyone leaves I summon courage to ask Yves if I can put my mattress here on the dining room floor. He looks at me askance and hesitates. I quiver in my sandals – this request obviously at odds with pilgrim etiquette. But I am mistaken, he introduces me to

Guillamo who is walking back to Rome having already completed the journey to Santiago. Guillamo is a loner, evident from his silence at the table and downcast eyes. A half smile crosses his lips as we shake hands before he retreats towards the corner of the room and turns to wheeze a loud hacking cough into his hands. Yves looks at me and shrugs his shoulders, 'Actually Guillamo is sleeping here.' Try as I might I cannot hide my despair, then Yves continues, 'But you can have the kitchen, as long as you wake before breakfast.' I thank him as though I've just been offered a five star room in a *parador*.

The priest invites us to a 'little concert and prayer' in the choir stalls of the church. We follow him to the drying room at the end of the corridor, a quaint box of space strung from top to bottom with pilgrim washing. I part lines of socks and underwear to reach the door on the other side. Feeling a little like Alice Through the Looking Glass I enter another world, candlelit and ethereal. Two lamps illuminate the main retablo way below us, a wavering golden light in the dark womb of the central nave. It is as if all the apostles have come to life as they flicker in the privacy of night when the main doors of Santa Maria are shut.

Seven hundred years of prayer and the scents of frankincense, oak and candle wax permeate the air. We settle back into the acoustic arms of Santa Maria listening to the priest play his guitar. My mind weaves in and out of his music until it seems each wandering thought floats with each resonant chord into a sea of calm, devoid of self. A blessing prayer is read in turn by Spanish, French and German pilgrims then the priest flicks a light switch and we watch the gathered apostles dissolve into darkness. I make my way back into the time tunnel, breathing in the lemony tang of laundry soap, and am reminded a washed mind is just as important as clean clothes for tomorrow's road. I make my bed on the kitchen floor and am rocked to sleep by the lullaby of the refrigerator.

9

Heaven has a Price
Viana to Ventosa

Fig branches hang over the fences of old stone houses, low enough to brush my cheeks, ancient branches laced with lichen and heavy with fruit. This leafy Eden at the foot of Viana's fortress walls, the scent of its late summer gardens and ripening fruit, transports me back to holidays in my grandparent's garden. Nin, in her apron with a bowl balanced on her hip, reaches up into the fig tree they planted half a century ago for the plumpest and purplest ones, harvesting just enough for a year's supply of jam. Grandpa is busy in his shed on the other side of the hills hoist. Oiled tools line the walls above cans of paint, all a pale pistachio green for some reason, the same paint used for the lattice surrounding their Queenslander's verandah and every piece of wicker furniture he can lay his hands on. Fig harvest was also the time

Grandpa raided the hives he had scattered over the paddocks around Laidley. Dozens of frames would be stacked in the middle of his shed, thick with clotted gold, ready for the extractor. He was always cracking jokes, rocking back and forward in his shoes, thumbs at rest in the braces of his baggy trousers. 'Come here, chickens,' he would say to my brother, sister and me placing a square of honeycomb into our cupped hands. 'Don't tell the Queen Bee.' Leaving a sticky trail behind us we'd run terrified and giggling up and into the forked branches of the fig tree, chewing our honeycomb gum in between mouthfuls of the figs Nin had missed.

Here in the privacy of a Spanish lane, I am seduced again and pick a handful of mauve-seamed figs for breakfast. Breaking each one in half, the mythical womb of Gaia, a galaxy of soft purple seeds. And it is into the origins of Gaia I go, respite from the nine flat kilometres stretching between me and Logrono. The gentle unhurried pleasure of a medieval town and backyard gardens give way to wastelands of bitumen, a soulless artificial lake, smoke spewing factories and the drone of traffic running parallel to the path.

I adjust the pack to my hips. Gone is the familiar padding of flesh; I now need the cushioning of an extra shirt between me and the waist belt as a buffer. All this walking is making me lean, nonetheless my girth remains on the side of generous, and at the ripe age of nearly fifty I'm at last beginning to feel pleased to be shaped like a pear. Like those terracotta figurines unearthed from

Paleolithic sites across Europe – well maybe not quite so endowed – those pendulous breasts, prodigious hips and pregnant bellies. Earth Mothers. Sustenance still had intimate links with the natural world when these primordial images were fashioned by the Greeks into pantheons of gods and goddesses. They began with Gaia rising from the earth, her immaculate conception through sea and sky the precursor to a mythical cast of archetypes.

I look to each of the four directions and see only denuded land; a plain that must once have been pounded by the hooves of antelope and deer. I think of Artemis, wild goddess of the hunt and of the moon, guaranteeing her people a cache of meat from migrating herds, and of Demeter bringing to life seeds planted each spring equinox into thawing soil.

Nothing grows on the barren ground around me and my feet are beginning to burn from an unforgiving concrete path. Every joint jars and slams against the other. A pilgrim greets me from a small rise where he sits chewing on a straw of grass as he vacantly surveys the sprawl ahead of us, a highway through countless car yards. I am tempted to rest with him but continue. Driven. I'm not sure whether it is this environment or the accumulation of kilometres and long days but I am tired and hanker to arrive, anywhere but here.

An operatic voice booms in the distance resembling something between Figaro and a German drinking song. A pair of dogs begin to howl and suddenly I am confronted by a large mutt. He licks both my knees effusively with a wet rasp of tongue then turns as if to say, 'Come on, she's waiting.' In the shade of a fig tree and two beach umbrellas an old lady stamps the *credencials* of a group of pilgrims. Their lanky lead singer sits on the stone fence opposite, lapsed into a heart wrenching version of O Sole Mio. I turn to Felicia, for this is the famous Felicia, grand matron of the Camino, who looks up at me with twinkling eyes. '*Hola peregrino.*' She rolls up the sleeves of her faded blue cardigan and slides me a bowl of figs and a glass of ice cold water.

For more than sixty years Felicia has lived in the low roofed ramble of stone buildings behind her offering *Higos, Agua y Amor,* Figs, Water and Love, to each and every pilgrim entering Logrono. She adjusts her glasses to the bridge of her nose and stamps my passport. Her grey hair is tomboy short. Loose strands of silver wisp about her plump, kind face. I leave a donation and shoulder my pack; my footsteps down the hill fall strangely into the rhythm of the baritone's song and it takes me another fifteen minutes before I can get the tune out of my head. But the distraction of it is no help for my unsettled mind. I am at odds with myself today.

I cross the bridge over the river Ebro, no longer a lyrical mountain stream but a river marked by industry. I feel a bit the same. I turn into Calle de San Gregorio to find two blue arrows pointing in opposite directions so I rest on a bench and pull out my tattered map. The way ahead: six kilometres of cement… brings me face to face with the plotting of a pseudo pilgrim. I contemplate… a bus ride.

The familiar tap tapping of sticks rings off the cobblestones and I look up to see a large disheveled woman lumbering towards me. 'Do you know which is way?' she asks in a breathless whisper, her face flushed with heat and a hint of desperation. 'I am look for bus station. She expires into a heave adjusting her giant pack back into the middle of her shoulders. 'Bus station?' I say, is this a message from God?

We trundle into the main square and find a café with views across to the Church of Santa Maria la Redonda. Its barricaded doors are plastered with signs, closed for restoration. I am not even disappointed. The idea of a deck chair, a cat stretch and soak in the morning sun is far more appealing. We eat apple pastries with our coffee and discuss the politics of travel. My guilt at the idea of taking a bus is assuaged by Hilde. Her ankles have swollen beyond recognition and she will bus the thirty kilometres to Najera to rest for a few days. 'It doesn't matter how Santiago comes to you. In your heart, is important.' Hilde's English is thickly accented with her native Belgian. Her quiet demeanor and what seems an unconditional acceptance of circumstance puts me at ease.

My yoyo mind stops bouncing and I see the extent to which untamed thoughts have sapped my energy. How – this road is ugly, too much traffic, why don't I catch a bus, but that's cheating – feeds upon itself until I am walking across my own bed of nails. But then to judge even this state is to be trapped by it. Better to see it and let it drop away. See it again and let it drop away. I remember one exercise given during a meditation retreat. We followed our Tibetan teacher outside and circumnavigated the temple. Above his head he tilted a mirror, inviting us to watch the reflection of sky in its frame. Sometimes we stopped and waited as a drift of cloud passed across its square of blue. 'The mirror is pure awareness,' he said. 'Clouds are your thoughts. Watch them and as they go, let them go.'

And like two clouds Hilde and I gather up our belongings and disappear from the plaza. We cross a park where old men sit in threes and fours, coiffed ladies teeter on heels toward cafes and boutiques and business men in tailored suits swing briefcases as they stride to work. Rush hour in Logrono. We walk against the tide to the bus depot, Hilde in her floppy hat and baggy trousers one leg rolled up to her shins and the other unrolling to a nonexistent ankle and me with a tangle of hair, my shirt unironed and inside out and oh so unfashionable knickerbockers.

I hang on to the seat in front of me and my eyes glaze over as the bus lurches onto the street, its engine coughing a blanket of exhaust. It is the strangest feeling riding this green beast, accentuated whenever we pass a walking pilgrim. I see two in the distance heading west, their bodies leaning forward into each pitch of their poles and my feet ache to touch the ground again instead of this shuddering steel. Thirteen kilometres to Navarette. It would have taken me three or four hours but instead I alight at its plaza in twenty minutes. I wave to Hilde until the bus disappears.

A group of Japanese pilgrims greet me with a perfunctory bowing of heads as they swing out the doors of Iglesia de La Asuncion and I swing through, into a church containing one of Spain's most outstanding Baroque retablos. My eyes slowly adjust to the dark of this cavernous space and I catch glints of gold and a dim pantheon of saints, angels and men. The entrance door creaks open and the sound of a coin clinking into a box amplifies into an echo. Bright spotlights switch on. For a fee we have a view of heaven.

Centred on a luminous stage is Mary in a white veil with God a giddy height above surveying the retinue of saints in multi-storeys of niche arches layered between panels of oil paintings whose depth of cobalt and vermilion look as rich now as it must have four hundred years ago. I am drawn in like a guest, moving from room to room with my eyes until eventually I feel as though I am wrapped in the same gold suffusing the saints. The light timer ticks away and I return again to the woman preparing for ascension, from the miraculous to the divine.

In the Book of Revelations, Mary is described as a woman with child, travailing in birth, and pained to be delivered. She is clothed with the sun, and the moon under her feet and upon her head a crown of twelve stars. Despite the raiments of a goddess she labored as a woman, blood staining her straw bed, so the son of God could be born into the lives of men. How then to reinstate Mary as Immaculate Queen of Heaven? It is hard to believe that her Assumption was given papal decree in only 1950 under pressure of a petition signed by eight million people. And what does official acknowledgment, of something already so fundamental to the faithful, mean anyway? In every church along the Camino prayers are sung to Christ and to St James for the safe journey of pilgrims. But here I touch the silver body of Tara against my skin and follow, in the last seconds of light, the gilded path leading Mary heavenwards. I am reminded again that all the comfort and protection I need emanates from these two female archetypes.

Somewhere in the retablo is a statue of the Senora del Sagrario who, it is said, has a splinter of the True Cross embedded in her body but before I can find her the light extinguishes with a clunk. I fumble for some coins but in the end give up and instead squeeze out of my pack and find a pew to sit. Enveloped in the dark I feel the pulse behind my eyes fade as the tension of looking for something subsides.

I remember my first experience of guilt. I stole a tomato from our neighbor's garden. She complained and I was reprimanded with a warning, 'God watches everything you do. If you sin you must ask for forgiveness.' The meek and mild Jesus I had dutifully prayed to for blessings each night at the foot of my bed was now my redeemer. He had died on that cross for me. This was bittersweet. My misdemeanors may escape the scold of a parent but never would I be free from the judgment of the man up there. It was my first conscious taste of alienation: a splitting into two that was to be vicariously compounded each time my parents fought. As I became more aware of the world outside my estrangement grew. I was thirteen when newspaper pictures of gaunt children, their eyes fly-ridden and bellies distended, arrived on our kitchen table and that night, an assault of aerial shots of an Armageddon flickered black and white into our middle class lounge room. Biafra 1967. The next day I climbed into my parents' bed and wept in my mother's lap. She searched for an answer but could only stroke my forehead and it was then I began to notice the face of the Buddha.

'He comes from India,' my grandmother told me, 'the one place I have always wanted to visit but your grandpa doesn't like to travel.' A seed was planted and a decade later I dived headfirst into my first meditation retreat and a love affair with the country my grandmother could never know. What a revelation to find myself cross-legged on a cushion listening for the first time to the Eightfold Path, a teaching essential to Buddhist practice. There clearly was the possibility to understand suffering and the road was mapped. Those were the heady days of my beginners mind, a bit like a honeymoon, before the realization of how infinite the layers of mind are and how each time I get back onto the cushion I start again. Breathing in. Breathing out. As I sit in this darkened church another piece of the puzzle slots into place.

Where do all the preconceived notions I hold come from? From my grasping mind; its need to know and to label so I feel safe and in control. Or should I say, so I think I am in control. But all this does is separate me from direct experience, moment to moment, of the constantly changing relationship between my five senses and the world. Can I see gold without naming it? Taste a grape without already thinking about putting the next one into my mouth? Feel the pain in my shoulder without wanting it to disappear? Listen to a high pitched snore in the bunk bed above without the tension of waiting for the next one? Responsibility for my happiness lies entirely within me. And my suffering? Each sensory encounter invites a response: like, dislike or neutral. Two of these responses open up a Pandora's box of possibilities for as long as one thought feeds into the next.

A Tibetan teacher once gave a talk on suffering and explained how wisdom and compassion are two streams within Buddhist teaching. One without the other, he said, is inherently flawed. Understanding suffering, whether it comes through long hours sitting on my meditation cushion or in the midst of a Biafra, can only evolve through a commitment to, and, simultaneously, complete acceptance of each present moment. Of who I am or who the one is that stands there in front of me. Real compassion is not a sentiment, it is deeply endowed with wisdom, with patience every time I open that box of possibilities. Open it mindfully, step into it with kindness, with a love as perfect as I can invoke. One step at a time.

I remember the inscription over Los Arcos's graveyard

gate. I was what you are. You will be what I am. All of life is a mirror. I am held in the world every breath I take and I surrender to it each time I breathe out.

Even with my pack back on I feel five pounds lighter. I trace my way through a maze of streets down to the bottom of Cerro Tedeon, past a shop front displaying ceramic bowls and jugs thrown from the red clays of Navarette's soil, the same clay turned and fired since Roman times. Beyond the town's fringe of concrete apartment blocks and rundown houses stretch vineyards and a horizon of hills honeycombed with *bodegas* where wines are cellared and mushrooms cultivated. I jaywalk a crossroad and greet an old man sitting at a bus shelter. 'El Camino?' I ask holding out my hands. But he ignores my question and instead strings commendable clicking sounds together between tongue and teeth, nodding his head in approval at the sight of a lone woman walking the Way.

'Me,' he pats himself on the chest, '*sesentiocho anos*,' and together we count out six sets of hands plus eight. He then draws himself up to full height and, drinking from an imaginary cup, asks 'You, *el vino?*'

Ventosa is another seven kilometres and it must be close to midday. '*Si, mucho*, I like.'

'*Valle*, come,' and I follow him back across the road to an old garage. The saloon style doors open on half attached rusted hinges. He strides over to a barrel and fills an empty jam jar with homemade Rioja rosé. As I take my first sip he makes fists with his hands and smiles as if to say this will make me strong for the road.

'*Si*, I make,' he says and I thank him. He calls me over to another barrel and slides off the lid. I peer down into its dark and hear an ooze of slathering and squelching, an orgy of fat black snails slipping and sliding over each other. There must be a hundred of them. I let out a pitiful yelp and back away. '*Uno moment*o,' he chuckles and pulls from a cupboard an example of Navarette's red clay ceramics. With a lewd grin he holds up a water pipe, molded into the shape of two balls at the base of a very erect spout. My sixty eight year old host's eager allusion to his prowess leaves me too mollified to even consider a reply. I check the doors are still open, take one last sip then make a hasty retreat. I can't believe I actually thanked him for the wine and curse myself. Worse than a fish thanking a fisherman for his bait. I fast track it to the end of town, walking my humiliation till it burns itself out into the open air of the hills.

Entering Ventosa, where the old stone and rendered concrete homes tower three storeys high, where in the listless heat of a late summer afternoon not a soul is awake, it is as though time has turned in upon herself. Is there really life behind those doors or am I moving through a landscape as ephemeral as the hollow sound of my boots and poles?

The wind vane atop San Saturnino's bell tower is still as the air and the *refugio* nestling against its fortress wall, with a red tiled roof and red geraniums spilling from each window box, has an open door. A copper fountain tarnished to deep ultramarine by time and light sits at the entrance, its water pouring into an elegant scalloped bowl. A breath of wind creaks the wind vane and rustles through a lavender hedge sending wisps of clean sharp perfume my way.

A Spanish pilgrim renovated this *refugio* four years ago after walking the Camino fourteen times. On the fifteenth he fell near Ventosa injuring his back and decided to stay. I take off my pack and hand my passport over to the man at the desk. Is this him I wonder? His manner is officious, bordering on stern, but all around him I feel care and attention to the smallest detail. Behind the desk is a framed piece of Japanese calligraphy and near the stairs a photo of Paulo Coelho dressed in full pilgrim regalia. I choose a top bunk by the window closest to the lavender. Breathing in the spritzed air I know I will sleep well tonight. There is rose scented pump soap in the bathroom, a real bathroom, and I feel like a queen. Above a sparkling white vanity is the first mirror I've seen in days and though there is not an aristocratic bone in the face that looks back at me the steaming water pummeling my shoulders and pouring down my aching back washes any care, queenly or common, away.

It is mid-afternoon and Ventosa's one bar is empty except for a couple of farmers. I order a nip of pacharan and take my chair out to the village's small triangular plaza. An old couple sit together on the balcony of an apartment on the other side, framed by the leaves of a grapevine, terracotta pots of geraniums and strings of peppers. Capsicums are synonymous with the end of summer and from a large bowl at their feet the man picks them up, one by one, and hands them to his wife. She pierces each with a large needle and threads them onto string. It will snow here in a few months and I imagine a Riojan potato and chorizo casserole bubbling on their stove, sweetly spiced with these same red peppers, soaked and sliced or ground into an earthy paprika. There is a rhythm in their work and an intimacy that stings my heart and I suddenly crave David's company. The sun inches its way to the horizon and the couple slip into shadow. In this small village their marriage is marked once more by a season's harvest as they move towards their own winter. I want to share the pleasure of the sun on my skin with David before it disappears. What is the season that marks the passage of us? It is strange to think we have known each other for more than half our lives; it feels more like spring than a ripening of summer.

 I wander back to the *refugio* and curl up on my bed pretending the pillow I hold is him. I take a deep breath of lavender and begin to see how my own lack of identity prevents me from growing in our relationship. It is as though my dash across Spain is a statement of independence, a cry for recognition. And what is this guilt I feel for the days that have slipped by without thinking of him? All it does is split me further into two; away from wholeness. My alienation spins full circle into gratitude for him. I am no longer at odds with our departure, how he dropped me at the station with a kiss that barely brushed my cheek and left before the airport bus pulled away. My world crumbled. It was a tug-of-war time, those final weeks of preparation. I knew he did not want me to go but I had become like a woman possessed. If I had succumbed to his silent disapproval I think the dichotomy raging inside me would have shredded any hope for a relationship. So why am I grateful? In every email David writes there is an empathy that permeates my being. It is as if the words flickering on the screen give me everything I have ever asked of him. 'Tell me that you love me,' I would sometimes say, 'just once.' But he never did. 'Actions speak louder,' he'd reply, or respond with a smile, a tickle and a bear hug. And really, how can I understand him without first knowing myself?

'I love you,' I whisper from one side of the world to the other, squeeze my pillow and fall asleep.

Through siesta-soaked eyes I notice a small picture of Ventosa's Virgin in the office and ask if it is possible to see her but it is not, she is ensconced inside San Saturnino and nobody knows who has the key. Someone taps me on the shoulder. Lara! We link arms and climb up to the church anyway, hoping for a divine intervention. Hope however is not enough to penetrate these windowless walls. I can only imagine the songs and celebration filling Ventosa each July when she is carried from her thirteenth century fortress into the streets; the golden ears of wheat are ready for harvest and a dance is given in her honour. The Dance of the White Virgin.

Lara calls herself quasi-catholic and we discuss the

parallels of Pagan fertility rites, a Virgin and a village harvest. I remember the grass of wheat in the arms of Eunate's Madonna and pictures of Demeter, Goddess of Harvest, carrying her sheath of grain, printed on packs of biodynamic bread at home. The seeds of ripe wheat must die before giving life – a fitting symbol appropriated by the church. From the Roman Book of Prayers, clergy chant: Mary the Grape, Christ the Sacred Wine, Mary the Wheat, Christ the Living Bread. And each Sunday, those familiar words, how can I forget: Take this, this is my Body. And I would let the paper thin wafer melt on my tongue never stopping to think beyond the literal version fed to us in preparation for our first communion.

The sun drops from the edge of our world and a cool wind whips up from the plains. We wrap ourselves with our arms for warmth and head down to the bar. The menu is a creased page full of variations on one theme: garlic sausage, fried eggs, chips, salad, bread and wine. At the table beside us sits a father and daughter. At first we don't recognize each other. Our transitory meeting this morning began in darkness. It was Sebastian who dropped coins into the light box at Navarette. I thank him for illuminating all that glory and we fill our four glasses. '*Salud!*' To a serenade of eggs spluttering in oil Lara trills away with Sebastian in her animated Spanish while I get to know Ana in faltering English. She is a shy nineteen, taking a break from her studies in Barcelona. From time to time Sebastian looks across to her with a mix of tenderness and pride, encouraging her attempts at

English, keeping her close in the fold of family for one last year before she flies. Wine flows, the night progresses, and the bar fills with farmers and cigarette smoke.

The sleepers in my room are silent. An absolving silence. A cool breeze blows in the window and I close my eyes. A black dog bounds out from beneath the lavender bush and from the rustle of silvery leaves white butterflies, hundreds of them, fly from cover into the night. Quiet as snowflakes. In their wake fall papery cocoons. I turn towards them and lie still as a chrysalis. Butterflies cover my eyelids, fluttering their wings against the warmth of my breath and the last sticky traces of their birth evaporates into the air. I wait and watch as they leave me for one night of stars. They separate each from the other and disappear into the Milky Way. Riding on the current of this shimmering river is a woman swathed in white silk, dancing. In her left hand she carries, not wheat but a lotus flower. The thumb and ring finger of her hand join to make the shape of a delicately opening eye, a gesture of union, compassion and wisdom. White Tara dances through my sleep.

10

The Falcon and the Dove
Ventosa to Azofra

Handel preludes the dawn. Violins, trumpets and a choir rouse us, 'Hallelujah.' Soft fingers of a god brush the sleep from my face. Breakfast is laid out in the dining room downstairs: homemade preserves, buttered toast and freshly brewed coffee. We eat silently together, each absorbed in the footsteps of yesterday and those ahead of us today, reminded, it seems, by the angelic voices that fill this house, of our reasons for rising so early to join the Way.

I tie my shoe laces slowly. Double the knot. Pick up my pack and swing it behind me, centre the weight of it and adjust the waist belt. Each movement takes on a slow, detached quality and I savor a certain sweetness that comes in the simplest of acts. There is an uncluttered Zen like feeling here, more sanctuary than dormitory, a quiet that infuses my preparation.

On previous Vipassana retreats, by day five or six, we have all slowed down to a snail's pace. An outsider could be forgiven mistaking us for a bunch of heavily medicated inmates. But entering a world devoid of speech and eye contact allows us to fine tune our awareness. We begin to notice the subtlest thoughts rising bubble-like to the surface, and from these the intentions that are born. The deeper we go the clearer it becomes: our lives are conditioned by habit. Opening a door for example. I walk towards the door and as I come close to it my hand automatically reaches for the handle. But is it automatic? There is intelligence and habit at play in this barest of acts. I touch the handle and turn it. I push it open. And my walking, even this, is something learned then taken for granted. At least until the ability to walk is taken away.

I look up to the wall behind the *hospitalero* who all this time sits unobtrusively at his desk. 'Who is she?' I ask him pointing to the postcard of a woman, her hand resting gracefully over her round belly, demure and knowing at the same time. 'You will find her in Leon,' he replies, in a voice empty of any inflection. I thank him and walk out the door, his dark pool eyes and her gaze, pregnant with possibility, imprinted on my mind.

I gather handfuls of spiked dew from the lavender hedge to wash my face and run through my hair. Rain during the night has turned the clay path to shining umber and soon I am walking up into a mist that drips like a fine shower from the oaks, kermes and gall trees. Sharp spikes of dwarf juniper cling to the rocky ground either side of the track as it narrows and climbs toward Alto de San Anton.

Hundreds of stone cairns dot the hillside, from elaborate monoliths taunting gravity to one or two pebbles on a boulder. There are communal cairns growing like a litany, each new placement of rock beseeching the company of another until nothing but a piece of gravel could be balanced on top, and others that have been created at one time as one complete prayer. I find a smooth round stone and choose a pyramid of three rocks. The air is as soaked with prayer as it is with mist.

From the pinnacle of San Anton I can see Najera, seven and a half kilometres of plain away, nestled into red cliffs and cut into two by a silver sliver of water. It's an easy descent down from the clouds and I lose myself in the rhythm of one foot following the other until I meet an old couple by the side of the road. She wears a floral apron over her black dress and a thick pair of orthopedic stockings. So absorbed is she in her task that I am invisible but from her husband, who rests against his walking stick at the edge of the field, I receive a gentlemanly tip of beret. I stand beside him watching this age old Riojan pastime of harvesting snails. With a trowel she digs into the soil then gently levers them out. Her husband regards each chink of snail hitting the bottom of their metal bucket with an air of serious satisfaction. He turns to me, rubbing his portly stomach, '*Tomate, chorizo y escargot...bueno, mucho bueno.*' What I would give to join them tonight for a bowl of Riojan stew. Chorizo sausage and fresh snails simmered to tender with vine ripened tomatoes.

In the back streets of Najera the only signs of life come from small café windows where workers blow smoke rings and sip short black coffee before their day begins. Paint peels from empty shop fronts and my reflection in their windows is a grimy blur. From Romans to Muslims to Christians and Jews, Najera has weathered cycles of prosperity and decline; the most recent being its fame as a furniture making town. Across the River Najerilla lies the heart of old Najera, a shadowy maze of narrow cobbled streets looking as ancient as its sandstone back drop. Gnarled conifers and oaks cling to the cliff tops of rock faces luminous and vermilion in the morning sun. Caves, like vacant black eyes sculpted from centuries of water and wind, keep constant vigil over Najera's red tiled roofs and ochre walls, and I am a pilgrim passing through in my clay-caked boots, for a brief moment absorbed into its sienna tones.

A falcon in pursuit of a dove once flew into one of these caves. The falconer, King Garcia, the miracle goes, found his bird sitting placidly with the cooing dove before an ancient wood carved Virgin and child. At her feet was a jar of fresh lilies and a lamp. I imagine him, breathless after his climb, dropping his leather gloves to the ground and falling to his knees. To celebrate he founded the Order of Knights of the Jar and built the Monasterio de

Santa Real to mark the spot but today, pasted onto the dark wooden panels of a Gothic door, I read another Closed for Restoration notice. Inside, the tombs of kings and queens lie so their feet are embedded in the mountain and outside, I stand for a moment locked into my own frustration. This was one place I had wanted to visit.

Out from the shadows of Najera, through a ravine lined with pine trees, my feet sink into a soft bed of pine needles. For centuries so many quests for holy grails and alabaster jars. Why and where do they lead? How is it possible that in the etheric trace of Christ's blood or a Virgin's tears there lies the possibility of salvation? What are we granted by walking eight hundred kilometres to the tomb of a saint? What am I doing? 'Clack, clack,' is the answer from above, a stork fusses over her nest precariously balanced on the monastery's bell tower. Above her a wind vane shifts an inch and I come back to the real meaning of today: moving forward and the clean scent of pine needles released under the weight of my footsteps.

The first house I pass in Azofra has a vine leaf trellis dripping with grapes and two storeys rendered in clay. This is the colour of La Rioja, of mountains eroding into red rivers and summer floods bringing mineral rich waters to thirsty vineyard soils. It is a colour you can taste: soft, mellow and full-bodied with a vanilla bouquet. What more enticement do I need to put down my pack and take off my boots?

Concrete benches are planted like minimalist stone

sculptures in the gravel garden of Azofra's brand new *refugio* and who should be sitting on one but Ana and her father. I make my way over to them in an elaborate circular dance following a very precise arrangement of white paving stones. I feel a bit like Monsieur Hulot tapping his way to the front door of his sister's house and want to vamp it up but decorum prevails. This *refugio* is maintained by the local council, not the church, and is a sleek update to a tradition begun by Dona Isabel in 1168 when she established the first pilgrim hospice here.

The doors open at one o clock so we find a restaurant for lunch. Sebastian tastes the house white then orders soda water. I look on askance as he explains if the wine is not good, best to dilute. Perhaps this is one of those impatient wines that has skipped the oak barrel for quick maturation in a stainless steel vat. When in Spain... We make merry on soda water bubbles, eat crisp lettuce with our grilled *pollo* and converse in a faltering concertina of French, English and Spanish.

I send praises to the council of Azofra. There are only two beds in each simply appointed room and to my delight I am to share with Johanna of the haystack and shared tomato – how many days ago did we meet? We are comfortable in each other's silence as we unpack our belongings and make our beds before sleeping away the afternoon.

The bar in the plaza is full to bursting. My ritual pacharan on ice seeps slow and warm into my muscles. Half the men are smoking fat cigars and the group beside me sip an amber liqueur of citrus and fire from shot glasses. A matchstick hangs from the corner of my neighbour's mouth; his boots are coated in dust and the stubble on his cheeks looks a few days old. After a morning tending the fields, their tractors cooling behind the green doors of each farmhouse shed, locals drink to the afternoon and to the crops hanging heavy on their vines. Half the world is here and making so much noise I can hardly hear myself think. Over there in the corner with a face as sunburned as the farmers is my Austrian bedfellow, the one I left for a fridge way back in Viana, smoking tailormades and playing cards. Another pacharan comes from behind and I look up from my notebook into the mischievous eyes of a tall pilgrim. Where have I seen him before? One glass is sufficient, for medicinal purposes, but I cannot refuse and soon my aching body feels as though it has soaked for a long hour in a hot anise scented bath.

My fair skinned donor sits outside with an olive skinned girl and they invite me to dinner back at the *refugio*. His voice is familiar. Logrono, *Higos, Agua y Amor*. It is the baritone and that is what I will call this affable Dutch giant forever after. At dinner I sit beside his new found love, Beatrice from Mexico. There is general agreement among pilgrims that on the Camino you have a good chance of finding yourself. In some circles another assumption follows – romance will find you. Beatrice and the baritone have perfectly matched wits for their unlikely convergence of Netherlands and Latino and I like them both immediately. Ours is one of many feasts to fill the dining room. A succession of platters and saucepans filled to the brim with bean stews, soups, spaghettis, breads, cheeses and all manner of make-do combinations fill each long table and everyone is welcome.

opening of my eyes to watch the sea of silent, stationary bodies around me. Oh how looks can be deceiving. Someone in the room would doubtless be reeling from a knee pain worse than death, or their mind absorbed in yet another rewind of a distressing encounter or what-if scenario or an erotic fantasy or anchored like lead in a fog of boredom. I was in a meditation hall filled with all manner of mental gymnastics! Then I would close my eyes again, ready, like a deep sea diver, to observe the next piece of me to surface and possibly unravel. It was impossible to know what dramas, pains or paradises awaited.

I still find it helpful to remember an analogy of mind and water given by a teacher on an early retreat. A tormented mind is like a storm charged sea, its waves crashing and foaming. But let the churn of silt and seaweed settle and you can look all the way down to the ocean floor, see slivers of sunlight playing on its rippled sand, the dart of silver gilled fish and the silent glide of a sting ray. You can swim effortlessly to shore. And as you come to know your mind, even if the surface of you is chopped and capped, you will remain anchored in the calm of that deep sea.

What is it that gives us buoyancy and depth? Could it be as simple as a foundation of goodness? How do we begin – is intent the spade that makes that first dig into the ephemeral world of manifesting thoughts? And what about gratitude?

This is how my mind wanders this morning.

The road stretching ahead is a bleached crumble of earth and the sky faded blue. Long summer grasses bow with the weight of their ripe seed heads and the whole world beyond this wild weed microcosm is a harvested wheat field. Somewhere and somehow in this pared down landscape I become lost. Literally, physically, lost. There are people about, stalking the hills in the distance, but not pilgrims. Gunshots ricochet from valley to valley followed by the barking of dogs. Keeping the sun on my back and hoping for the best seems a better option to venturing too close. I come to a bitumen road and spot a familiar profile plunging ahead, staff in hand. We are walking in the same direction so I can't be too lost. It is just that I find myself on this unforgiving tar while he walks through green fields. I make one attempt to cross but the ploughed ridges of earth are high and irregular and filled with the prickles and points of severed wheat.

Shielding my eyes from the sun I look up to the high pitched call of a bird. I wipe the sweat from my forehead and it is as if I am there, gliding on the upsurge of a thermal, looking down at three figures. Two equidistant from the third who stands still with his arm outstretched, a black wolf hound at his side. The two moving toward him lean into their staffs; a man wading through a dark green field of potatoes and a woman along the straight lines of a tarred road. Each step shrinks their triangle. I hear a whistle and am lured back down to earth.

We meet in the still point of a falcon's eye, the man, the woman and the falconer. The bird's chestnut wings flap then settle close to his body. I smell the raw scent of blood and watch as the falconer offers him a piece of meat. Were it not for his Reebok shoes and prescription spectacles our confluence might well be a medieval one. Falconry arrived simultaneously in the fifth century from the Moorish kings of Northern Africa when they invaded Spain, and the Goths who rumbled along the Mediterranean coast from Eastern Europe. It was soon adopted as sport of sports for noblemen and today many of the Arabic terms for falconry remain.

I listen to the tinkle of bells attached to the peregrine's legs by leather *pihuelas*, each a different note, as he settles down onto the soft buckskin of the falconers glove, his *guante*. I watch the peregrine's white tipped wings slowly fold behind him. His bird is a fine hunter, squat and broad shouldered like a lean Sumo wrestler. The falconer, observing my admiration, turns to his bird with pleasure, mimicking the way his neck glides from side to side fluid as an Indian dancer as he tracks our every move. I let out a laugh of delight and the peregrine hops up and down unfolding his wings, '*Por favor, mueva un poca a poca,*' the falconer motions to me. 'Move back a little,' the pilgrim translates, explaining how hawks sometimes shy of women.

My companion into town is from Galicia. He walks the same pace as me – as if we have a train to catch. In a sense he does, having only three weeks to spare. When he learns I am from Australia he shakes his head. 'Eucalyptus is a very bad problem for us.' He works as a parks ranger and is grappling with the noxious spread of eucalypt trees originally planted in Galicia for paper production. I am suddenly home again, traipsing through the bush listening to cicadas and the crunch of tinder under foot, breathing in the scent of smoke and lemon gum, collecting fallen strips of white bark from paperbark trees perfect for fashioning imaginary boats and bowls.

Piles of potatoes caked in red dirt, line the road into Santo Domingo de la Calzada, named after the eleventh century monk Domingo Garcia, patron saint of engineers and public works. One night by the banks of the River Oja he had a dream and the next day he left his hermit life to begin work on the notorious Camino path across Rioja, transforming it into a safe passage for pilgrims. Domingo preferred to work quietly and out of sight. He had previously been rejected by monasteries as too stupid and felt his presence jejune, unworthy of company. But angels, according to the legend, did not agree. I imagine Domingo sweating in his cassock, clearing paths single-handed with a humble sickle. Whenever he stopped to rest an angel picked up his blade and continued the work. Once this had been accomplished he turned his energy to building a hospice for pilgrims and soon a village was born and a bridge, then a hospital, a guest house and a church.

We walk beneath a gathering of stone hunchbacks and monsters, a musician and a man in combat with a lion, into the rambling cathedral of Santo Domingo, a spacious layering of stone metamorphosed over five centuries. A group of tourists from the *parador* next door file in with their cameras and guidebooks and I catch from the corner of my eye an elderly husband nudging his wife as he points to us, the *peregrinos,* in our crumpled clothes and sunburned skins, as much an attraction as the church. I feel secretly pleased to be on the other side of the lens. Yes I have a guidebook and camera too but today, two hundred kilometres into my journey, neither are of any importance. I am just happy to have walked here and to be touching the same stones as the centuries of pilgrims before me.

Below the tomb of Santo Domingo is his crypt. I can almost taste the air as I walk down the stairs, cool like the scent of a freshly swept dirt path. Somehow I prefer this unadorned tomb, to the Gothic excesses above. My mind can settle without being tugged from one marble embossed story to the next. Here it is easy to understand the Benedictine vows of simplicity and how they are deemed to bring one closer to God. If Santo Domingo were to rise from his grave I suspect he would feel proud to see the continuous trails of pilgrims and he'd probably have a chuckle at the pair of chickens pecking away in the Gothic hen house near the entrance to his beloved cathedral.

High above a paneled wooden door is a gilded decoration looking more like the crown of a queen than a chicken coop. Inside, behind lace ironwork live two hens. Every fourteen days they are exchanged for another pair in memory of one of the Camino's most famous miracles.

HELEN BURNS

In the fourteenth century a family of German pilgrims stopped in Santo Domingo. A local woman took a fancy to their handsome son, Hugonell, and *wolde have had hym to medyll* with, carnally. He declined her offer and, to his horror, was arrested the next day for the theft of a silver goblet she had planted in his bag. Imagine his distraught parents as they heard the judge pass his sentence: Death by hanging. They were powerless and had no choice but to continue their pilgrimage, praying all the way for his soul. On their return they were overwhelmed to find their son still hanging on the gallows, alive and well. (Never let reason get in the way of a good miracle.) Some say it was St James who supported Hugonell's weight all that time and keeping him alive. Others swear it was the work of Santo Domingo. Elated – St James had heard their prayers – Hugonell's mother and father rushed to the home of the judge to tell him their son was still alive. The judge, knife and fork raised ready to tuck into his supper of roast chicken, retorted that their son was as alive as the chicken on his plate. In that instant the chicken sprouted new feathers, stood up, clucked and flew away.

To this day Santo Domingo de la Calzada endures a string of pilgrims ever hopeful for a stray feather fallen from the cathedral's coop, a talisman ensuring them fortuitous travel to Santiago. I linger a few extra moments, listening to the scratching of chicken feet but nothing floats my way. *Donde la gallina canto despues de asada*, where the hens crowed after being cooked, is the town's motto and I wonder as I leave whether those two chickens will escape the fate of a roasting pan after their holy interlude.

I am windburned and sunburned by the time I reach Granon and my throbbing feet feel like hot lumps of iron, tight and swollen inside my shoes. The seven hundred year old Church of San Bautista sits like a fortress in Granon's main plaza. I walk around it twice before discovering a weathered door with a bronze staff and scallop shell for a door knocker. I strike the shell, push open the door and climb a spiral of stairs into the bell tower where a tall German man gives me a detailed tour then assigns me to the loft. I take a mattress from a perfectly stacked pile in the corner and make my bed under timber beams. A print of a regally dressed St James seems to approve the shipshape precision of this *refugio*, all the more contrasted with each tired arrival of sweat-soaked, thirsty pilgrim.

Mouth watering scents of vanilla and warm pastries waft up the street from the Jesus *panaderia*. A gathering of locals wait their turn to order. The door squeaks open and we make way for an old lady carrying a garlic studded leg of lamb on a tray. She passes it to the baker and he opens the oven door. A rush of rosemary and roast lamb scented steam billows out into the shop as he adds her herb anointed tray to the community stove. Standing in the midst of a village's Sunday tradition I feel suddenly out of place, a dumbstruck, shy stranger. I yearn to be invited home to lunch, to be one of them. Instead, tongue tied, I point to a pretzel and am hastily served.

Across from the church is a bar, empty except for a few men playing cards. They all drink martinis so I order the same. The distracted barman slides a glass to me while shouting across the room to a newly arrived group. What I really want is a plate of food but I've lapsed into a mute. Far from the saintly countenance of Domingo I nevertheless have empathy for those who suffer the jeers of stupidity. In my case, self inflicted. I can hear the sizzle of something in the kitchen, but by now feel completely disenfranchised.

Church is out, the bells are ringing and within a few minutes the bar is full. Amongst all the finery of stockings and high heels, lace shawls and Sunday suits I spy another pilgrim. Carmen's English is non existent. We suck on our olives and share a basket of bread in a kind of silent communion as the chatter all around us and the chink of ice in a hundred more martinis rises to a crescendo.

With only one change of clothes, laundry at the end of each day is a necessity. In the tower of San Bautista this cleansing rite takes on heavenly connotations. Through a door at the end of the loft a dark set of stairs leads to two old washtubs in an unadorned room of dust and stone above the church's vault. Washing completed I climb higher again to find space on lines hung between four giant church bells stained with a season of swallow droppings. Through Sunlight soap-scented shirts and trousers I look down through the arches across a ripple of red tiled roofs to plains of harvested wheat, a ribbon of purple mountain and a sky turning from smoke haze to swirls of pink and elysian blue. Suddenly I am not alone anymore. Here in this belltower, built high enough to catch a whisper of wind, the breath of an angel, that shroud of isolation I felt in a room full of people dissolves as naturally as a stain soaks away in water.

San Bautista's bell and Granon's terracotta rooves.

A familiar voice wakes me from siesta and I look down to the dining room to see none other than the baritone and his senorita, Beatrice. We set two long tables under the watch of St James and the *hospitalero* while in the tiny kitchen his wife prepares dinner. Strains of a drunken song from the plaza below gathers momentum as we sit down to eat. I sense an agitation in our host as he stands at the head of the table commandeering each platter carried from the kitchen. 'Whatever you do don't mention *ze* war,' the baritone whispers above a chorus that has now collapsed into out of tune profanities and guffaws. Apparently these bards are also pilgrims, very inebriated ones, and by the grace of some *refugio* decree our commandant had refused them beds. Another song is launched and one pilgrim's offer of a bottle of wine for the table is immediately rejected by the *hospitalero*, who now paces the room painfully torn, it appears, by his duty of care. 'Here we turn water into wine,' the baritone whispers to our group at the end of the table as we twirl spaghetti around our forks, break bread and stifle giggles.

12

Crossing the Mountains of the Goose

Granon to San Juan de Ortega

For the first hour I walk in the dark, linking footsteps with Roberta from Italy. I am glad of her company as the drinking trio of Spanish pilgrims, in their slept-in faded jeans and tracksuit pants, leer at us as they alternately overtake then fall behind. I feel their heavy lidded eyes boring into my back. When we finally summon the courage to greet them, one replies with a gruff mumble and the others with a leer. This encounter feels like an affront after the light hearted steps and B*uen caminos* of so many pilgrims so far. I am uncomfortable and cannot look into their dark, bristled faces. They stop again at the side of the road and lean back onto the swags atop their old style canvas backpacks, silently chewing long strands of grass.

I am thrown back into the real world where things are not equal. I've become used to physical discomfort – hot feet, aching hips. But here I am confronted with an ill at ease mind. I find myself picking up pace in an attempt to lose them. I even start to leave Roberta behind. Perhaps my fear equates to survival but it also takes me out of my body, away from the simplicity of left foot, right foot into a state incapable of experiencing night turning into day – tiny flecks of golden light on the horizon, the call of one bird to another in the dark thickets of blackberry bushes beside the path. And I become incapable of seeing these three men as good men. Where then, is my human sensibility? As I plough ahead the memory of one woman rushes back to me.

She is rolling across fiercely hot paving stones in a circumambulation of a South Indian temple. Her tangled hair saturated with coconut oil, dirt and sweat clings to her body in long dark strands. Another woman stays close adjusting her cathartic roll, keeping her near the ancient walls. Her incomprehensible chant pits the thick monsoon air; the only word I recognize is Shiva. I stand at a distance with burning feet, listening, falling as if in a trance, into her wailing mantra. Purification or penance or both? Self-inflicted, or not, pain acts like a short circuit. It cuts through mundane, habitual ways of thinking and acting and brings us immediately to the place where we hurt most. A place fertile with opportunity. The image that had stayed with me yesterday returns. On the forty ninth night of the Buddha's fast he vowed to stay awake and in the morning he opened new eyes. The world was the same but his place in it was not the same. He took the bowl of saffron milk offered him, drank long and deep, then sat with a small band of monks and explained the Four Noble Truths. In the fourth truth he gave them the Eightfold Path. It was a way of living; a way to approach the constant ricochet of craving and aversion. Right Understanding, Right Thought, Right Speech, Right Action, Right Livelihood, Right Effort, Right Mindfulness, and Right Concentration. Not quite the Ten Commandments but nevertheless the Buddha's code for conscious living.

In the woman's primal turning and in the fear I have of these three men – what is it that can hold us, keep us safe and at the same time open? Hers was an image of Shiva, mine now is the serene face of the Buddha. My mother's was the compassionate face of the Virgin Mary, and my father? Well his solace lay in the sea, in whiskey and pipe smoke, and, I like to think, his three children.

But still, despite my ruminations and visions of beneficent beings, I continue to walk as if my life depends on it, willing myself toward the horizon, taking giant strides foolishly thinking I can separate myself from what is.

And so it was for me in Burma, sitting in one place for one timeless month. Despite the environment, perhaps because of it, I fell unwittingly into a cunning mind trap. The meditation I practiced has continued in a strict tradition, unadorned and unchanged for centuries. Unlike the retreats I had sat in the West, here, there was no token coddling for body or mind. The monastery was an oasis of noble silence set behind high concrete walls in the outer suburbs of Rangoon, on one side a busy road and next door a panel beating shop. The same schedule is followed every day of the year. Alternating one hour periods of walking and sitting meditation begin with the first bell at three thirty in the morning. There is a break for breakfast at four thirty and lunch at ten thirty followed by a rest period then back to the meditation hall. A cup of tea with a sliver of jaggery sugar is served in the evening and the last bell of the day is rung at ten thirty.

April in Burma is very hot; cumulonimbus clouds billow across the sky. Sometimes they grace us with a mango shower, an affectionate Burmese description for a tease of light rain heralding the coming monsoon. But it never comes and we are drenched by an ever increasing humidity. Each day I would fill my water bottle from the dispenser outside my room unaware that it had not been properly cleaned, at least for a western stomach. The inevitable happened and I was to spend many periods in between meditation squatting on a toilet as I continued drinking the same water to avoid dehydration. Over the next week, sleep deprived and unable to eat, I descended into delirium, thinking at one point my bed was a bowl of giant fruit – lychees, rambutans and watermelon. My physical deterioration accentuated each thought until one morning, for the entire hour of the first sitting, I became progressively consumed by panic that I would not be able to stand up and walk out of the room when the bell rang.

I had backed myself into a corner, lost sense of what was appropriate and what was not. A monastery is in many ways like a sanatorium for the mind. The Sayadaw dispenses medicine to the yogis: be attentive, note each and every thought and each and every sensation. The fact that I was sick made no difference – I noted the cramps in my stomach, the giant fruit salad on my bed, my tears and my fears of slipping into a nervous breakdown. I noted them when I could but as my body weakened so did my resolve and ever so quietly I slipped into muddied delusion. I thought I was practicing as the Sayadaw had instructed but my mind had dulled and my noting was nothing but habitual repetition. There was no clarity and no room for discrimination. Eventually I broke my silence to ask for a doctor and was taken to a clinic for a series of drips and at this point, thank you very much, told to go to the kitchen and fill my drink bottle from a cauldron of water kept boiling for foreign students.

In a few days I felt normal enough again. My thoughts were less gross, they drifted light as feathers then disappeared. They danced themselves out on the surface of my mind making barely a ripple. I began to see the play of my senses – taste, touch, hearing, sight, smell – and how they triggered my mind. I would hear a sound not as an identifiable sound but just as a pressure or tingling or pulse inside my ear. Then I would label it – birdcall, hammer on metal, bell. Almost imperceptibly, practically simultaneously but not quite, my mind would jump in with a like or a dislike or a memory that might trigger a new strand of thought. Each resulting thought evoked a further physical response, sometimes as subtle or fleeting as one pulse across an eye or the twitch of a muscle. It was a slow but natural transformation stepping out from the confines of my mind to an awareness of it. A recognition, delicate, like the uncurling of a new leaf into a rainforest dense with vines, the sprawl of tree roots and limbs twisting and turning toward the sun they so desired.

It had been a painful week but one that taught me no matter how much I suffer I have a choice – to be drawn in, to drown in the drama or simply be present keeping all the time a light vigil of awareness. Those moments of panic that had accumulated into fear were a kind of mental deconstruction. I was amazed to later find an exact textbook explanation for what had happened to me. The state of *wretchedness* I had faced had a name, *Sammasana nana* and it needed to be experienced before the next stage of meditation, *Udayabbaya nana*, could begin to arise – insight into the rising and passing away of physical and mental phenomena. Like an onion, layer by layer, attachment to who I think I am peels away.

What sense is there in running? I slow down and begin to hum *Om Tara tuttare ture soha*, then blend into it, Hail Mary full of grace, until both prayers become seamless, one after the other, carrying me into Castille. I stop to rest beside Villamayor del Rio's fountain and breathe in the scent of sweet charred smoke wafting across the plaza. An old lady tends a bed of charcoal in a tall soot-stained corrugated drum, turning red capsicums over and over until they are blistered black. She dips them quickly into a bucket of water before dropping them onto a cloth. She smiles at my request to take a photo and adjusts her apron so that its pink stripes fall in neat lines across her grandmotherly midriff. I zoom out the lens to include her front door flanked by a glorious blaze of red, pink and white geraniums spilling from nine terracotta pots. Life blooms still in the medieval hamlet of Villamayor. Like many of the villages dotted along the Camino the young have long gone to cities leaving the elderly to harvest the fields. And when they die their ancestral homes are more often than not boarded up, ill-considered for holidays and hardly attractive real estate. By the census of 1830 when the Camino had all but died, Villamayor's population had dwindled to one hundred and twenty five. Now I could count its inhabitants on a few hands.

From the other side of the plaza comes a raucous concert of pig snorts and grunts. I venture closer and peek into the front door. Accustomed to the morning light all I can see are the silhouettes of black bodies and curly tails in a wheeze of stamped dust but I do not tarry. Mid-inhalation I am literally propelled back into the street. The smell, an intoxicating mix of pig, urine and hay, is so cloying it might well have been fermenting there in the dark since that 1830 census.

Ah, the clean air of the open road. I gulp lung-fulls and stride ever westwards, my extra speed, less to do with three rough and tough men, possibly more due to that unexpected dose of methane. The trail narrows into a path skirting steep cliffs, once the haunt of saints and hermits. Belorado comes into view. With a healthy population of two thousand it seems a positive metropolis. At the Church of Saint Nicolas I give thanks for surviving the perils of cliffs, pigs and hung-over pilgrims. The town clock peals ten times, a signal for coffee.

The entrance to Plaza Mayor is strewn with the telltale signs of a night's revelry. Empty wine bottles are being scooped up from the roadside by an ancient looking garbage truck, a far cry from the days when Belorado's Jewish population nominated two of their own to sweep the streets in return for cow pasture and firewood. If the sound of ten bell chimes has not begun to wake the locals surely this smashing of glass and screeching of brakes should, but the only sign of life in the plaza is a small group of pilgrims reclining outside its one open cafe.

Beatrice and the baritone have mysteriously arrived before me and sit, not a care in the world, with a bald French man, Claude who was in the bunk bed below me way back in Ventosa, and Alex, a tall young German with studious eyes. I remember passing Alex outside Najera. He was singing to himself. We discuss the prospects of *refugios* in the next few villages and I decide to head on another twelve kilometres to Villafranca Montes de Oca for no other reason than its lyrical translation, Village of the Mountains of the Goose.

I meander through fields of summer grasses to the

tiny village of Tosantos and am invited in by the *refugio's hospitalero*. He brings me a cup of tea and sits me down in a small living room. Alone and stationary my mind seizes the interlude and goes into overdrive. Why do I choose to walk by myself? Why do I shy from people and never seem to know what to say? Small talk seems so small … and on and on I go until, as my feet cool down, so does my head. I lean back into the sofa and close my eyes. From the next room comes a murmur of voices and the sound of a broom sweeping the floor. Outside the trill of a bird and a rustling of trees in the wind.

That lovely swish swish of the broom; I am back in Burma. Each morning two women swept leaves from the quadrangle outside the meditation hall. It was a comforting sound sometimes having the delicious effect of sweeping my mind empty too. There were over a hundred of us meditating, men at the front, women at the back, all Burmese with the exception of three Korean women, David and me. We were a collection of ages – monks, nuns and lay people, mothers and daughters, fathers and sons. Some had been taking part in the same schedule for years, others ordained for ten days, their fresh shaven heads dimpled and white against their dark skin and monastic robes, brown for men and pink for women. Though meditation is a solitary silent affair, living in such close quarters felt both intimate and supportive. Words were superfluous.

I take a sip of tea and notice a shelf of books under a framed St James, an odd assortment of paperbacks in various languages and states of repair left behind by pilgrims. Jane Austen sits beside Cervantes, Paulo Coelho beside Tolkien. *Cantico Espiritual*, I read on the tattered spine of a thin book. It sits squeezed between a Bible and *Carne Tremula*, a Spanish edition of Ruth Rendell's *Live Flesh*. I take it down from the shelf. To my delight there are English translations scribbled in some of the margins – verses written by the sixteenth century mystic St John of the Cross, inspired from *The Song of Songs*.

San Juan de la Cruz is one of Spain's most accomplished and loved poets. He cared little for church politics choosing instead a simple, contemplative existence. He also had a penchant for long walks. It is said he traveled close to eighteen thousand miles all over Spain, most probably, given his inclination, *discalced*, shoe-less, and dressed in a coarse homespun habit as was the practice of his mentor and friend St Teresa. I wonder did he venture into these hills and break bread with the monks who chose to live in caves and remote monasteries far from Inquisition eyes. I imagine him, with his friar's haircut, an indomitable free spirit less than five feet tall; passionate about the need to live as a recluse in order to be close to God.

His views, interpreted by many as demeaning to the church, did not escape the Vatican and on papal order he was arrested. In the nine months of his imprisonment by the shoe-wearing friars of the Unreformed Carmelites, St John was confined to a cell six feet by ten illuminated for a short few hours each day from a crevice, just three fingers wide, high on one wall. Once a week he was taken into the refectory, where, as they recited their psalm *Miserere* the friars took turns scourging him with a cane. What would King David have thought, I wonder, of his penitential verses being sung in time to the lashing of a man's back.

'He would be better off in the hands of the Moors,' St Teresa said, beside herself with worry. But out of that torturous time St John composed rapturous songs. I flick through the book and all but swoon when I come to a translated verse in a long hand scrawl at the bottom of a page: with his serenest hand my neck he wounded / and suspended every sense with its caress / lost to myself I stayed my face upon my lover having laid from all endeavor ceasing / and all my cares releasing threw them amongst the lilies to fade.

I look out the *refugio* window. The romantic in me wishes I had time to climb the mountains on the horizon, take up residence in one of those hermit caves. From a distance they look like unfathomable gouges into the hard heart of rock, alluring, mysterious. Cobwebs, bats and dust aside, surely a sojourn in one of them would unlock the doors of my house; make it ready for the guest to enter.

St John's life as a mystic epitomized the apophatic or negative way, a term flung about by scholars in their debate on the parallels between Christianity and Buddhism. God, they say, is no benevolent being riding clouds in the sky. Only by describing what he is not can we begin to understand what the divine is. Only by stepping through the looking glass of our *self* can we move beyond ordinary perception and usher in the guest. In *Dark Night of the Soul* St John wrote: From this arid night there first of all comes self-knowledge, whence as from a foundation rises this other knowledge of God.

I imagine God as a light streaming into St John's cell. So illuminated does the room become, no dark remains, no shadows and no-self. But these grand ideas of dissolution, the insubstantiality of self and dissolving into the divine, are all conjecture until then. All the hours I have invested cross-legged on a cushion, eyes turned in, are, as St John suggests, building blocks. The path to liberation begins with knowing myself.

Another destination – or is it the same – presses my feet back into their boots and I make my way out into the sear of midday sun. With twenty two kilometres under my belt I have usually hung up my shoes by now. The sky begins to drop from a clear blue dome into inclement clouds. What ironic freedom it is to not have the choice to hustle indoors at the sign of rain. I tie a scarf around my forehead to soak a growing trickle of sweat and strike the way. Small whirly-whirlys whip up dust round my feet and crickets, out of nowhere, break into a pulsing chorus: an ode to the elements and the comfort of aloneness.

There is an old soul feel to this path that on the surface looks barren and windswept. Countless pilgrims have etched the earth under my feet and, as if on queue, the ruins of San Felices de Oca appear. Here, ninth century Mozarab Christians, in their exodus from a Muslim ruled south, built one of their most celebrated monasteries. Now all that is left is one arch in a crumbling beehive of bricks. I shelter against the shade of its eastern wall to devour a chunk of bread, averting my gaze from a sorry looking garden of weeds, toilet paper, plastic wrappers and drink cans. This is either a locals' hang out or pilgrim toilet stop. Alex and Claude wave as they pass, the wind dies down and all is quiet.

Sic transit Gloria mundi. I imagine the Latin chant of a barefoot monk sung from within these walls as the last flame dies from the burning sheath of flax he holds: Thus passes the glory of the world. There is no difference whether these words are uttered in a chapel where gilded angels languish and wine is sipped from a silver chalice or here, twelve centuries later, amongst the weeds and ruins in a world awash with late summer raindrops.

In Pali, the language of the first Buddhist scriptures, this same truth is pared down to one word, *anicca*. I was twenty when I first heard it, over and over, on my first ten day silent retreat. I had dived into the deep end of a pool and could barely dog paddle. The first three days blurred into one painful interminable hour after another. At the beginning of every meditation, from a small cassette recorder at the front of the room, came the deep, unwavering voice of our Burmese teacher, *Anicca, anicca,* changing, changing. Our bodies turned into incubators for testing this truth as we methodically tracked sensations head to toe and back again. If observed with a quiet enough mind, pain in an ankle or knee that at first felt like a solid mass of unbearability, became instead a dynamic flux of tingling, throbbing, burning, heavy, light, sharp, dull and so on and on until, unbelievably, it simply disappeared. These first experiences seemed to me nothing short of miraculous and I stored them away to memory. There were times in later retreats when, as I delved deeper into old knots and calcified habits, pain did not shift so easily but at least the seeds of possibility had been planted. I had established a foundation for my practice, not of expectation but of faith.

I muse about acorns growing into oak trees as rain-scented clouds move in over Villafranca, one short kilometre away. Mist tumbles into its valley smothering the ghosts of Romans and the clang of iron forgers over smelting fires that once rang by the river Oca a thousand years ago.

An abandoned school house has been transformed into a *refugio*. In a bunker like dormitory I find a disheveled old man with a haunted, mad almost, look of exhaustion splayed on a bed, boots and all, staring vacantly at the ceiling, and in a corner a couple whisper to each other with their backs to the door as if they want to shut the world out. I choose a bed between them and spread it with a blanket. In an attempt to ward off a growing despondency I lie down to the whine of the bed's springs and turn to face the flakes of plaster threatening to fall from the ceiling. A cloying smell of damp wool rises to greet me.

Just as my gloom begins taking a tighter hold, cheerful young voices come trilling down the hallway. Alex, Claude and a German couple have set up a picnic under the stairwell. I offer what's left of my cucumber and baguette, Claude slices paper thin pieces of *jamon* with his penknife, Alex proves a connoisseur of local cheese as he presents to the table a sheep's milk Zamorano and a soft goat Mato and Frida and Karl produce more bread. Perfection.

But I still feel ill at ease about sleeping here – it's as if the ghosts of schoolchildren still pace the damp concrete corridors of this makeshift *refugio*. My feet begin to itch and then the thought occurs – I don't have to stay, I can keep walking. What a revelation! San Juan de Ortega is only another twelve kilometres and there is plenty of daylight left. Weather predictions and deliberation about staying continue at the table as I shoulder my pack and wave goodbye.

A rough gravel track snakes up behind the Church of Santiago through heavy mist and the silent cover of twisted oaks and tall pine trees. I feel like an untethered horse and take big breaths of sweet cloud-soaked air. The top of the track levels out before tumbling to the bottom of a valley then up again. A group of cyclists pass like fiendish red backed insects. They lean into the wind and I watch them, horrified, as the wheels beneath them spin into a high speed descent.

Om Tara tuttare ture soha, I sing into the clouds of dust they leave behind, playing with the tune and the spaces between each word. Today it is a prayer for them as they disappear and then a prayer for the world they have left behind, a silent self-contained world where from a kernel comes a seed then a forest measured not by effort but by the natural passage of time. There is no recklessness or impatience here, only synthesis. Leaves take in carbon dioxide and breathe out oxygen; I breathe in oxygen and breathe out carbon dioxide, *Om Tara tuttare ture soha.*

Karl, Greta and Claude catch up to me, they too had felt uncomfortable staying on at Villafranca, and for the next few hours we interweave. Karl tells me, through the fat raindrops splattering our hooded heads, that he must return to Germany in two days for his job in an architectural firm. 'Maybe I will walk more next year,' he says wistfully. After only a short couple of weeks I have become so immersed in this life that I have forgotten there is any other. But then I remember, it is thanks to home I can be here. I only have to look around to realize how interconnected everything is, and how transitory. One minute I get it and in the next I forget.

An army of scalloped and cloak-clad faithful could march ten abreast along this high mountain road but it feels a lonely place. Wayside clumps of bright orange broom and heather do little to mask the desolation. Occasional delicate sprouts of crocus break through the gravel path like a tease of nature, ensuring I am mindful of each step. To crush a flower underfoot? Tantamount, I think, to rubbing salt into this solitary silence.

Before long it is as if I am walking through a river of pink petal stars and into the tears of God. On and on the rain falls. On and on the road goes and my body begins to slow down and to sink into itself. Wells of sensation rise to the surface, thick and larger than life, as though from the tired limbs of a sleeping giant. The image of an ancient water wheel starts to turn over and over in my mind as each thigh bone burns and swivels like dead weight in their socket. My hips ache – I didn't know hips could ache – and the soft tissue under my skin plaits into a vice-like belt, tightening with every step. I go into each sensation then out again to the water wheel and to the flowers and the rain, to the weight of the pack on my shoulders, to my mind slipping into despair at ever arriving, to the water wheel, to my hips, to my bones. The rain coagulates into grey mist and my mind gnaws away until all I am left with is right foot, left foot. Breathing in. Breathing out.

My relief at the sight of San Juan de Ortega's tower could never be compared to that of a medieval pilgrim arriving in mud caked moccasins after a long day adrift in the wastes of Montes de Oca. Perhaps the bell I hear is the same deep peal ringing out the last rays of sunlight that guided him here. And if he was to arrive by twilight on the auspicious day of a spring or autumn equinox he would fall to his knees in the presence of a Virgin, angels and the miracle of light. At the foot of a capital in the monastery's Romanesque church a graceful stone Mary, Milagro de la Luz, awaits her moment of illumination: a single ray of light arcs its way up from the lower apse wall to rest for a hallowed moment over her womb. San Juan in his devotion to the welfare of pilgrims had, for the glory of his God, also mastered the mystery of a turning earth, capturing the moment in stone and light.

But when, on any other day, we pilgrims hobble and limp those last miles to the monastery it is more likely the regaling of a miracle that impels us on. The deformed *peregrino* Vadovin, for example. With twisted limbs he had dragged himself along the Camino and was cured here. Vadovin then walked the remaining miles to Santiago with the agility of a child.

An elderly lady dressed in black, silver hair held back with a silver net, makes a note of my arrival and vaguely waves me up a wide set of stairs. I have stood still in a queue for less than five minutes but this is all the time it takes. Every muscle, tendon and ligament in my body shuts down and it takes a huge effort to lug my pack back onto my shoulders. With both hands on the banister I steady and pull myself up the stairs. Vadovin would be impressed.

If the *refugio* at Villafranca was a bunker, how can I describe this? I wander through a maze of rooms choked with bunks and pilgrims in various states of disrepair. By now most beds are taken and I look for the impossible – a well sprung unmarked mattress, preferably near an open window and away from bathrooms, with a soft feather pillow that doesn't bear the depression of a head from the night before. I search up and down narrow aisles stepping over packs and spread-eagled limbs, finally settling for a bed in a corner. Half way through unfurling my sleeping bag the man on the bunk above turns in his sleep, farts and exhales with the violence of a diesel semi-trailer. Desperate I bury my head like an ostrich in the pillow before noticing a dark dribble of stains on its cover and the dank smell of mildew rising from its centre. Someone flushes a toilet on the other side of the wall and the plumbing works itself into a frenzy. If I've walked an extra twelve kilometres for a better bed there has to be one.

I gather up my sleeping bag and drag my pack behind me until I come to a vacant top bunk next to a thoroughfare that at least affords a sense of space and is a good two rows from another bathroom. On the bed below a petite young Frenchwoman searches the ample depths of her frilled floral toiletry bag for a mirror and lipstick. How civilized! Yes, this is more like it. I take the sprig of heather from my pack and offer it to her. It is as though, in the labyrinth of these dark damp rooms, there is an air of lost and injured soul unused to the offering of strangers and she looks at me as if I am pointing a loaded gun in her face. But she takes it, '*Merci,*' twirling it into the auburn curls of her fresh shampooed hair. With my last sliver of soap I tip toe into a shower booth where cold water gushes from the hot tap, shocking my body into a semblance of life. Suddenly awake I am not the least deterred by the debris of hair and wrappers and used cotton buds left behind by others. Cleanliness next to godliness. And are we not, as pilgrims, all on a quest for saintliness?

Wine flows from the Taberna Marcela, a hole in the wall coexisting within the monastery compound. I hobble into its front room a few steps away from rigor mortis but all is forgotten when I find Roberta and Carmen with her brother, Manolo. We shout the day's adventures in three languages over the din of a full house. Beneath their dark eyebrows the same gentle light shines from Carmen's and Manolo's eyes. Carmen has had a wine or two and no longer shy, babbles away in Spanish while her brother huddles over his beer looking more like a bohemian Romany as he constantly pushes his long dark hair behind his ears. Fair skinned Roberta reclines in her chair like a Cheshire cat and I remember our yoga stretches together in the loft at Granon yesterday as if they had happened a lifetime ago. She tucks into a plate of salad and shrugs her shoulders when Carmen, hearing she is vegan, looks at her plate in horror. 'I manage,' is all she says with a smile.

Spaniards have a close affiliation with meat; sausage and *jamon* go into just about everything. I feel like a bit of a heathen, attacking fried eggs atop two ominous looking rounds of black *morcilla*. I confess to being only half vegetarian these days, if there is such a thing, and even less so in Spain given the food on offer. Nevertheless, I hesitate when Manolo explains the sausage on my plate is made from blood, a specialty of the house. Some gastronomic circles go as far as saying pork spiritualizes the stomach, whatever that means – but it is good and all the better washed down with a glass of Castilian red.

I climb the monastery stairs in a blur and search for

my bed. The air is thick with the scent of rising damp from a groaning sea of sleeping pilgrims. Half-conscious I snuggle my rubbery drunk body into my sleeping bag observing with some surprise how softly sprung the mattress is. Something feathery scratches my cheek, a sprig each of heather and gorse tied together with a strand of grass. Who? I wonder, before falling back onto my pillow, not needing to know. I close my eyes and rest in the winged arms of Montes de Oca, mountains of goose, and a thousand and one crocus, their pink petals curled into delicate buds for the night under the watch of all the other wildflowers and a sky of milky stars.

13

The Path to Your Door

San Juan de Ortega to Burgos

A Nordic lament pierces the dark. Earplugs work well for heavy breathers and the discreet snorers but only muffle the impacts of a terrified sleeptalker. Is he surrounded by a pack of wolves? I roll over, as if turning my back to the noise will help, losing an earplug in the process. While I fumble about in the gorge of my bed his lament changes course. Backed by a chorus of other gurgling, snorting sleepers, his voice penetrates my left eardrum like a botched pilgrim version of *Miserere. Libera me de sanguinibus, Deus:* Deliver me from blood guiltiness, O God.

Well might these Santiago bound dreamers chant this confessional prayer and so should I. I start to curse the air and all who exhale audibly into it, working myself into a state of irritation making further sleep impossible. The eerie hoot of an owl solos into the choir and I begin to suspect present company includes a few vagrant spirits of pilgrims and priests sheltered here these last nine centuries. The *Miserere* continues. T*unic impotent super altare tuum vitulos:* Then shall they offer bullocks upon thine altar, and I plunge into visions of pagan sacrifice, anything, to rescue me from this unmerciful ship of medieval souls.

I have no idea what time it is but have no hesitation in joining the bob of torch lights and getting out of here. These predawn evacuees are usually a select mix of those with a deadline for St James and plain avid walkers, decked out in serious boots or European sandals and socks. Let no man or woman interfere with their military regimen of miles.

Moonlit puddles of rain cover the wide path leading away from San Juan and for the first few heavenly kilometres I empty its damp must from my lungs. There is a benevolent God after all – I breathe in her cool, conifer air. After limping about in a state of semi-paralysis last night, I can hardly believe how nimble I feel. Maybe San Juan De Ortega is a place of miracles or maybe it was just the *morcilla* sausage.

Soon the forest gives way to an open plateau of low heather and pasture where, in the pre-dawn fog, ghostly shapes of several curious cows gather near the path. Looming behind them, looking more ancient than San Juan is a lone oak tree with a waning half moon caught in its branches like a smudge of pearled light.

A conference of huddled bodies have gathered at a crossroad. One girl walks in a circle, head down, searching for a sign, while a man paces back and forth dialing his mobile phone. 'My wife left before me and now maybe she is lost, or I am lost. She is not answering,' he says, more frantic by the minute. We all agree that at such a major intersection it is strange there is no scalloped shell marker.

'Maybe it's a joke,' a young American boy suggests, 'a local playing tricks with pilgrims or…' I look to the girl beside me, drawing arrows in the dirt with her boots, and brace myself for a launch into conspiracy theories but we are saved by the arrival of a weathered old man rolling a cigarette as he walks. With a final lick he holds it in the corner of his mouth and takes his walking stick from under his arm. It hits the ground with a jangle and for a moment we forget our plight. An assortment of bones, shells, charms and two crucifix dangle from the crook of his polished staff. They remind me of the random notes of a wind mobile but this eccentric collection of symbols has rhythm. A step by step sort of music always arriving, a quaint percussive accompaniment to one pilgrim's slowed down pace in a world gone mad with speed and the need to get somewhere else.

He lights up, rolling back and forth on the balls of his feet in tell-tale sandals and socks, looking rather pleased with all the attention, then in a chorus of tinkles and clangs he points to the left with his stick.

'Keep ze sun onz your back,' he proffers in an exhale of smoke.

'But there is no sun,' I say.

He inhales slowly, fixing me with eagle eyes, 'Zen follow ze moon,' and with that proceeds, minstrel-like, down into a valley thick with cloud. We watch him like some kind of apparition.

The distraught man missing a wife is unaffected.

'Her name is Rosa,' he pipes in. The old man has gone but we still stand, stymied in the mist. Someone suggests he wait for a while in case she reappears.

'If you see her tell her here I am,' he says, his Latino heart palpitating under his impeccable safari clothes. He doesn't look the type to stay at San Juan, more a candidate for a *parador* with white aproned maids and complimentary dry cleaning. Money might buy comfort but never peace of mind; owning a mobile phone is no guarantee either.

Each of us take turns to hug or pat him on the back before we continue our appointed way.

'Ello. Ello!' he keeps shouting into his phone as we descend.

'Ello?'

Like beads re-threaded on a rosary, intervals of open road fall beside us.

What must it be like to walk the Camino with your partner? During the period David and I had planned to go together I harbored one dilemma: he walks so slowly and I walk fast. How on earth could it work?

We played a kind of old married couple cat and mouse game until the day it was agreed I would travel alone. I knew instinctively David did not feel the same urgency to go but to verbalize this felt like jeopardizing something sacrosanct – our relationship. Living with one person year in year out, borders become blurred, habits leak into each other. Like the sand on a beach between high and low tide, soaked soft yet firm enough to hold footprints. We can look down and see the individual marks we make; the different depths our weight makes in the hollows our heels leave behind, the spread of our toes and the slight shifting of sand at the edges of the balls of our feet as we move forward. Then the sea rises again washing a thousand grains of sand back into the images we made. The individual marks of us disappear. A mystic might say those grains are the work of God. The sea serpent slips away and Adam and Eve return as one to their garden. But I wonder, in a mundane world, is it more a case of lost identity.

Let sleeping dogs lie. Is that what I had been doing? I like to keep the peace, turn my cheek, take the path of least resistance. It's easier. But the idea of walking this pilgrimage had grabbed me by the scruff of the neck. The dogs were waking. By refusing to let go, the balance of us was tipped. If I looked at myself through David's eyes I had become headstrong. A woman possessed. But for me, there was exhilaration. I had cracked open my shell and my wings were testing the velocity of the wind.

A chill breeze blows from the valley below and I speed up to keep warm. The village lights of Ages come into view as the fog of night evaporates and a new day appears through loose woven threads of mist. I think back to nights at home, that time before sleeping when we would meditate together. Try as I might in the last few days I have been unable to conjure the details of David's face but now I am there. In the pitch dark of our loft he comes back to me. I can see him, in half lotus, sitting to my right. Those piercing blue eyes. They could metamorphose from passive deep pools calling me in, to eyes that saw right through me. There were other times when they were elusive and I felt locked out. When I think about it, each was a response to something happening inside me. That's the play of relationship, the dynamics of it. I would come home after a weekend away; chattering, scattering my things about the house, settling back into the familiar and he'd sit on the periphery of my small whirlwind, my opening of the room's windows he had closed, waiting for me to settle down.

A statue of White Tara, her hands held in gestures of generosity and protection, watches us as we sit silently in meditation together. Secrets, illusions, the tensions of the day, they all bubble to the surface when I attempt to be still. Then I have a choice: like a hungry fish I can bite the hook and lash about in reruns and rewrites, or let them fall away like a child's tower of pick up sticks. When the illusive moments of dissolution arrive there are no bells or drum rolls. No words... there is something else. When we climbed into bed afterwards, there was lightness to our touch, a *jouissance*, an unbandaging of us, and then as we took turns to nestle into each other's shape, sleep came, deep and dreamless.

I stop to rest at a set of picnic tables and fill my water bottle from the Ages fountain. I am left with a sentimental kind of optimism that one day we can walk the Camino together putting to rest, at least for the moment, the idea of a hare and tortoise-like challenge across Spain.

Tucked away in a side street is a café and either side of its pearly gates lie the packs and poles of a legion of pilgrims. Inside manna is being served. I savor each chocolate-laced spoonful of cappuccino froth with a fresh baked baguette and sit back content to watch the eager comings and satisfied goings. It all seems so civilized after the night at San Juan. Mr. Latino walks in, beaming, with Rosa on his arm. She is as immaculately dressed as him with a sweep of blonde hair falling across her shoulders and I leave Ages with a glad heart.

Wild herbs thrive in the barren wayside at my feet, yellow dock leaves and the seed heads of plantain, a blood purifier and poultice for bee stings and poison ivy. Eight kilometres of tar loom on the last leg to Burgos. I dread the thought of a trudge through industrial suburbs and car yards. This is the modern day pilgrim's dilemma. I am neither Catholic nor Buddhist enough – there, I've confessed – to resolutely walk every inch of the way. I had heard it is possible to catch a bus and, to add to my demise, I had also jotted down the address of a Burgos *pension*. The idea of a night sleeping solo in crisp white sheets – maybe this is my Rapunzel moment?

I catch sight of a pilgrim ahead. There's something

familiar about that pack wobbling precariously to the right and the way he walks, halfway between a limp and a jig, a jog and a lurch. Winnie the Pooh comes to mind, scaling giant trees, hanging from balloons and fending off wild bees, all feats that pale in comparison to the prospect of finding honey.

At the one bar village of Orbaneja I find him splayed on a chair drinking a bottle of lemonade. Ivano! The fig tree near Puenta la Reina. '*Buongiorno*, do you remember?' He looks up, at first in consternation, then breaks into a high pitched laugh. I pull up a chair and order a cider then, with the help of the barman who can make some sense of Italian and my pigeoned English, and Ivano who seems to have a rough command of Spanish, we engage in a sort of Camino *lingua franca*. Ivano lights up at the sound of 'bus' and '*pension*' and asks if I have a phone number. It's already in my pocket. He pulls out a mobile and dials his secretary in Venice – she speaks perfect Spanish – asking her to book a room. I am curious to know what it is, exactly, that Ivano does. A designer of fantastical jewelry, perhaps, down some dark water lapped lane? Or glass goblets embossed with gold leaf, velvet masks hand stitched with feathers and rhinestones. Or maybe a banker.

'*Dos* rooms, Ivano, *dos*, two,' I hold up two fingers concerned for a moment he might be thinking of sharing. '*Si*,' he nods, placating me with a wave of his hand and we wait for her to call back.

Without our waiter as interpreter conversation dilutes

to smiles and sign language as we head toward a night of luxury. There is lightness in our steps together; we are relieved of words and therefore the sharing of our history. Ivano is a slow walker; sometimes I saunter along beside him and at others stride ahead. I decide on a shortcut under a fence and across a railway line. I can see Villafria's backstreets on the other side. Ivano considers the invitation but continues along the main road adding a good five hundred metres. 'Meet you there,' I call across the field.

We wait for the next bus into the city and in fifteen minutes alight in the centre of town. *Pension Pena* is only a few streets and three flights of wooden stairs away. I am as excited as a child on holiday. There is a full size towel on my double bed, a mirror, even two coat hangers in the wardrobe and a little balcony just big enough to stand on with a view to the street below. We arrange to meet later for a walk to the cathedral. I take a shower in the bathroom down the hall – a long hot shower – before falling into a deep siesta in the privacy of my very own Burgos palace.

After combing out a week's worth of knots from my hair I knock on Ivano's door. I hadn't bothered with the usual ponytail, enjoying instead the sensation of my hair falling free down to my waist, the cleanest it has been for weeks. This was a mistake. Ivano takes a step back, looks me up and down then blushes. '*Bella,*' he whispers. I am dumbfounded for a moment thinking maybe this is just a chivalrous Italian style greeting but, as we amble down the fashionable Avenida General Sanjurjo, Ivano keeps looking across at me, doe like. I try not to notice. Without the weight of his pack his walk takes on a loose limbed gait, more puppy than bear, and I pretend not to hear the occasional whisper under his breath that sounds suspiciously like a*more, amore*. Any other time I might be flattered. Today though, it all seems a bit incongruous and I start to feel trapped like a kookaburra in a Venetian cage. But I can't laugh it off; his heart on a sleeve has such innocence all I can do is look straight ahead while casually twirling the wedding ring round my finger.

In the shadow of Gothic cathedral spires I am saved not by a bell but by the baritone and Beatrice. We join them for wine and olives. They walked today from Villafranca and report that the truck stop café served up a memorable meal. The baritone has a lucrative job selling shipping rights to oil companies and deals are done by mobile phone even as he walks the Camino. Today a particularly large contract was sealed and to celebrate they are staying in a four star hotel just around the corner from our little Pena Palace. Burgos, with its grand cathedral, is something of a milestone for pilgrims. It is a city known for rich collections of art, the leafy boulevards along its river and an abundance of café culture. In high spirits we quaff a second wine and order tapas of marinated sardines and tongue zinging piquillo peppers stuffed with salt cod.

Beatrice sees the dilemma of Cupid's arrow each time Ivano shifts his chair a little closer to mine and I shift mine a little closer to hers. 'Come on you,' she says to

The Way Is a River of Stars

him, 'let's go for mass.' I feel as though we could be sisters, she the vivacious redheaded Catholic one that, I find out the next day, has also spent time with the same Tibetan teacher whose blessing pouch I wear. Her laugh and trilled Mexican accent is infectious. She has that singular quality of making everyone at the table feel at ease. I silently thank her and watch as they disappear arm in arm into the southern portal of the cathedral under the gaze of its twelve stone apostles.

The baritone leans across the table. 'Why are you so sad?' he asks. I am taken aback then laugh, a nervous laugh. 'Excuse me? What do you mean?' He grabs my hand and I feel as though an old, old soul looks straight through me. 'I've been watching you. Something is holding you back.' His words feel like a shock and I begin to cry and am soon shaking for fear I'll completely lose it – break into uncontrollable sobbing here in the middle of the plaza. All I can do is return his gaze and shake my head. 'I don't know. Nothing?' It's a lame reply and my stomach ties itself into a double knot. My whole body is on fire. He sits silently until my tears stop then whispers, 'This is your chance, whatever it is you can let it go. You can.'

Defenseless and strangely quiet I am suddenly a ghost back in our little house by the beach watching David go about his day without me. Both of us, in this imagined moment, lonely or simply alone? Though I feel invisibly strung to him through both affection and habit I have also felt relief to have this time apart. It suddenly seems a paradox and I feel cornered by the baritone into somehow reconciling the two. A dull panic curdles my thoughts. I look over to my friend, his carefree nature returned like a lost rabbit out of a magician's hat. He pours water into our wineglasses, 'Look at us,' he smiles, 'we are the same age, courting fifty. Life is short.'

Grateful he doesn't press for a reply – it would be a lost cause if he did – I come back. Back to the touch of my chair, the plaza and the cool glass stem in my hand as if returning to shore after being swept into sea by the pull of a deep, invisible tide.

I walk by a stone fountain, past the vacant stare of a pockmarked boy riding a fish, and look up to the limestone spires that have shimmered white under each setting sun for five centuries. They mock the winds, my glossy brochure says. And time too, I think, as I marvel at these eighty four metre towers of stone piercing the sky, still beautiful even as the polluted air of a modern Burgos scars their delicate tracery. I read on, The Cathedral of Burgos is alive, a Gothic temple dedicated to the Holy Virgin Santa Maria and her Immaculate Conception. I look up to its rose window, a rich glow of light, suspended under an arcade of eight kings and above them, the two towers. But it is the statue of the Virgin Santa Maria my eyes go. She stands midway at the base of the lantern spires as if she is the mediator between man and heaven. Either side, sculpted in large stone letters, is the declaration, *Pulcra es et Decora*, you are beautiful and fine.

Inside the lavish baroque surrounds of St. Tecla's

chapel I spot the backs of Beatrice and Ivano as they walk up to the priest for communion but I want to be alone and turn instead to the glass doors on my right. A few people kneel inside a long chapel, and I am drawn in as if caught by a slipstream. The Capilla del Santismo Cristo is home to The Black Christ yet against a scarlet red wall hangs the palest of bodies wearing a velvet skirt on a crucifix painted the same emerald green. His closed eyes, gaunt bearded face, the bruises and dark trickles of dry blood covering his arms and torso overwhelm me. Waves of heat flood my body again and I stop halfway to sit behind the hunched back of an old man. As soon as I am still the heat subsides and in its place I am slowly wrapped in what feels like a cloak of absolute acceptance, surreal coming from an image so violently wounded.

Those unexpected tears, where had they come from? I am there again in the plaza, hovering above our table and its empty wineglasses filled with water, looking down at the long lean body of my friend reaching out to me, watching my response, my pyre of confusion. The baritone in, I am sure, misguided affection seemed to be hinting I should leave David. He had, after all, recently left his wife of eighteen years, sold the house and was as a result a happier man. But the idea of leaving a relationship that has been part of me for almost half my life had thrown me into a kind of panic. Equally fearful though was the prospect of continuing together. Here in the presence of a medieval Christ, a most unlikely place for a Buddhist, I could see for the first time clearly and objectively the tired repetition, the repeated salvage of a comfortable routine from the same mistakes. How each time I played out the martyr, the disempowered damsel unable to speak her mind because she doesn't know her mind, and all in the name of keeping the peace. This realization doesn't come from a logical place, it is more an energetic recognition of the patterns engraved into my body. Letting them go feels more physical than mental. At first my exhalations seem charred but the longer I sit the finer and more subtle the release becomes until the pure quiet air that I breathe in is the same that I breathe out. More tears come, this time devoid of qualm. Absolving.

Candles always burn here to an image of Christ, said to have real skin and nails, and hair that needs shaving every eight days. It is the same image sculpted by the Pharisee Nicodemus who helped embalm Christ's body with myrrh and aloes after taking him from the cross. And so it is, credence is given by the faithful, myths overlap the real and miracles are worked. But I feel as if I am in a place where believing is not important. Allowing and being is. Words form like a vibration at the base of my throat, 'It is never the other,' they say, 'it is in you.'

There is a verse from the Hebrew Song of Songs: Rise up, my love, and come / the rains are over and gone / the flowers bloom in our land / the time for pruning has come.

What mystery, only by pruning a rose bush do roses come.

Mass has finished and Beatrice and Ivano walk in through the doors to sit at the front. Their faith and belief in the sacrament of communion brings them closer to God. What is my communion? 'It is never the other, it is in you.' Strange words, a riddle perhaps, that could be misconstrued. But no, in a sweet painful twist, there is a truth so obvious that I almost laugh out loud. It is as if all the cells in my body stop for a moment then start to spin again on a different axis. What happens to me is of no consequence, what matters is how I deal with it. Here though, the riddle turns in upon itself and the *I* of it disappears.

Remember following the mirror? Those big blue reflections of empty sky? I watch myself walk across an imaginary frame like some kind of mirage carrying bunches of roses into my cluttered house... the time for pruning has come. This, in the hands of two haiku-dueling Zen monks, is taken one step further. 'The mind is like a clear mirror, don't let it gather dust,' said Shenxiu to which Huineng replied, 'There is not a single thing where can dust collect.' Words come and I scribble them down: holding one of the angel's wings, I am tired of looking from the outside in, now is the time to look from inside out. This is the other wing!

Letting go, even of wings, I feel more whole than ever before and more ready to love.

I walk out from the shadows of the cathedral spires into a

late afternoon sun, light like a length of muslin pegged against the sky, my body rinsed, spinned and turned inside out. As I make my way back to the *pension* a woman stops me, asking for directions to a *refugio*. I have a vague idea and try to explain but underneath our words it is as if we share another language, female – open. It's a dreamlike encounter, as we look one to the other, that comes from our solitude and our bodies – hearts becoming whole and limbs aching in the same places. We wish each other luck and both start to cry as we hug. That is all we do. A fleeting encounter carrying more meaning and depth than many a long term acquaintance.

I continue along the river and spy Ivano sitting on a bench. At his thonged feet the water is a mercury dapple of willow reflections. His eyes are closed and his face turned up and into the rippled light moving across his skin as if he is feeling its caress. I put my hand out over the water to see what light on skin feels like – the quiver of a leaf left after a bird has taken flight from it – then slide onto the bench beside him.

He has not eaten and insists I join him, he knows the perfect place. Inside the doors of a dark beamed inn we settle into winged back chairs of polished oak at a table set with linen napkins and real roses. This is an *asadore*, a traditional old fashioned Castillian restaurant and I feel very under-dressed and, uncharacteristically, not at all hungry.

Ivano orders for me despite my protests but what arrives is perfect. A light almond gazpacho. His plate comes a few minutes later, lamb roasted in a wood fired oven. With a wine glass of the lightest El Bierzo red I am content inhaling the marriage of garlic, lemon and paprika, rosemary, thyme and oregano. Those doe eyes and insistence are as strong as ever but I am less concerned now. What use is there being defensive? He is a good and kind man and even though he refuses to acknowledge my marriage ring, 'Italia, you me,' I enjoy his company. It is frustrating though not to be able to communicate as I am still curious about his life, possible wife, secretary, villa; his reasons for being here.

We wander home under stars and the elegant light of old world street lamps, climb Pena's three sets of stairs, hesitate on the landing for one awkward moment then say goodnight. If I had been eighteen or twenty eight, I would have followed the path of least resistance but I am almost fifty. Today has been a day of keys and padlocks, tears and, hitherto, an unknown gravity. I lost my balance, I tumbled and floated and found my feet again. Be true to yourself. Exist with and not because of your lover. This is the galaxy I find myself in and as I let my body rest, close my eyes, its stars swirl milkier than the Milky Way through my heart.

The sound of sweepers and steel shutters opening on the street below coax me awake. I stretch out under my white sheets in my double bed lifting the top sheet then letting it fall featherlike onto my body. Again and again. Princess for a night I was, for nine velvet gloved hours. Had there been a whole packet of peas under my mattress I would not have cared.

The door to the room opposite is open. A blanket lies half on the floor, the bed linen tossed and wrinkled. Ivano has gone but I am not ready to leave.

I wander the streets without my carefully packed world, metaphorical and otherwise, strapped to my back. I find the post office and collect the package mailed to myself way back in Madrid. A new notebook, a sachet of shampoo, a quarter of Dr Bronner's all purpose peppermint soap, one third of a guidebook's pages and a tiny tube of rose hand cream. So thrilled am I to be in possession of such treasures that I trip on a paving stone across from the bridge and fall flat on my face. A sorry sight I must look with two bleeding knees but the small group of Burgonians waiting for the lights to turn green don't seem to notice. I blush for nothing as they stare ahead into the vagaries of their day, their desks and office chairs, their in-trays and out-trays, the small words that passed between lovers the night before, the kiss still fresh upon a daughter's cheek, the sensitive over wrought wife wanting what he is impotent to give, the rendezvous that will take the place of today's siesta.

I watch the blood seep through my trousers, roll them up and head towards the cathedral. Around a corner I crash head on with Stefan – intense, owl eyed, round faced Stefan from Austria. He has been walking since midnight from San Juan and is a misplaced soul here on the wide paved streets of a metropolis. But there is a smile and look about him that has the satisfaction and worldliness only a twenty year old can know.

'Where are you staying?' he asks.

'In a *pension,*' I reply, and without thinking, 'do you want to share a room?'

He lights up, 'I was just thinking maybe we could.'

Well there it is, what madness I think to myself inviting this gorgeous young man into my room. Think of him as Hamish my eighteen year old nephew, they even look alike. And you sleep in roomfuls of men every night so what's the difference, I continue, my mind doing what it does best, wriggling in and out of the situations it creates. We walk back and the Pena's senora is only too happy to give us Ivano's old room with two single beds.

There is a pleasant familiarity about the streets as I wind through plazas and parks, past boutiques and *panaderias,* tiny bars and the *asadore* from last night back to the cathedral. Through the Puerta del Sarmental, past the conception of a Virgin and her coronation. Past the ticket counter. Pilgrims admitted free.

Amongst a rack of brochures and guides I pick up a small bookmark containing words from a Pilgrimage Prayer, printed on behalf of helpers of disabled children on their way to Lourdes. It was not a prayer written for any particular pilgrimage. A pilgrimage is a pilgrimage no matter what the destination.

The path to your door is the path within / Is made by animals / Is lined by flowers / Is lined by thorns / Is stained with wine / Is lit by the lamp of Sorrowful dreams / Is washed with joy / Is swept with grief / Is blessed by the lonely traffic of art / Is known by heart / Is known by prayer / Is lost and found / Is always strange – the path to your door.

Is blessed by the lonely traffic of art? What does that mean, I wonder, as I pass one sumptuous chapel after another. The answer lay closer to home than I could ever have imagined. I find out much later, thanks to the sharp eye of an editor, that the prayer was written by Australia's most endearing poet-cartoonist, Michael Leunig. Was he looking through the eyes of one his ducks or a whimsical lone man dressed in an overcoat with a teapot on his head? What would Renaissance painters have made of that? I gaze up at their huge canvases, patinas of glistening oils draping the gorgeous bodies of angels and martyrs. There are Flemish tapestries and tableaus of stone, Baroque frescoes and Rococo altars, marble tombs and wooden tombs encased in copper and encrusted with jewels, and a carved walnut door. Seven female saints, Adam and Eve and the Annunciation, depictions of stigmatas and royal marriages, archbishops and urinating angels, Jesus on the road to Calvary, El Cid, and two versions of Santiago himself, Matamorous style, riding his stallion and wielding a sword and as a humble *peregrino* looking a little haggard among all the glory. And above – plastered domes carved and brightly painted, Mudejar domes, delicate weightless ceilings of stone tarted up with a bit of Gothic, and a star ribbed dome at the very centre blessed by the effigies of prophets and more saints. Thin shafts of dust drizzled light plummet down illuminating it all, and those of us looking up in wonder, blessed by the lonely traffic of art.

In the Capilla de Santa Ana, at the base of a fifteenth century retablo, a tree sprouts from the heart of a sleeping Jesse. The image does not quite gel with the angels and saints crowding every other chapel. This is an Old Testament story and for me the image speaks of a world more pagan than Christian: a place where the nether realms of sacred glades and tree spirits conspire against the miracles and resurrections of men.

I remember walking into a rainforest at home early on a summer morning and noticing lines of tiny ants filing up and down the lichen stained trunks of guioa trees. Each tree was studded with sap, tearlike extrusions translucent as amber and smooth to touch. The ants circled each one, a processional feast, I thought, this sipping from the blood of trees.

What affinity the Druids must have had with the natural world, their priests making incantations to the soul of an ancient oak. And how things change. In a tale from medieval Europe the heathen women of a village pleaded with Christian missionaries to stop cutting down their temple of sacred trees. 'The Gods of rain and sunshine will be destroyed,' they cried. Eight hundred years later – not such a radical protest.

I look up to the Virgin holding the Christ child on her lap at the top of Jesse's lineage tree, ancient fertility rites now safely cleansed by her immaculate conception. This temple of excess has something for everyone ...is always strange – the path to your door. I read the last lines of Leunig's prayer before circling the cathedral again, stopping at the door of the Black Christ to remember, in the end, how profound and simple truth can be.

Pigeons congregate in the evening and so do we in the plaza outside. They for crumbs and us for wine. Beatrice, the baritone, Stefan and a new face, Asterix. I wince at the name as much as his accent, a slow Californian drawl, but in the end am charmed by the presence of this tall, silver mustached hippy on the loose. For our last Burgos supper we find a bar down a side-street crammed with locals. Beatrice hustles to the front and yells our order across the counter, laughing, questioning, commanding. Spanish is a language that loves to express itself.

Five fried eggs, hot chips, salad and a platter of melt in the mouth salt squid arrive. We sit on tall stools and raise our glasses with greasy fingers. Comrades for life.

14

Shorn Sheep

Burgos to Hornillos de Camino

A shivery wind blows in through the open French doors of our room. Stefan has gone and I have a rendezvous with Beatrice and the baritone in twenty minutes, my first walking engagement on the Camino. We meet in a corridor sized bar packed with coffee-swilling, cigarette-smoking men in suits. Odd, given the hour is hardly past dawn. But by the time we reach the outskirts of Burgos the streets resume an empty, familiar quiet.

We are one third of the way to Santiago. A *meseta* stretches the next two hundred kilometers, a bare, flat, desolate scraping of land feared by some for its loneliness, detested by others for its boredom and loved by the rest for its three hundred and sixty degrees of pristine nothingness. I am not sure where I will fit. Ahead, as if heralding a taste of the pared down world to come, a line of poplar trees rustle in the wind and late summer leaves spiral to the ground with a sound like shhhh.

Our chattering falls away and the baritone strides ahead into the poplar forest on his poplar legs. Without the waggle of tongue and ears I am more present to the small details around me; part of my environment rather than a separate entity moving across it. When Beatrice and I begin talking again we discover we have both spent time with the same Geshe, a Tibetan scholar and teacher, she at Dharamsala's Library and me on a mountaintop in the Border Ranges of home. We share tales of his teachings. Before volunteering at Mother Theresa's hospice in Calcutta Beatrice spent a month studying with him in the foothills of the Himalayas. 'Geshe gave me the courage to be with dying people,' she says. 'There was no conflict when I began working in Calcutta. A verse I memorized from his teachings says, "May I give all help and joy to my mothers. May I take all their harm and pain secretly upon myself." And the nuns at the hospice would say, "See Jesus in each person you care for." Chanting and praying both I felt as though the more pain I took in the bigger my heart became. Never did I feel, okay enough, I can't take anymore.'

I tell Beatrice about the time I first met Geshe in my early twenties. Fresh from a period immersed in the austerities of Vipassana, Vajrayana Buddhism felt like a feast for mind and eye. We'd spend hours visualizing a pantheon of brightly coloured *dakinis*, Buddhas and *bodhisattvas*. There were bowls of nectar, rainbow bodies, sweet incense, giant lotus flower thrones, oceans the colour of lapis lazuli and amethyst mountains.

Step by step Geshe led us through the *sadhana* of the Medicine Buddha. We visualized his body as blue. His right hand, held in a *mudra* of generosity for the healing of all affliction and his left, holding a begging bowl, a symbol of the need for contentment if we are to be cured. In order to transcend suffering, first we need to understand it. Part of the Medicine Buddha teachings contain vast pharmacopoeias of alchemical potions using flowers, leaves, roots, barks and precious metals but our task was to loosen the habitual grip of our mind. It felt more like inner alchemy as Geshe instructed us to merge into the mind and body of the Medicine Buddha.

On the third day we sat for an hour meditation. It was a perfect morning. Outside a string of prayer flags hung motionless from two giant brush box against a cloudless blue sky. Someone tip toed into the hall, a muffled whisper echoed across our silence. At the end of our sit Geshe told us one of the participants, on her way to the retreat, had crashed her car into a tree and died. Her twin boys both survived without a scratch. We all knew her and it felt for a moment as if we all held onto the same breath. Geshe asked us to pray for her and her sons. He was unflinchingly calm in the way he held us until we were able to breathe again and walk out into a day that was still the same blue and strangely blameless.

For the rest of the week there was an urgency to our

practice. The glamour I had associated with our visualizations, the offerings of flowers and sweetmeats to the Gods, mantras and *mudras*, was no more or less meaningful than any other Buddhist teaching. It was not what I practiced but how.

Beatrice nods and we fall into a comfortable silence, our footsteps in time. I think back to my mother; how her Catholic upbringing, with its elaborate layering of ritual, continues to live under her skin. How we can never be separated from what forms us. Listening to the chants of Tibetan monks or breathing in the wood-spiced smoke of Tibetan incense I feel immediate resonance just as she must, hearing a Gregorian choir or breathing in frankincense.

In an hour we reach Tardajos. Its shuttered houses look sallow in the slow rising sun, its wide streets forlorn. St Francis of Assisi stayed here on his way to Santiago and, in the year of her death, Saint Teresa took communion in the Church of Santa Maria where farmers still pray to the Virgen de las Aguas for spring rains.

'What do you know about Saint Teresa?' I ask Beatrice.

'She was a rebel. At seven she ran away with her brother. She wanted the Moors to cut off her head, as a sacrifice to Christ. Then at twenty two she ran away again to join the Carmelites. She had so many visions and raptures that some accused her of being possessed. Can you believe for two years she took equal place beside Saint James as Patron Saint of Spain?' She pauses for me to digest this startling piece of information. 'That is, until the Cathedral of Santiago put up a fight and the pope had to withdraw his decree.'

I'm shocked. Not that I have an investment either way in who gets to be highest saint on the ladder but it seems a touch fickle – politics on a path to *campus stellae*, the field of stars. We link arms, two women united for a day, walking a road to the bones of a Saint called James.

'*El Castillo Interior*. Do you know it?' she asks. I shake my head. 'This was Saint Teresa's second book, *The Interior Castle*. In it she described the soul as a diamond with seven storeys inside.'

'Seven?' I reply. 'That's the same as the number of chakras in Tibetan Buddhism.' I am astonished to find a parallel concept in the visions of a sixteenth century Catholic saint. Beatrice's eyes twinkle as she quotes a favourite line, 'There are many ways of being in the same place.'

'Come on ladies, make a move,' the baritone calls from a distance. So wrapped have we been in the intrigues of Saint Teresa we've dawdled the whole way through town.

Beatrice blows him a kiss and waves him on. 'Oh, and then there's the part where she warns her nuns about the dangers of falling for their confessors.'

Linking arms and quickening our pace we laugh our way to the end of Tardajos where the baritone waits, greeting him with a salute, a stand to attention and a bellow of 'Yes, sir.'

'You Dutch people,' Beatrice admonishes with a flirtatious flick of her red hair. 'Always so on time.'

We catch up to a woman hobbling in a pair of threadbare sneakers. I wince as I watch her, with her makeshift wooden staff, set each foot down carefully, so carefully, as if she walks over hot coals. Beatrice asks in Spanish if she is okay. Blisters cover the soles of her feet and fester between all of her toes but she refuses to stop. Santiago awaits. Her attitude is neither stubborn nor pious. Her suffering, so palpable it hurts us, has humility and faith, and I don't doubt for a second she will walk every inch of the way.

Beyond the village of Rabe de las Calzadas looms the *meseta*. I walk to the crest of a hill with a sense of curiosity and anticipation. The sky looks bigger, the air feels dry and thin. Seven years of Zen practice, I hope, have loosened the cogs of my mind enough for me to appreciate a week's walk through literal emptiness. A sharp small pain shoots down my left shin.

There it is, a monotone golden tapestry stretched tight to the horizon. You can see for miles. Eight and a half kilometers away are the pinprick of conifers and matchbox roofs of Hornillos del Camino. Tiny dots, pilgrims, freckle the dirt road sweeping toward it like the arc of a fisherman's line hurled out to sea. Another small sharp pain, this time, down the right shin.

My attention fluctuates between the two, exhilaration of the expanse ahead of us and the awful awareness that these new sensations in my legs are more than phantoms.

The high altitude air washed clean by all this space is quaffable. I listen to the banter of two lovers and learn that when the baritone takes off to the next village, leaving Beatrice to work her magic with whoever she joins, he will leave in the middle of the road a bottle of water or a wildflower with a small note attached for her to find. She looks up at him, half again her height, as he prepares to stride ahead, 'You better wait for me at the next village.'

I fall behind both of them, taking progressively smaller, tenderer steps. In my well worn in shoes and moisture wicking socks, and succumbing to just one tiny blister all this way, a sense of physical invincibility had crept in. But as each foot touches the ground an ominous sensation grows in a part of my body I had never considered a risky attachment. Beatrice and the baritone are soon two stick figures in the distance and by the time I reach the outskirts of Hornillos the pressure from each step transfers up my legs to points where, with acute precision, it feels as if particular cells are being sliced into two by a scalpel. The sensation ricochets from one leg to the other, compounding, until each incision tears the person I think I am into pieces.

As if to mock me the ruins of a leper hospice appear in a tumble of weeds. 'Unclean, unclean,' I hear in the hot rippling of wild grass. Is it the hallucination of my pain ravaged mind or the real voice of a disembodied woman trailing the wind outside the gates of Hornillos de Camino? She clacks a warning with the two pieces of wood in her numbed hands and its sound cuts through my self pity. How many pilgrims passed by this hospice of San Lazaro on their way to safe haven, averting their eyes from the rags and disintegrating bodies of these outcast souls? Our little sufferings – how they mask us to the plight of another and how they chain us to ourselves. I realize that for the last hour of limp-limp I've been consumed with aversion for the pain. An aversion that turns in upon itself to a craving for its disappearance.

I face the road back to Burgos and see the faint silhouette of the woman with blisters shimmering in the midday heat. I know it is her, she moves so slowly it seems she doesn't move at all. Her small shadowless body breaks the cycle of my mind games. The Camino is a way of stone as well as stars.

Beside a three spouted fountain with a plaster rooster in eternal crow at its top a handful of pilgrims loll about on white plastic chairs like seeds spilled from a pod. Beatrice looks at my limp and we both know I won't be going any further. Perhaps I could summon the energy and the heart, but not the legs. Watching them walk west arm in arm I feel suddenly sad and terribly alone. The baritone turns back and calls, 'Go get yourself a bed,' as if to shake me out of it.

It starts to rain as I finish washing my clothes in an old tub at the back of the *refugio*, a quaint assortment of rooms tacked onto the church. Then it pours. I settle onto my top bunk and try not to breathe too deeply. The man below has just draped his socks over the end of his bed; the smell puts the pigpen in Espinosa to shame. There is only one thing for it. Chocolate.

I offer some to an elderly Italian couple who share the bunk beds across from mine. They are frisky as newlyweds having for the first time two beds joined at the side. We polish the chocolate off and collapse into giggles and pigeoned gibberish as we devise a makeshift clothesline with our walking poles. Underneath our artfully displayed underwear we settle into the sweet oblivion of siesta.

Perched on the church steps pilgrims shelter from the rain like a flock of bedraggled birds. I am amazed to see the Argentinean tango dancer from Puenta la Reina holding court in their midst but no sign of her *ninos*. In two weeks her skin, hanging in loose old lady wrinkles from a body of sinew, has turned from olive to near black. With a captive audience and perfect stone ceiling acoustics she sings to us and the empty plaza in a visceral voice.

Hornillos de Camino has an intimate internalized feel with its one general store, one bar and population of sixty nine. Not unfriendly, more uninterested in catering to anything outside of its own ten century history. We become that. Lazy figures on a porch waiting for the sky to clear, comparing blisters on feet and other predicaments, invisible or otherwise, and our own much smaller histories – the people we have met, the ruins visited and the ones passed by. Dreams. Loose clouds on currents of wind. The rain abates. Some shoulder their packs for another few hours of walking. Others arrive, soaked to the bone.

Two familiar shapes appear at the end of the street. One of them lanky and energetic. It could be Don Quixote and the other, squat and round with a bandy legged gait, his faithful Sancho Panza. But no, that's too tall a stretch of the imagination, it is instead the tall and beautiful young Ana and her kindhearted father. There are no beds left but the mayor who doubles as *hospitalero* gives them mattresses on the kitchen floor. We escape a gathering of noisy spaghetti cooking pilgrims for the warm, crowded and even noisier dining room of Bar Manolo. *Tortilla de Chorizo y Pimientos, Lomo de Cerdo con Leche* and *Pollo con Setas* grace our table with wine good enough to drink neat. Ana has the tortilla, her father the pork roasted in milk, a popular old world way of tenderizing meat and a favourite of his back in Barcelona, and me the chicken with wild mushrooms. It's a repast that makes us forget the sleeping arrangements ahead.

In an early scene of Don Quixote his niece attempts to dissuade him from leaving home. 'Many go for wool and come back shorn,' she admonishes.

What she considers negative would be an auspicious outcome for a pilgrim. Why walk eight hundred kilometers? In the beginning it is as if Santiago de Compostela is the gold at the end of the rainbow but as the miles go by you watch yourself cast aside possessions, the unnecessary shirt, the pages of a book. 'Just a minute, let me check my diary' – is mercifully ditched too. Who knows where I will end up today and who cares? I do shudder though at the thought of those stinking socks on the bunk bed below mine. But in the end a bad smell is just a bad smell. In the big picture it pales in comparison to how much a mind can let go and how much a heart can hold.

We walk out into a night dappled by moon and cloud. There is something about the scent of old stone houses and streets after rain, washed clean, as if the smell is new like bricks fresh from the kiln, shining cobblestones gathered from riverbeds settled into soft beds of mortar. Streets untrod and untarnished by trails of medieval pilgrims or the kicked dust of twenty first century boots. The night is too pristine to waste.

I wander to the graveyard on the edge of town where the only shadows thrown by the moon are of trees and crooked tombstones. The iron gate is open, rusted into position. I lean back against it and look up at the sky. This is a *meseta* kind of quiet. Quiet that settles into your bones and wraps you like a mother wraps a child. Clouds shapeshift across the moon and I imagine Freston, phantom thief of books, riding his dragon cloud into the Don's house to save him from further hallucinations, wounds dealt by giants, and bruises had falling from horses. All a conspiracy to snap Quixote out of his dreams.

A lone slow walking stranger in a leather slouch hat snaps me out of mine.

'Can I join you?' he asks as he sits down beside me looking straight up to that same dragon cloud, now more like the face of an old man.

We become so mesmerized by the parade of beasts and birds, a phoenix and a two headed swan, a wolf and a witch's hat that soon it is as if, sitting in the gateway that separates the living from the dead, we are swallowed and spat out on the other side of time.

'Where have you come from?' I ask.

'Somewhere past Castrojeriz,' he replies. 'I slept out.'

'But …' and then I understand. He is walking in the opposite direction. And that is why he feels different. There is not an ounce of anticipation in his body.

In the early days of the Camino reaching Santiago was only half the journey. There were no trains or planes for a quick exit home. You turned around and walked into the dawn for as many days as you had walked with the morning sun on your back. A few days ago I passed a couple also walking east. They had a donkey and were dressed like an apparition of Joseph and Mary. They had that same slow presence about them. No grasping in their eyes.

I listen and I learn. Not just the name of a character in the next village and his quaint bar or the last Templar knight or the ghosts that live in the mists of Foncebadon. I learn that once you come to the end of all your desires, when there is no longer such a thing as a destination, you come to a common place of uncommon beauty.

15

Seven Ingredients
Hornillos de Camino to Leon

I leave a sleeping Hornillos, past its sentry of tall pine trees out to the edge of a dark quiet world. The pain in my legs is no better, if anything worse. With the slightest pressure the exact same points halfway between both knee and ankle inflame as if pierced by a red hot needle. As soon as I lift my foot the sensation changes from sharp to dull. The other leg then cries for attention. I walk slowly, delicately. Can I make friends with this?

A church bell peals three times and three times twice again calling up the sun and three hundred and sixty degrees of gold. It is the Angelus, the Peace bell, rung at morning, noon and evening as a call to prayer. *Angelus Domini nuntiavit Mariae*, a prayer asking for the blessings of Mary: Pray for us, O Holy Mother of God, that we may be made worthy of the promises of Christ.

The bell's chime strikes the body of the world, an exquisite sound. Discomfort in my own small body pales and as my back slowly warms with the rising sun I walk on as if in a trance. What does it mean to be made worthy, I wonder. That I empty my mind-body of every ounce of self? In Zen retreats once each day the teacher gives *dokusan*, a private face to face interview with students about their practice. Usually a formal encounter it begins with a bow and ends with a bell. It is the only time a student speaks during a retreat. Generally *dokusan* lasts no more than five or ten minutes, it is considered a precious time and not to be wasted. The teacher might ring the bell mid-sentence if a student lapses into theories or conjectures, self-loathing or self-loving. The bell is a symbol of clarity and as such can shake a student out of aimless navel pondering into the enlightened moment of *satori*. In Tibetan Buddhism the bell represents the feminine principle, the wisdom of emptiness, an oceanic womb where all things are born and into which all things dissolve.

The Angelus prayer continues: We beseech thee, O Lord, pour thy grace into our hearts.

How can I receive this grace if I am already full? Each morning at the end of a Zazen meditation we would chant the Heart Sutra: *Ze Sho Ho Ku So Fusho Fu Metsu*. All things are essentially empty, not born, not destroyed. *Fu Ku Fujo Fuzo Fu Gen*. Not stained not pure, without loss without gain.

I feel like a tiny spider, eight little legs spinning,

swinging dew drenched threads between Christian prayers and Buddhist chants, singing bowls and church bells all awash in a water coloured land that knows inherently the mystery contained within every night and day, every seed and tree. Is there any difference between the warp and the weft, the heart of a woman and the world she sees reflected in it?

So here is the *meseta*. A harvested earth and a sky twice the size of any I've ever seen. Tiny prairie birds scamper out from clumps of missed wheat to skim across the fields chicka-chicking on very important business before disappearing again into a vast straw coloured canvas of nothingness. I add prairie birds to my list of uninvited but often entertaining visitors; the monkeys, wild horses and rampaging elephants that corral in my unconscious ever ready to pounce. This is the perfect place to set them free and though it takes me half the morning to walk the ten kilometers to Hontanas I feel as emptied as the sky.

Most of the villages up till now have sought protection from armies and thieves on hilltops. For the first time I descend. Hontanas lies sheltered from harsh summers and winters in a natural bowl of the plateau. The bell tower of the fourteenth century Church of the Immaculada Concepcion rises above its sunbleached roofs but there is nothing immaculate about the cemetery of white goods and oil drums littering the entrance into town. I take a photo, framing it so that the old fridges and washing machines won't impinge the romance of an otherwise timeless scene, forgetting that memory singes us and cannot be dismissed so easily.

One and two story homes share the same walls; small kiln bricks and larger hewn blocks hint at different generations of building. Tufts of dead grass grow from crevices of abandoned houses like old beards and slabs of lichen stained rock wedged into outside walls as stairs hover like giant fungi at the entrance to crooked doors.

'You'll find him in the first bar on the right – the small dark one,' my cloud watching companion from last night had said and sure enough through a tumbledown door I enter the dim lit domain of the famous Victorino. A few pilgrims are here, taking in the peculiar ambiance of dust-coated strings of chillies and garlic, dog-eared matador posters and an odd shaped collection of glass beakers and trophies. I am, it appears, in the presence of a champion. A framed picture and newspaper clippings taped to the wall show him pouring a long stream of red wine from the spout of a beaker onto his forehead. The wine then flows down his nose and into his mouth.

Behind the bar Victorino himself stands like the seventh dwarf in a checked shirt bursting at the buttons, slicing through long baguettes and a chunk of *jamon*. He mumbles a greeting, gives a nicotine toothed smile when I ask for the next *bocadillo* then pours a dubious looking glass full with red wine and slides it to me. I had not ordered this but drink it anyway thinking it might dull the pain in my legs. I attempt to concentrate on the advice of the girl sitting beside me while, from the corner of my eye, I watch Victorino's dirt-stained fingernails rub half a tomato into my bread.

'You must stop walking,' she says and a debate begins. A Swiss woman swears that shin splints, for this is what she says I have, will not heal unless I stop. A Spanish girl disagrees saying I should just keep going and it will work itself out. But Victorino is the deciding factor. He brings over black coffees, looks at my legs then says he is going to a funeral in Corrion de los Condes. He can give me a ride. From there a bus leaves for Leon where there are *farmacias* and a hospital.

Pilgrims come and go from the bar and the monkeys and prairie birds take up residence inside my head. Even if I continued to walk, at my present pace, it would take another month to reach the end of the meseta. And what if I risk permanent damage by continuing? Then there is my non-changeable air ticket home. A short bus ride here and there does no harm but to skip a good third of the Camino? Sacrilegious! In the two hours I wait for Victorino I seesaw between despair and denial. Just when the landscape seemed to be creeping into my soul and the rhythm of the days and the silent workings of saints, this has to happen.

'Exactly. Perfect,' chimes a bell-like voice inside my head.

Victorino, now dressed in a blue suit with trousers falling short of his ankle socks by a good six inches, throws a dozen baguettes onto the back seat of his old van to make room for me in the front. I climb in. He slicks back the few strands of grey hair falling across his pink scalp, dusts flour and breadcrumbs from his jacket and with a splutter we lurch into first gear then with another, into second. We head out of town at a speed that feels positively reckless.

Any philanthropic leanings I imagined my driver might have whittle away in the next few kilometres. Between horn honks for every pilgrim we pass he turns and leers at me repeating, with a gravelly, more lecherous by the minute voice, *'Guapa, guapa.'* He tries again with *'Bonita,'* taking one hand off the wheel to pump his arm. I slide closer to my door and laugh him off thinking, what the hell have I got myself into this time? Isn't he supposed to be going to a funeral? I attempt the wedding ring tack with a matronly glare but this only hots things up. *'Me gusta mucho, bueno,'* he chuckles in reply as if to say, 'I've captured me a feisty one.' I resort to the snub as any other response only serves to egg him on and for the remainder of our journey stare out my window across a flat, lifeless panorama broken occasionally by the lonely silhouette of a pilgrim. In less than an hour we cover the distance that would have taken three days to walk.

An unabashed Victorino ushers me into a busy café at the Carrion de los Condes bus stop. He orders coffees and I pay, the least I can do as thanks for the ride. I notice him focusing on a lottery ticket display behind the counter and buy him two. Harassment aside, a cup of coffee seems hardly enough recompense for petrol. He appears happy with this and we return to the van for my pack. With it hitched half onto my back he demands ten euros. I am dumbstruck and then furious with myself for being so gullible. First for accepting a so called funereal ride that turns out to be more a case of hostage to lewdness and then to fork out half a day's budget on two lottery tickets. In my best combination calm-rage voice I let leash my defence. His face freezes into a scowl and he demands again. Our Mexican standoff is cut short by the arrival of the bus. I can't believe I give him anything, but I do, placing five euros in his hand before stomping away.

Still shaking with a mix of indignation and humiliation someone grabs me from behind in a great big bear hug. Ivano! I attempt to match the same delight on his face but fall a little short. Out of the frying pan and into the fire. Then who should I see but Hilde. How funny, our last parting in Navarette was from a bus. Hilde is as unhurried and accepting of circumstance as she was when we first met; her flushed cheeks and that lopsided floppy hat cast their spell again. Thoughts of Victorino banished, I hug them both. Back in the folds of The Way – whether we walk or ride a bus is simply not the point. Another tap on my shoulder, tall fair Alex, lone singer, connoisseur of cheeses. 'So you did get my flowers,' he says with a twinkle. Confused at first I follow his eyes to my pack. Tied to its straps are the sprigs of heath and broom left on my pillow all the way back in San Juan de Ortega.

We clamber aboard; the injured and the tired, the time constrained ones and the had enough of the *meseta* ones. It seems I have joined a whole new sub-culture, *peregrinos del autobus*. Any minute we'll launch into a multilingual version of the Yellow Submarine as we full speed diesel our way to Leon. I feel the same odd sense of displacement though, traveling a distance that would take another five days of walking in just over an hour. But the view from my window stretches barren and brown for miles and the Camino is a relentless gravel line running parallel to the road. The few lonely pilgrims I glimpse look fragile against the harsh straightness of it all.

Hilde, Ivano and I head for the Convento Santa Maria de las Carbajalas, run by the Madres Benedictinas. Alex heads for the municipal *refugio*, lured by rumours of internet and television. Hilde hobbles, Ivano lopes and I limp up and down a maze of streets in the old city, retracing our steps several times before finding the Convent spanning the length of a deserted plaza.

Through gates large enough for a horse and carriage is a complex of dormitories, each room filled with steel bunk beds. But there is redemption, men are in one room, women and married couples share another. God bless the Benedictine nuns. They follow a Leon tradition begun in the Middle Ages when curtains were hung between beds and no more than two bodies per mattress were permitted, it being: A dishonest thing to have women and men in a single dormitory, given the people who come to the hospice are not, generally, of high calibre.

The nuns are kind. At this stage of the Camino, most pilgrims have walked at least four hundred kilometers and, as one nun says to me, 'Suffered a little for Jesus.' She has no objections to me staying extra nights so my legs can heal and gives me directions to Leon's hospital where pilgrims are treated for free.

In the waiting room I sit with a man in deep conversation with the coins he holds in his hands. A nurse calls him by name, like a child, and leads him away. I have been moving from place to place every day and have forgotten there are those who, even in the town where they were born, have no place other than the comfort of strangers and the world that spins inside their head. I know I am making an assumption about him but is his awareness so different from mine? I too live in a world of illusion, maybe the only difference is that mine has windows. It is in the end the same quantum leap, the same answer to a deceptively simple riddle, that takes any one of us to the threshold of our true home.

Alex walks in and we are pointed to a pilgrim clinic. A doctor examines the multiple blisters on Alex's feet then bathes them with iodine and applies bandages. I roll up my trouser legs with nothing to show but she pokes here and there, writes me a script for anti-inflammatory pills, suggests an ointment and commands rest. I feel better already. We wind our way back through the streets of old Leon and plan to meet at the cathedral in the evening.

This is a royal and courtly city, packed with plentiful riches, says the *Codex Calixtinus*. Couples wander down the streets, women in twin sets and shawls, the men in tailored shirts and pressed trousers. Bars, bakeries and ice cream parlours are abuzz as shoe salons, sombrero boutiques, fine china and antique shops open for evening trade. I order *chocolat caliente*, perfect for dipping warm *churros*, long deep fried doughnuts dusted with icing sugar. Twilight falls in soft layers of palest pink and the air is infused with the perfume of promenading ladies.

Drumbeats notch this sensual overload up ten decibels. The street clears for a feast of noise, a troupe of beaming foot stomping Samba musicians playing in time to their whistle blowing, somersaulting leader. Steel surdo drums, smaller repenique drums, cowbells, tambourines and cymbals. It's a *Carnivale* that brings a smile to an old lady leaning on her walking stick. The little boy beside her is so mesmerized he stops licking his ice-cream. And me, well, shin splints or no shin splints, their rhythm is impossible to resist and I join the growing crowd of dancers who follow behind, stop-starting along Descalzos Regueral Cervantes all the way to the cathedral. I am a woman possessed, shaking out my shoulders, setting free my hips; moving into the heart of the beat and out again until my body forgets itself.

Just as a bride arrives at the foot of two golden Gothic spires so do we. As if to challenge the drummers, church bells peal four clear deep notes from high to low over and over. The band strikes up again and the stone *Virgen Blanca* standing at the centre of the main portal is smiling. Above her an angel weighs human souls on a pair of scales. To the right ghoulish little men stuff sinners into boiling cauldrons and to the left a parade of happy souls are ushered toward the gates of paradise. Jesus sits above, both hands raised in triumph. As for the bride, adorned in white silk, her face is as radiant as the Virgin's. I follow her through the doors of the cathedral. Inside I am swallowed by light.

La Pulchra Leonina, House of Light – one hundred and twenty five stained glass windows twenty and thirty feet high, fifty seven circular ones and three gigantic rose windows. If I were to put my heart into that angel's scales I swear she would feel only the weight of a feather. Transfixed, I turn around and around in the middle of the nave before floating down the ambulatory past the main chapel to the five smaller ones radiating behind.

And there she is, the woman I had seen on Ventosa's *refugio* wall, so lifelike she takes my breath away. Virgen de la Esperanza, I read, sculpted in the thirteenth century. Her hair is covered by a Gothic circlet and veil the colour of ripened wheat, her body is draped in a midnight blue cloak embroidered with flowers. Ever so lightly she rests the long slender fingers of her right hand over her swollen belly. The sign below says: He came as the son of a human mother: Galatians 4.4. I look up to her ivory face, the tip of her long nose and cheeks blushed bright rose-pink, her clear brown eyes framed by raised fine-lined eyebrows. Innocence, dream, astonishment, love – all of these suffuse her. If ever a Virgin deserved the name Esperanza, Virgin of Hope, it is her. And if ever there was a rumoured miracle of a beating heart inside stone I would swear here, it is true.

Drifting back to the main retablo my eyes return to the last of the day's light streaming through its expanse of stained glass. Twelve apostles circle the still point of the highest rose window. The colours of their robes, cobalt, magenta and daffodil, dapple the cathedral floor. Who were the artisans that blew molten glass into cylindrical shapes letting them fall flat to solidify on stone; who experimented with oxides and enamels; who cut and filed them to fit between strips of lead? What were their names, these men who lived seven hundred years ago, their bones now no more than the dust I see carried in the stained shafts of light? But the bodies they made – saints and falconers, regal ladies and proud donors, mythical beasts and hunters, pilgrims kneeling at the tomb of St James – they all come to life each time the sun rises.

What would it be like for a medieval pilgrim arriving in Leon from France or Belgium or Italy; the soles of her feet cracked and hard as old leather, lips blistered from a *meseta* sun or the snows of the Castilian plain? If she looked up, would she think it was God breathing into her through those windows?

Mass finishes and the silence around me stirs into a hum of voices and shuffles of feet. I catch sight of Alex leaving the chapel and am surprised when he tells me he is Catholic. More than surprised, I am strangely moved. Behind those thick lens glasses his blue eyes engage without the need to posses and I sense in the way he walks he is grounded and at home in his body. It is as if, when someone as young and intelligent as Alex embraces

Catholicism, new life is breathed into what many perceive as antiquated.

Along the Camino I have been enthralled by the worlds of sculpted saints, adorned and unadorned domes, a tympanum, a cloister, and here in Leon the Lady Esperanza and all around her these windows of light. They have opened the way, invited me in, to begin to understand and appreciate something that, for most of my life, I did not. I remember the first line of Leunig's prayer found in Burgos on the other side of that meseta – the path to your door is the path within. And as Alex and I amble from one end of the cathedral to the other I wonder if our meeting might be another door, another star, on this path we walk.

The drummers have gone. We turn down a narrow lane away from the evening crowd and follow the ruins of a wall whose foundations are close to two thousand years old. The route we take would have been familiar to Romans, Muslims and Jews and merchants from as far as the Middle East. Fleeces from sheep grazing on Leon's southern plains were traded for Byzantine silks and precious stones. Christians then Muslims, then Christians again, ruled Leon until, in the thirteenth century, Burgos stole the show. There were tales of a Gothic wonder, Our Lady of Burgos, the construction of its spires and portals a miracle of faith and architecture. People left Leon in droves. Had it not been for the Camino, Leon might have fallen altogether. The present cathedral replaced a Romanesque one, to equal if not outshine any other on the road to Santiago. And the humble pilgrim, after months of flea-ridden beds, could look forward to five star accommodation in the famous San Marcos hospice, today a *parador*, an entirely upgraded establishment fit for wealthy tourists and high class pilgrims.

On a terrace lit by lantern light, under the shadow of horse chestnut trees, we eat olives and woodfired pizza. Local families fill the tables while children race about on scooters and pushbikes. A toddler with a tomato smeared face plays hide and seek under his parent's table. We ease into our chairs, silently musing the lazy evening we share, away from cathedrals, *refugios* and roads forever strung with pilgrims.

But there is one question I have been wanting, waiting, to ask and with Alex I feel I can. 'In churches along the way, you know how there is often a mass before a pilgrim's blessing? Well, I take mass sometimes. I was confirmed as an Anglican a long, long time ago but, as a practicing Buddhist, I wonder am I committing some grave sin in the eyes of the church?'

'Or in the eyes of Buddha?' he asks.

'I hadn't thought of it like that,' I chuckle.

'I don't know what a priest would say, in his heart. The pope though, that's another question. But for me, as long as you are aware of what you are doing and it is done with good faith … show me the sin in that. It is between you and God and I have a hard time seeing him turning anyone away.'

We fall quiet again and as I chew my food I start to

chew one word.

'Faith. It's a loaded concept don't you think Alex?'

'Blind faith, for sure. This is probably the place in any religion where people lose touch with themselves and with what is morally right or wrong.'

I agree. And we talk on into the night about the implications of belief. How faith is a belief in something greater than ourselves. And how faith begins. Is it devotion that first hauls us out of the sea of self? My first religious memory is of a plastic nativity set brought out each year and given pride of place under our Christmas tree – Mary, Joseph and the three wise men. It was a story as magical as any fairy tale for a small child. I loved that little tableau and though each year it looked worse for wear, chipped paint, cracked plastic, my devotion would inch up another rung, from the mother who bore me to a benevolent God in the sky.

Faith kept me on my meditation cushion. 'Think of it as trust or confidence,' some teachers said. I remember in early retreats finding myself uncomfortably stuck, whether in pain or the bog of inertia when for hour upon hour nothing *happened*. Doubt crept in – what a waste of time, so many things I could be doing, I should leave – and on and on my mind connived. It was faith, developed over time, that helped me hold these doubts at bay. Everything changes, *anicca*. This was the only permanent thing I could rely on. I had clocked up quite a few hours over the years experiencing this startling fact and slowly my original devotion, the idea of a smiling Buddha sitting on a lotus throne, grew into faith based on a cerebral understanding. This in turn was grounded by each moment of mindfulness whether on my cushion, in walking meditation, brushing my teeth or lacing a shoe.

In second century India Nargajuna wrote *A Precious Garland,* a text of five hundred verses, as advice for the happiness of his King. In the fourth verse he wrote: Having faith one relies on the practices, having wisdom one truly knows, of these two wisdom is the chief, faith is its prerequisite.

In a similar vein, the medieval philosopher and theologian Saint Anselm wrote: I hold it to be a failure of duty if, after we have become steadfast in our faith, we do not strive to understand what we believe.

Ten minutes to curfew! We wish each other a good night. I tip toe into the Convent's chapel just as the Benedictine sisters are beginning their nightly service. They stand either side of the altar, all of the nuns in black except for the white wimple and veils of two young novices. One of the sisters is so old she hardly has the strength to stand. Her purple veined hands never stop trembling as she holds herself up with a rail yet her voice lilts high above ours as pure as the Angelus bell that chimed this morning, a *meseta* away in Hornillos. Fifteen centuries ago St Benedict initiated his monks and nuns into the chanting of prayers seven times a day – God could not possibly ignore such persistence.

We sing a Spanish Salve Regina. 'Hail, Holy Queen enthroned above, O Maria! Hail, Mother of mercy and of love, O Maria!' The lights go out and we are plunged into darkness. Climbing into our bunk beds, the only sounds are whispers between husbands and wives. The rest of us close our eyes, blessed by the *great silence* of a Benedictine night.

I am woken in the morning by two women swishing disinfectant up and down each aisle, their mops ringing in steel buckets. '*Tranquilo*,' one says as I get up to move my pack from the floor. She swings it to a top bunk and motions me to stay. I roll over feeling deliciously naughty lying here in this huge room as every other pilgrim marches on.

My expectations of a peaceful night were dashed early. The woman in the bed beside me was a steam train, each breath in like a slow 'I think I can, I think I can,' chugging up a hill, filling her balloon-like lungs in preparation for the breath out and then a rip-roaring belt down the other side. She was a small woman too. For a while all I could do was lie in bed shaking my head in disbelief. The tension between each breath grew unbearable. I kneel to you, dear reader, in confession. I took one of my walking sticks and began to poke her, a gentle poke, but for a few entertaining minutes this was enough to settle her down. In the end though I had to devise a more self contained strategy. I plumped up the foam of my earplugs, tied a towel around my head, buried under my pillow then counted cloud jumping sheep. I have vague memories of fifty eight.

I drift in and out of sleep but soon my feet start to twitch. Promising myself to take it slow I venture out into deserted Sunday morning streets until I reach a market in a medieval square. Under fringed umbrellas, makeshift tarpaulins and maroon marquees stalls sell *son todas nuevas*, all new season produce and this being autumn, what a feast! Crates of green, red and black capsicum, turnips, shallots, hessian bags of green beans and tiny dark Pardinas lentils, sunflower heads full of speckled seeds, red apples and purple figs, a rooster on a lead and crates full of canary yellow chickens.

A loudspeaker crackles to life with the music of a brass band and the cheese and sausage vendors crank up their sales pitch. At eye level is a glorious array of *embutidos* swinging from hooks, enough to turn the stomach of a Moor or Jew. Perhaps the pride of place pork takes on a Spanish table goes back to the days of re-conquest by the Christians after years of enforced abstinence. In a frenzy of national pride chorizo quickly found its way back into paellas and chick pea tagines. And in the days of the Inquisition the tables turned again. Clandestine Jews and Muslims needed to at least feign affection for the scent of sausage or risk expulsion.

The leathery skins of salt cured *jamon serrano* hang heavily and are sold by the leg or in paper thin slices – anything thicker is impossible to chew. There is *lomo embuchado* a pork loin marinated with smoked paprika and oregano and chorizo sausages, *dulce* and *picante*, sweet and spicy. I pass long black *morcillas* looped into circles and remember the night in San Juan de Ortega and my miraculous recovery the next morning. This Leon market is carnivore heaven. The *piece de resistance* is *jamon iberico*, the cured dense flesh of a hairy black pig that forages in cork forests. Two samples are held out for the inspection of a tall silver haired customer. He adjusts his glasses to the bridge of his nose and purses his aristocratic lips while the vendor points to the delicate marbles of fat running through each. I relegate my purchase to a few slices of humble Serrano made from a white pig and a quarter of the price.

What does seduce me though are the *quesos*, wheels of cheese three deep and four high on tables running the length of the next aisle. Many owe their legacy to Leon's reputation for wool in the Middle Ages when shepherds herded sheep across the Castillian plains each freezing winter so that they grew the thickest, most sumptuous of fleeces. It was the cheese crafted from their ewes' milk that sustained them. I face full moons and half moons and wish Alex was here to guide me. A red aproned man cuts me a shard of Zamorano. '*Similar al manchego,*' he says as I let it melt in my mouth. This cheese is matured in local wine cellars and its rind is a musty grey. It tastes nutty at first then a loam of dark underground air and oak barrel lingers in my mouth. I work my way through samples of San Simon smoked cheese, a wonderfully mild goat Garrotxa and the sycamore leaf wrapped Valdeon blue, salty at first then sweet on my tongue. An old man, looking like the father of all cheeses, steps his assistant aside and takes a sliver from a thin orange wheel. 'Do I eat this too?' I ask pointing to its crusty rind and he nods effusively. '*Queso de La Serena.*' This is the cheese that will clinch the sale. Made from raw merino milk and curdled with wild thistle flowers it has a creamy taste and velvet consistency, a tang and an intriguing hint of bitterness. I break the largest euro note I have and figure on picnics for the next couple of days, not to mention cheese scented clothes, as I pack four tissue wrapped chunks like rare truffles into my bag.

I rest for the remainder of the day, swallowing antiinflammatory pills every three hours, praying for another miracle. It is hard to know if my legs are healing or the drugs are just masking the pain. I join a group of pilgrims over instant coffee and sugar coated biscuits left out by the nuns. There is the inevitable discussion about the next few days of walking and I learn there are substantial sections out of Leon that tag beside a highway, not to mention an hour of industrial sprawl beforehand. I decide to take the bus to Astorga, two days walk away, vowing this will be the last time. The very last time.

Tacked to the wall behind us is a faded photocopy listing Seven Ingredients for a Pilgrim. The first is *Silencio*. The Way is not for speaking but for listening, to your interior, to all the creation that surrounds you and to God.'

The second, asterixed and underlined, is *No Tener Prisa*. Do not be in a hurry. In a letter to David last night

I talked about time. How five weeks were not enough and that things, interior things, were slowly coming to the surface. How I wanted to live from the inside, not the outside, and how I wanted us to be authentic and that there wasn't any time to waste. I read number two again, out loud *No tener prisa*. The words begin working like a mantra, finding a place beneath the surface of my day to day mind. My leg will heal in its own time, if I need to take another bus again, well then so be it. Life unfolds by itself, let God's will be done.

These two Benedictine ingredients stand sufficient, like the flour and water of a fire baked damper. But if you add another two, yeast and honey, then knead into it three more, oil, eggs and a pinch of salt, the loaf you break open is fragrant and light with a golden crust.

The bell rings for tonight's prayers. Before I go I write the last five ingredients down, to knead and to chew in the days ahead. *Soledad* – solitude, *Esfuerzo* – effort, *Sobriedad* – sobriety, *Gratuito* – gratitude and *El Romanico* – the language of Romanesque stones.

16

Water Pouring into Water

Leon to Astorga

A pilgrim is no more or less transitory than those who move about in bus terminals on early mornings, trailing suitcases on wheels behind them, sipping *café con leches* and eating *tortillas* at the bar, their paper tickets to home or to work or to visit a distant relative, a christening or a wake, folded into two and placed in a pocket ready for the conductor. I perch on a stool, breathing in the same stale cigarette smoked air, happy to be on the move again, compass set to West. After two days marooned in one place I am impatient to set sail, the *meseta* and the Victorinos of the world behind me, the green hills of Galicia ahead. My first tentative steps, though tender, are hope-filled and relatively pain free.

The bus to Astorga speeds through fields of lavender. Gone are the papery dark heads of sunflower fields.

Forested mountains seem like visions against the sky, and this from the eyes of someone who walked only two days on the *meseta*. The Camino Frances and the Via de Plata, beginning in Andalucia six hundred and ninety kilometres to the south, join in Astorga for the remaining two hundred and seventy to Santiago. It's as if the changing terrain marks a rite of passage, like a destination on the game board of a God – You have reached a crossroad where north and south meet, gather your strength; before the arms of St James enfold you there is one more mountain range to cross.

Roll the dice again and take as your reward dinner at The Gaudi Hotel.

A young Francis of Assisi walked the Camino. Details of his journey are scant but Astorga's San Roque hospice is one place that claims him as a guest. In the folk tales of *The Little Flowers of St Francis*, however, more can be learned through the eyes of the thirteenth century Franciscan friar Brother Giles, who, with the blessing of his teacher, made the same journey. In the spirit of Saint Francis he preached penance and love for all creatures and stayed in remote places, better to give himself to watching and prayer.

He fasted all the way with the exception of a supper of beans found on a barn floor. Once a man called out to him and thinking it was an offer of alms Brother Giles walked over but instead was invited to a game of dice. Mockery and insult were commonplace in the back streets of medieval towns. In a later chapter Brother Giles compares vices and sins to: Venomous and mortal poison, but virtues and good works, salutary medicine.

As a child I shared my mother's love for St Francis. In my mind he was like a biblical Dr Doolittle. Later, in my early twenties I found the perfect gift for her, a print of a haloed St Francis in Giotto's *Sermon of the Birds*. We were not at that time the best of friends. Dad had died and, in an attempt to separate herself from painful memories – words uttered in the last years of their marriage that could not be undone, and the gossip of a small country town – she moved to Brisbane. But a change of scenery can be just that; the pain remains. I was no different and in my denial I fled to the other side of the world for a year. Returning pregnant, I miscarried on my first night at home. My mother, still trapped in her despair, skimmed over this when I tried to tell her, as if I must be mistaken. I will never know if this was a case of denial or more the pretence of respectability. I made a secret of it too, burying the reality of a life just poured from mine, and the estrangement between us grew. Any mention of joining her for church seemed to me, given the words flung between us and those we were incapable of expressing, hypocritical. I ran the other way.

But the morning when she unwrapped her gift I remember clearly. Holding the painting up she looked at me. 'You remembered,' she said.

When I was a child she used to recite *The Prayer to St Francis* at bedtime. Its verses came flooding back as I watched her fingers trace the gold hem of his robe: Lord, make me an instrument of your peace, where there is hatred, let me sow love; where there is injury, pardon.

The distance separating us was still too painful to be resolved but the picture of a saint blessing a flock of birds offered us a window of grace, where we could look into each other's eyes and ask: That I may not so much seek to be understood as to understand.

Slightly dazed from this unsolicited surge of memory I walk into the long shadows of Astorga's cathedral, a literal patchwork of eight hundred years. Only a few buttresses and a cornice of carved leaves remain from the original Romanesque church. It was replaced by a Gothic cathedral and then for the next three hundred years Renaissance and Baroque artists put their stamp on it. A century later Juan Bautista Grau y Vallespinos, Astorga's new bishop arrived eager to keep up the tradition. In true maverick style he started from the ground up commissioning a brand new *Palacio Episcopal* next door to the cathedral. His good friend Gaudi was assigned the task of a palace to bring Astorga into the twentieth century. The townspeople were horrified at the lewd fairy tale extravaganza of white granite turrets and towers taking shape before their eyes. They were pious enough to keep quiet until after the bishop's death but then let loose. An incensed Gaudi left for Barcelona swearing never to return and after a stalemate of twenty years another architect finished the job. No bishop since has had the courage to take up residence and it is now a museum.

It lacks the wild play of mosaics and whimsical detail

typical of Gaudi, but what I see fires my imagination. Rapunzel lets down her golden hair from the highest window as gallant knights ride white stallions up to its Gothic doors. A king and queen drink from pewter goblets in the banquet room while two wolfhounds chew on the bones they throw. As if to complete the fantasy I look back across to the cathedral and see a contemporary sculpture of a black steel chair standing tall enough for a Goliath in the middle of the plaza. Pink alyssum and petunias grow from its seat. Astorga, it seems, is an ongoing canvas for *artistes*.

The San Xavier *refugio* stands opposite the Convento de Sancti Spiritus where nuns have been cloistered since the sixteenth century. I knock at the door, crossing my fingers they will they let me in. No pilgrim on foot would be showing their face this early in the morning. 'Welcome *peregrino*,' Eileen says with an Irish brogue. She takes my passport not at all perturbed that I have come by bus. 'There are already a few of you here and some that are staying an extra night. You can go in the loft with them.'

She dismisses my profuse thanks but when I comment on how beautiful the *refugio* is, stops everything to tell me how they have only recently opened and that the building was once a palace built just one century after the nuns moved in across the road. 'More Moorish than Spanish,' she says. 'Put your feet up on the terrace above the garden, relax, you'll feel like you're in Tangiers.'

I walk across a polished wooden floor to a bed with a plumped up pillow and neatly tucked white sheets. I take more care than usual unpacking my bag, as if the attentiveness shown to the comfort of others asks the same of me.

Saint Francis Xavier, this *refugio's* namesake, is a popular saint in Spain. A co-founder of the Jesuits he left a legacy of Catholic converts in 16th century Indonesia and Japan. But as I walk barefoot down the hallway to a sparkling white bathroom, passing a pilgrim sponging water from the floor, I think the choice of name has probably more to do with the Jesuits' belief in effective love. Love shown in action with no personal preference rather than an affective love, more about the feel-good self.

Sunlight streams onto the terrace and I join the girl from the bathroom stretched out on a bench with her friend. We bathe our feet in tubs of water and epsom salts left out for pilgrims along with bandages, iodine, panadol and a whole lot of creams and salves for worn out feet. Sophia and Janine are fresh from high school in Germany; they could be sisters with their fine auburn hair and porcelain skin. Sophia's eyes are a clear sky blue and Janine's a deep dark brown. They can't believe I am from Australia. An email had come this morning to say that Sophia is accepted into a university on the Sunshine Coast. My brother lives just ten minutes away from that campus and they ply me with questions about the sea, the bush, the kangaroos, the Barrier Reef. We make a circle of arms and legs and massage each others feet. Janine suffers the same shin splints as me but hers is exacerbated by swollen ankles. It is their third day here and slowly, ever so slowly, she is improving.

'You must come with us tonight for hot chocolate. Astorga is home to the best chocolate in the world. We're German and we know what we are talking about!' Sophia laughs and adds, 'There is a clock in the plaza you have to see when it chimes.' I am genuinely surprised by their invitation, still not used to being included in circles so young, and delighted at the idea of watching time pass in such angelic company.

I wonder about the Camino – its full catastrophe of characters walking, sleeping and eating together in places often so confined even the closest friendship can be challenged. Age, country and religion, not to mention the quirks and habits each of us acquire over a lifetime are, if not transcended, tolerated. Is there any reason why, if this is a reality here, it can't be a template for other places, other times? Perhaps I am trying to reduce life to too simple an equation. Perhaps a pilgrimage is a classroom. We learn there is the possibility for a different level of community, a real communion. We then have the opportunity – responsibility – to carry this home.

Acuerdate de mi juicio, porque asi sera tambien el turyo. A mi ayer, a ti hoy, is carved above the window of a 14th century cell where prostitutes were once jailed: Consider how I have been judged, for your judgment will be the same – me yesterday, you today.

'*Hola peregrino,*' they cried through slits in the wall of a building squeezed between the two churches adjacent to the cathedral. Whenever they heard the familiar tap-tap of a staff they called out, 'Have mercy. Some bread for us?' Pilgrims slipped food to them out of either charity or the hope that their own souls might be redeemed, or both. I walk past its padlocked door unable to reconcile this element of the church –the fear of God and the possibility of eternal suspension in a Bosch-like world if you fall prey to an unconfessed moment of lust or any other of the church's myriad sins. Madonnas and compassionate images of a Christ – yes. All the miracles and magic, the three wise men, the immaculate conceptions and the assumption – yes. But not the terror in a child's eyes looking up to her scripture teacher as she describes the horns of a red devil and how the fires of hell burn in great caverns and caves below the earth.

I scurry from the shadows of Santa Marta and San Esteban to the sanctuary of the Cathedral, past the giant's black chair and through the southern portal where a graceful Virgin sits below her benevolent God. Am I just a hopeless romantic? Incapable of taking the black with the white, evil with good? Then I realize – my fixation on hell as a purely Christian concept is just another pigeon-holed view. How easily my mind falls into its habitual *this* or *that*. Its grasping excludes an awareness capable of holding both. Both sides of me too.

This thought tumbles me back onto my meditation cushion and a Tibetan Buddhist retreat in a freezing Blue Mountains winter. Vajrayana has its own quota of hell realms and wrathful deities. A Rinpoche leads us in minute detail through a visualization accompanied by a theatre of bells, conch shells, horns and drums. We plunge into the Bardo, the nether world between the living and the dead where *dakinis* drink blood from human skulls and pierce the chests of demons with pitchforks. He reminds us again, 'Keep your mind natural and undiluted, self contained in its own nature, like water poured into water.' It is a terrifying spectacle, undiminished by the knowledge that if I open my eyes I am actually sitting in a candlelit room wrapped warm in a woolen shawl. But our teacher keeps us steady in the places our mind fears most. 'The Lord of death will drag you by a rope tied around your neck and cut off your head, tear out your heart, pull out your entrails, lick your brain …' He reminds us again we are safe. No demon can harm us as they are only projections of our own mind. In reality, 'We are naturally formed from emptiness, so there is no need to fear. Emptiness cannot harm emptiness.'

Inside the cathedral pure notes of a Gregorian choir float from its four corners. I look up to the Gothic vaults, stretched ribs of stone defying gravity as they arc and intertwine at an astonishing height across the breadth of the cathedral. They and the towering fluted pillars the length of the aisles to the main retablo have created an empty vessel into which the Latin chants are sung. A priest in a black robe hurries in behind me leaving one world, as I have, and entering another. I ask him who is singing. '*Core de monjes del Monasterio Benedicto de Santo Domingo de Silos*,' he replies and disappears through another door into the chapter house. These are the recorded voices Alex told me about. He took a detour from Burgos just to hear them in the flesh. I walk slowly from *capilla* to *capilla* and drop into that sensation of water falling into water. I feel as if I am gliding through the stained light filtering from each window, the scent of lilies and polished walnut paneling and air washed clean by wave upon wave of luminous voices. Melodies as old as the medieval hands of an apprentice inking psalms onto vellum manuscripts; fine as the measured dip of his feathered quill into pots of cinnabar and cochineal, malachite, ultramarine and gold leaf mixed with egg white.

A Japanese tour group file in to the pews in front of the main retablo and begin to pray out loud. The Santo Domingo monks move onto another chant; it's familiar, the same sung with the nuns in Leon, but this time in Latin, '*Salve Regina, mater misericordiae ... ocolus ad nos converte,*' Hail to thee, Queen, Mother of Mercy ... turn thine eyes upon us.

I wonder what it was like when man and woman first looked up to the sky. Perhaps the woman's belly had been swelling since spring. She rests his hand there, sharing the strange kicks and turns of a life inside, the tiny shape of a half formed fist. Perhaps it was then he first fashioned a woman from clay – long breasts heavy with milk and a full moon stomach. They prayed to her before a hunt for the meat of a bison and its fur to keep their newborn warm. Their great, great grandchildren prayed to her each time they planted grain and she shape-shifted her way century through century.

The same priest walks past again and I ask if the Madonna statue in front of us is ever taken out into the streets for a celebratory procession. He frowns at my disjointed Spanish and I cradle my arms as if carrying her and walk towards the door. '*Se venera en su capilla de la que nunca sa,*' he says shaking his head. One must venerate her only here, she never leaves the chapel. I am mortified at the way he now looks at me. Does he think I was asking if I could take her out? He scampers off to another room as if he can't get away fast enough.

'You'd probably like to go outside wouldn't you?' I turn back to her stifling an embarrassed giggle. 'Back to your roots, the celebration of a harvest, the coming full moon.' She sits unmoved, impeccable. As I swing out the cathedral's western iron doors I take the dancing limbs of a silver Tara out from under my shirt so she at least can catch some sunlight on this beautiful day.

'Pilgrims can have lunch at the Gaudi Hotel for ten euros,' Eileen had said back at the *refugio*, 'just show your *credencial*.' And there it is across from the Gaudi palace, an impressive three story edifice of brick and balconies. I pull my shirt down in an attempt to smooth out its wrinkles and run fingers through my hair. Hardly worth the effort I think as I catch a glimpse of myself in a window. The maitre de checks my pilgrim passport then ushers me in to an empty dining room as if I was just another lipsticked, airbrushed lady. I am unfashionably early for lunch.

'Vino?' the waiter asks with a deadpan face as he unfurls a starched napkin across my lap. 'Gracias,' I reply in my very best Spanish and in a few minutes he returns with a bottle of Tinto Bierzo Mencia.

Just as my first course arrives, so does the second lunch party. I am fascinated by the grandmother who presides at the head of her family and try not to stare between sips of wine and mouthfuls of entree, *la menestra de riano*, a delicate spring vegetable stew. What luxury to dine alone, no conversation to be pitted against the food and no interruptions to my clandestine pleasure watching the respect this weathered matriarch engenders. She wears a black velvet singlet that clings to her skin, a slim fitting skirt to match and sensibly heeled black sequined slingbacks. Silver hoops with a star hanging in the middle dangle from her ears, lobes stretched long from years of adornment. She places a small black phone beside her plate, keeping her hand at the ready – for a widower perhaps, as enamored as me, with her sense of style. She speaks of small things with the lover of one daughter. A second daughter, all three have the same piercing eyes and noble nose, peruses the menu for her two children dressed to the nines like frothy tulle fairies. A table for twenty eight on the other side of the room begins to fill. The clock strikes three. Let the banquet begin. Troops of waiters swing through the kitchen doors with giant platters of honeydew wrapped in *jamon* and bottles of wine wrapped in triangles of linen. Another matriarch heads their table, her face creased into a permanent two toothed smile, while the handsome young man to her left pours sparkling water into her half-glass of wine.

My gloved waiter returns with the second course, a Michelin-star arrangement of lamb shank and rack on a ring of mashed potato. The gentry and hounds inside Gaudi's Palace would be impressed. Rapunzel might even be allowed down from her tower. He pours me a second glass of wine as I languish in my fairy tale, savoring the way each sip transcends from cherry-plum to earth and mint. This ruby wine from the Mencia grape owes its origin to the cabernet vines of France and to French pilgrims on their way to Santiago. They tucked bundles of precious cuttings into their satchels and planted them deep in the crystalline soil of the Bierzo mountains, said to yield the perfect cabernet.

Course number three, a cheek of *crema de limon* in a pool of macerated red berries. I stretch out my legs and wiggle my toes inside their glass slippers, sated by the hum of voices and celebratory toasts in the slow unfurling of an Astorgan afternoon. I leave behind a galaxy of wine spills on the white linen cloth.

17

The Bright Blessed Day, the Dark Sacred Night

Astorga to Rabanal de Camino

It is easier for a camel to enter through the eye of a needle... After three days rest I am walking west again. My pack feels light and my expectations less. I feel strangely like that camel stepping into another world. I have gushed and gurgled like a river through Basque country, tracked a rhythm through vineyards, across wheat fields and over a mountain pass, lost my mind in Burgos and surrendered to my legs in Hornillos. Now I am three quarters there – a small part of me threaded through the needle.

'Tell me what is the sound of one hand clapping?'

'Without speaking, without silence, how can you express the truth?'

Zen masters gave their students *koans* like these as a

way of jolting them awake. Jesus challenged his disciples in a not dissimilar way. Through parable and allegory he asked that they step out from their self-made minds. For a camel to enter Jerusalem's narrow gates all the baggage tied on its back had to be removed and even then the camel had to get down on his or her knees to fit. In order to know anything, everything you know must be left behind.

Not far out of Astorga is Valseviejas, a small village, and at its edge the Ermita del Ecce Homo, a medieval hermitage dedicated to the words of Pontius Pilate. 'Behold the man,' he said to the bloodthirsty jeers of a crowd, introducing them to Jesus wearing a crown of thorns. I wipe a patch of one of the hermitage's grimy windows with my shirt sleeve, enough to see the dim shape of angels, an altar, a Christ and a Virgin. The Valseviejas villagers also call their small church, Chapel of Our Lady of Solitude in honor of the name given to Mary on the day she waited alone after her son's crucifixion and before his resurrection.

I revel in the solitude of a clear blue sky, the shiver of long dried grasses, the sharp bitter-green scent of wild yarrow and the flick of winter's tongue against my cheek. To keep warm I walk a little faster and overtake an older man, Brazilian, I think, from his accent. He calls out to me. 'Hey Mercury!' We laugh, and I wing my way on, head down against the chill of the wind.

I begin a soft chanting of *Om Tara tuttare...* letting each *soha*, each so be it, merge into *Om* beginning again, over and over, until my body becomes buoyant and I am a nameless passenger in a vehicle moving by itself. Out of the blue, out of my heart a whirlpool of tears come until I am walking towards a horizon of mountains uncontrollably, unashamedly weeping. As though by emptying myself the way is clear for this flowing of tears.

Love from my breaking open heart, is how I had ended my last mail to David. That is how I feel now – breaking open – but not just to him, to the sky, this way of stars, to solitude.

A shepherd moves out from the shadow of trees and waves to me as he herds his sheep into a stone corral. I wipe my tears and wave back with a feeling of immeasurable gratitude – for his greeting, for everything. Of the five remaining pilgrim ingredients I had written down in Leon, *Soledad* was the first and *Gratuito*, the third – I seem to have skipped *Sobriedad*, the second. With a laugh I acknowledge there will come a time for sobriety but not now. I lift each foot with a measure of tenderness for my body and gratefulness for the journey I am taking in it, and joy!

Purple heather and orange broom line the road leaving the village of Santa Catalina de Somoza. A tall pilgrim in a wide brim leather hat passes me as I leave the last stone house behind. He has loner written all over him but manages half a smile. I think of David, how he could easily have lived as a recluse, like those cave dwelling hermits of old Spain. I used to be intimidated by his utter self-containment until I realized I was taking it too personally. Only then could I begin to take refuge in the quietness of him.

El Ganso, the Goose – it is hard to believe this twelfth century village had its main street paved less than ten years ago. A flock of sheep baaa past me as I hug the walls of the eccentric Bar Meson Cowboy. Tacked onto its front are blackboards advertising *tortillas* and *empanadas*, *Sidra* and *Embutidos*. Out of its wild west swinging doors comes the unmistakable voice of Louis Armstrong: I see skies of blue and clouds of white the bright blessed day, the dark sacred night and I think to myself... I can't help it and join in, 'What a wonderful world.'

It takes a few moments to adjust to the light inside – the colours of the rainbow so pretty in the sky, are also on the faces of people going by – and am greeted with the subtlest nod of a head by the loner who passed me in Santa Catalina, looking more like Marlborough man, his feet propped up on a chair as he rolls a cigarette. Saddles, sets of spurs, bridles and sombreros line the walls and behind the bar is Mr. Cowboy himself transfixed by a soccer game on television. This is a man's domain and the coffee I am served is black, thick and strong enough to put hairs on my chest.

Rocket launched, I think as I head out into a prairie blue sky, adjusting the hip belt of my pack a notch, ready for one last stretch of road. Caffeine courses through my veins and I feel cocky as a cowgirl.

Walking mile upon mile through sunburned grass, greeting strangers and the black faces of white fleeced sheep, breathing high altitude air – my five senses step into the dance between each of the four elements. Weeping and laughing, filled with solitude and gratitude, moving seamlessly into myself then out again to the world witnessed with my feet, through my eyes, tongue, ears, nose and skin. Each intrinsic to the other, together arriving at the lip of the Grail.

Twelfth century pilgrims setting out for Santiago had, if they were lucky enough to be literate, one guidebook at their disposal, the *Codex Calixtinus*. My destination, Rabanal, is listed as stage nine with Leon the day's starting point, sixty kilometres away! I wonder how many accomplished that? Was this just a careless miscalculation by Amery Picaud, the monk in charge of transcribing the *Codex*? Maybe every pilgrim traveled on horseback? Or, in the church's enthusiastic promotion of The Way, was it a case of an ever so slight exaggeration. An unsuspecting penitent, *Codex* in hand, three centuries before the discoveries of Columbus, would be setting out for Compostela ignorant of the time it really was going to take on foot. Eight hundred and fifty kilometers in thirteen days? That's an average of sixty five kilometres a day, without the aid of ergonomic shoes and wicking socks. In its last pages the Codex dangles another carrot. St James is hailed as a refulgent miracle worker: The tongue of the dumb untied, the ear of the deaf unplugged, the possessed delivered... etcetera. The final phrase of this long one sentence paragraph turns full circle back to the coffers of the church: ...and foreign people of all parts of the world have rushed in large masses bringing in laudation their gifts to the Lord.

I find a small piece of quartz-laced rock near an abandoned television and keep it warm in my hand. This is my gift. To be given not at the cathedral but tomorrow at a cross embedded in a mountain of stones.

Rabanal's *refugio* is named after a local hermit monk, Gaucelmo, who dedicated his life to the protection and shelter of pilgrims. Back then it was called Hospital de San Gregorio and survived as such for several centuries. In the 1720's church authorities made a reconnaissance visit and ordered, for proper sanitation, that the straw covering its floors should be changed once a year! From the sparkling panes of glass in every window to the swept pathways and floors – not a piece of straw in sight, the meticulous attention to detail I find is worthy of a parish priest's house. And yes, this used to be the home of Rabanal's priest once upon a time too. Now it is managed by the London based Confraternity of St James.

'How ya doin?' Keith the *hospitalero* greets me with that unmistakable, unhurried drawl all the way from Sydney. Irish Eileen sits beside him helping with the passports having driven up to Rabanal with Gaspar for a visit. 'Hellooh Hailen. Glaass of wine?'

I had forgotten how good it is to hang out with the same language, to banter and joke, all the more irreverent given our roots – two convicts and one escaped. This is Keith's first time volunteering and Eileen's second.

'Are you walking alone? Are you married?' she plies

me with questions and I fire back.

'Me?' she replies, 'I was, with two grown up kids and a dog. The first time I walked I fell for a Spanish man. I went home thinking it was just one of those flings you have but when I got home the marriage turned rocky. So I thought let's walk the Camino together. Plenty of time to bond and patch things up. Well that was a disaaaster! We ended up divorcing. Long story short, third time lucky. The next time I walked I fell in love for real. That's what they say about the Camino, don't they Keith?' she looks over to him with a twinkle. I jump to conclusions thinking they are the loving couple but no, Keith is wandering the world loose and single after a breakup. 'Another Camino casualty,' Eileen quips, to which Keith shrugs his shoulders. 'Gospel of an Irish redhead. Does that mean I have to walk another eight hundred kilometres before a woman bowls me down?'

Sophia from Astorga walks in. 'We missed you last night and I promised you chocolate.'

I had fallen asleep after my feast at the Hotel Gaudi and Astorga's famous chiming clock had not tolled loud enough to rouse me. 'So I brought you some,' she hands me a bar of the city's finest dark orange.

'Janine has her feet up, back at the *refugio* and we think we will walk in a few more days. When Eileen said she was coming here I took a chance that I would see you.' I give her a great big hug and a kiss and break open the packet. Keith pours us all another glass of red.

Gaucelmo's forty six beds soon fill and a sign is posted

on the front gates directing pilgrims to the other two *refugios* in town. We bask in the sunny courtyard of this typical Maragato house with its L-shaped patchwork of stone, an orchard and a barn. Hermann from Germany joins us, another *Caminophile* having walked it, 'More times than I can remember.' I wonder is this the fate of everyone who sets out for Santiago? Is it like sea in a sailor's blood? Hermann has the air of an eccentric and the habit of twirling into curls the ends of his white moustache. He launches into tales of the Maragatos, the hardworking people who have lived here longer than anyone else. Their origins have been linked to the Visigoths, Celts and Berbers – all of them rovers moving in on a free-for-all eighth century Spain. Then in the 1950's small statues were discovered at the site of a nearby Punic cemetery. They were dressed in the same costumes brought out today for special occasions – hats bigger than sombreros, red garters and bell-bottomed trousers, suggesting the ancient sea traders of Phoenicia are the Maragatos' real ancestors. Until the nineteenth century they traded by horse and cart, from the *meseta* to Galicia, carrying grain to the coast and returning with salted fish.

'Lunch at Gaspar's anyone? They serve the best *Cocido* Maragato.' Hermann seems an expert on all things Maragato and I wonder if he sports a secret pair of red garters under his trousers? Inside the stone lintel arched doors is a bar where Gaspar himself presides, puffing a fat cigar. Hermann has already set his heart on the blackboard special, *Cocido de Moras y Orejas*. Eileen, after deferring to Gaspar, quietly suggests to Sophia and me, 'Unless you are seriously into pork, stick with the regular stew.' Gaspar holds up ten fingers to emphasize we'll still be getting the traditional ten kinds of meat on our plate. Removing the cigar from his mouth, he entices us toward the regular *Cocido* Maragato with one last detail: his cook is the genuine article and any stew he makes is guaranteed to be thick enough for a spoon to stay raised in it. 'One serve will probably do the three of us,' says Eileen. To even consider ordering anything else after Gaspar's oration, backed up by Hermann's, 'Nothing but the best for my *frauleins*,' is unthinkable.

Hermann takes great delight in pointing out the anatomy of all the bits in his huge bowl. Snout, ears, trotters. Our first course has its own fair portion of pork, this is Spain after all, but beef and lamb too. Suffice to say, about as meaty as you can get. Then, as we are close to finishing, a casserole of steaming potatoes, chick peas and cabbage is brought to the table and, finally, the soup. Hermann, silent for the last fifteen minutes, calls for more bread to mop up his gravy and regales us with another Maragato tale. Our served backwards meal is a tradition harking back to a time when men at war against the Moors were settling down for a three course repast. Halfway through their vegetable soup the enemy was sighted and they had to take up arms. How can a soldier fight without meat in his belly? Moral of the story – eat the meat first.

Thanks to a too full stomach and the serenade of

snorts from a man napping in the bunk above, my siesta dreaming turns into pig ears flying through space. Walking the fog of it off through the backstreets of Rabanal I nearly collide with two old women as they march past, each with a long upturned bench balanced on her head. A Maragato meeting perhaps? I turn down the laneway from which they suddenly appeared to find myself at the gates of an old stone stable and a house with timber planks nailed across its door. A low wall of stacked stones separates the periphery of the village from fields, mountains and a burnt orange sky. Lichen covers the rocks like a crocheted doily and seasons of fungi dimple the stone. It is as if this crumbling wall holds time at bay, quietly and tenaciously.

Inside the Romanesque Church of Santa Maria de la Asuncion is a statue of San Blas, saint of wool combers, wild animals and those suffering from throat afflictions – particularly cases of fish bones stuck in the throat. Perhaps his presence here is owed to a few miraculous cough-ups of very fine *bacalao* bones. Again the Maragatos move across Rabanal's stage returning from Galicia with their cartloads of dried cod. On every Friday and Wednesday and all through Lent this prized fish graced many a Catholic table, desalted in baths of water for one and a half days then cooked till tender with potatoes and pepper.

The Benedictine monks of this church quote the words of another saint, St. Anselm, in a brochure by the door: Look for God in the silence of your solitude... the pilgrimage is not only done on foot, it is principally done by your heart.

Rabanal's monks offer pilgrims the chance to stay a few days in their monastery for rest and meditation: To look for the yellow arrows which will guide you through the pilgrimage of your life. And for one moment I ache to stay, to be released from a date printed on an air ticket.

White plaster stained to ashen from centuries of candle smoke peels away from the chapel's dome revealing eight hundred year old bricks. At the centre of the apse hangs a simple crucifix and above the altar are the faded shapes of red, ochre and ultramarine stars and planets. I wonder how this chapel must have looked painted from top to toe but prefer it as it is now, stripped of images and ideas. My eyes have nowhere to go. Three Benedictine monks, the entire population of the San Salvador del Monte Irago Monastery, stand at the front.

They chant psalms, hymns and canticles in an antiphon of voices that echo softly back to us from the chapel's dome. Layer by layer every ounce of resistance in my body to this present moment is released. *Adsumite Carmen et date tympanum citharam decoram cum psalterio*, take up a psalm, sound the tambourine the harp and lyre, *clangite in neomenia bucina et in medio mense die sollemnitatis nostrae*, blow the trumpet at the new moon, at the full moon on our solemn feast.... *Et cibivat eos adipe frumentiet de petra mellis saturavit eos*. And he filled them with honey out of the rock.

We listen to the splash of wine poured into a chalice,

of bread as it is broken. Even the candle flames are still. We walk out into the night and, without exception, stop to look up into a river of stars stretching the length of our world.

Keith sits on the verandah having a quiet smoke. I remember the vocal gymnastics of the man napping in the bed above me. I make an attempt at seeing this memory as empty as is everything else in this ephemeral world. Am I kidding myself? I wonder, holding instead to the psalms still singing inside me. Or am I a thoroughly modern discriminating woman? I take a risk and ask Keith if it is possible to sleep solo on the floor of the library. He looks at me in mock askance then gives me a conspiratorial wink, one Australian to another. I tiptoe with my mattress out of the dormitory into a sanctuary of silent words.

18

The Tower and the Rainbow
Rabanal de Camino to Molinaseca

A bank of storm clouds tumbles over and down the mountains ahead. Today I climb to the highest point on the Camino where rumours abound of wild dogs and the roaming ghosts of pagans and pilgrims. But I feel confident. The pain in my legs has all but disappeared and Keith, at breakfast this morning, had allayed my fears. 'Piece of cake,' he said. 'Should I carry any extra supplies?'

'No you'll be fine.'

So on the outskirts of Rabanal, instead of facing the dark clouds I walk backwards watching an eastern sky turn gold. The silhouette of Santa Maria's roof appears above the trees and the stage is set. The sun, from where I am standing, inches up to shine directly through the keyhole of the bell tower. There is solstice at Stonehenge and solstice on San Juan de Ortega where that ray of light shines onto the womb of a Virgin. Had I been a devout Catholic I would now be on my knees. I watch the illumination of space around a bell, that vessel of pure sound into which all things dissolve and from which all things are born. Into the unprejudiced nature of light I sing, *Om Tara tuttare ture soha*, before turning to face the mountains.

The vestige of Foncebadon snakes along a stone path on top of the ridge, a village as bleak as the morning. Half an hour ago clouds were swirling above me magenta and crimson with dawn; now I walk through the damp drizzle of them, a thick mist the colour of dirty snow. The church is closed and so is the bar. I smile when I read its name, La Taberna de Gaia. Grandmother Earth serving coffee and *bocadillos*, an offering perhaps, in lieu of Gaucelmo's ruins, the once upon a time church and hospice for pilgrims, at the edge of town. But somewhere here, in this cluster of crooked stone houses, Gaia is sleeping, I am sure of it. Maybe she was the one up before sunrise painting the sky.

Sheltering under the roof of a deserted farmhouse I sense a presence and turn to see the stooped figure of an old man peering out from a doorway. I wave and he retreats like the head of an ancient turtle back into his stone shell, his roof of slate patched up with sheets of warped tin. There is an old saying: Who hasn't passed by way of Foncebadon doesn't know solitude or sadness. When winter comes Foncebadon's population reduces to two. It seems I am privy to one. I layer myself against the cold and wet, solitude I have but sadness, no. Among all these collapsed roofs and crumbling houses stands a magnificent tree crowned with clusters of red flowers. How could I be sad?

Snow depth poles line the ascent to the summit of Monte Irago where the *Cruz del Ferro* rises from a huge cairn of stones. It was Gaucelmo, like a mountain climber claiming his right to the top of the world, who planted a cross here eight centuries ago and so another pilgrim tradition was launched. Pilgrims still carry the extra weight of a rock, or pebble, from home as an act of repentance to be offered here. Some carry a prayer-infused stone for those unable to walk while others add the ashes of a loved one. I find my little quartz stone and wonder what my motivation is. Am I participating simply because this is the tradition, one so old that along the way ritual has overtaken meaning? The Celts were the first to mark high mountain passes with piles of stones and then the Romans. Here they built an altar to Mercury, a God remodeled after Hermes, Greek God of boundaries and all the travelers crossing them. I peel off my raincoat. Well if Hermes was here, Gaia was too. I laugh a little too loud, much to the chagrin of a prayer group gathered under the eaves of a small chapel. She sparred with Hermes on his chariot and then, triumphant, shape shifted into a snake. The poppy she held, for she loved red flowers, transformed into a ruby-red pomegranate endowing her with fertility and strength.

I close my eyes and a red skinned Goddess dances across them. The Tara I wear is white but she also manifests as red, green, yellow and blue – each colour symbolizing different attributes. White Tara is the remover of obstacles – attachment, aversion and ignorance. Red Tara transforms desire into compassion and love.

I rub the quartz between my hands like a fire stick then visualize all of those at home I care about. I breathe them into the stone. The stone is a beating heart in the palm of my hands and I wish into its centre bright flames of love. *Om Tara tuttare ture soha*, before placing it on the cairn.

'*Ultreia*!' Onwards and upwards the pilgrims' song goes, and I plough through the clouds wearing every item of clothing I own. I stop one last time to pull out a sarong for fear my ears will freeze and drop off, past caring how absurd I must look with a garish print of tropical flowers tied round my head. A woman I've not seen before passes, her rain splashed face breaks from concentration into a smile. Constant rain soon saturates my raincoat. My nose drips, my cheeks burn and my hands are so numb they can barely hold onto their poles and I am alive.

Through the fog I hear the muffled sound of a bell. Manjarin Refugio de Peregrinos, a sign reads, with a more recent plaque nailed beside it, *No Al Guerra*, No to War. Below, so the pilgrim knows exactly where she stands, are signposts to Roma 2475 klm, Jerusalem 5000klm, Santiago 222 klm and Machu Pichu 9453. I feel as though I've arrived at the centre of the universe as I enter the *refugio's* humble door. The hallway is so narrow I need to take off my pack before I can fit. A bit like those camels in Jerusalem.

Two wet bodies hustle in behind me eager for warmth and we squeeze our way further into a labyrinth of ramshackle rooms. From an annex a young man looks up from the silver scallop shells he threads onto leather and waves us on to the hearth of the house. I join more bedraggled pilgrims and rub life back into my hands over a brazier, breathing in the smoke of frankincense granules bubbling on its coals. We are quiet, hypnotized by the fire, and as my body defrosts I look up from our cauldron noticing small details about the room. Wrinkled red peppers and a net of chestnuts hanging from the ceiling. A bed with a straw mattress, a collection of chipped mugs, a plastic dishwashing bowl and a jerry can for water.

A man in army greens and leather boots clomps into the room. He has a white mustache and beard, and spectacles with lenses so thick his dark eyes are a blur. Paying no attention to us he potters about. He turns up a tape recorder filling the room with a Bach concerto and pours a cup of coffee from a thermos, stirring into it a heaped tablespoon of sugar. He slurps pensively then mutters to himself before disappearing down the hallway. This must be Tomas otherwise known as the last Templar Knight. The authorities in Leon don't think so. In their attempt to shut down his eccentric and unauthorized *refugio*, they threatened to cut off its electricity. Tomas began a hunger strike on the steps of their office until they acquiesced.

There are pilgrims who dismiss Tomas as a quack giving his Templar hospice a wide berth no matter how severe the weather. But for me there is simplicity and an economy of words here reminiscent of the early Benedictine monks whose same vows the first Templar Knights chose in 1118. It was the heyday of religious pilgrimage when travelers crisscrossed Western Europe from Rome to Jerusalem and Santiago. Sins confessed, respects paid and prayers offered; you turned around and walked back home. The Knights provided safe passage. They also waged a holy war against Moorish invaders; a dual role, not unlike the two contradictory images of St James. In a relatively short century of glory money poured into their coffers. It was this wealth, ultimately, that led to their downfall. Complacency and deceit unraveled the ranks, and rumours of sacrilegious activity were leaked – sodomy, reciting the mass backwards, and denial of the Christ and Virgin.

On the wall behind me is a tapestry of the Last Supper and a serene print of Mary holding a crimson heart. Below her is a drawing of Christ with a Templar cross bound around his forehead. Tomas, it appears, has taken the original pledge of the Knights and given it a home again.

With a flurry of footsteps he returns. A red satin Templar cross is stitched the length of his long white tunic. Two tall apprentices with ringlets of long black hair herd us into a circle with military precision. Tomas stands beside me, half a head smaller but with a presence large as the room. He hands me a Templar flag and two cards. Seven carnation stems, two of which still hold blood red flowers, are gaffer taped to the flagpole. I haven't a clue what is happening but am honored nevertheless. To the exquisite strains of *The Lark Ascending*, the spit of coals and a meowing cat winding its way between the legs of our circle, the ceremony begins.

Our knight and protector mumbles an introduction under his breath then begins a Gregorian-like chant. I close my eyes like everyone else and let his voice wash over me. My legs feel strong like linden trees, my body is relaxed and my mind open and receptive to the ritual that swirls round our circle as natural as the wind and rain washing the world outside.

A strong calloused hand covers mine and taps the flagpole three times. The ceremony is over. In my abrupt return to the room, the fire, and the presence of others, I drop the two cards Tomas had given me as I return the flagpole to him. Mortified, I pick them up. One is a postcard of the Cruz de Ferro midpoint in the arc of a rainbow and the other is a tarot card – lightning striking the top of a tower. What does this foreshadow, I wonder, a shiver at the base of my neck. A vague recollection of home surfaces, me cross-legged on the floor turning over this same card and reading, crisis often precedes realization. I give the cards back to Tomas but he only takes the Tower.

The author with Tomas, the 'last Templar'.

One of the apprentices pours us black coffee and I ask him about the prayers Tomas sang. 'Angeles,' is all he says. The girl beside me adds, 'He calls on the angels to protect us.'

I want to stay the night. But that is hours away. The final few metres of ascent before the climb down into Bierzo has disappeared into fog. I look for a rainbow. I defy the Gods to send one. How auspicious that would be. But all they deem is a slight parting of clouds at the top of the rise.

Before leaving I buy one of the silver shells threaded with leather. As I pull it over my head I see it has an engraved figure of St James inside. White Tara has company. I stay quiet for the next hour giving them time to get to know each other against my skin. The track down is a landslide of slippery scree demanding all my attention.

Wild lavender clings to the rocks and I rub their silvery leaves into a sticky paste and apply it to my shins, a symbolic gesture more than anything, as a familiar sharp twinge begins to protest the bone jarring descent. I pat my face with its perfume; the most prized of essential oils could never compare to the pleasure of this. Below, the slate roofs of El Acebo look like the frills on a dragon's back and beyond stretches a vast, verdant valley cupped into a goblet by indigo mountains. It is an intoxicating sight but more exciting is a lazy trail of chimney smoke and the scent of woodfired bread.

Pilgrims are shoulder to shoulder in the small front room of Meson El Acebo and locals have taken up the long tables at the back. I should be used to it by now but it still astonishes me when I bump into a familiar face. I am overjoyed to recognize the tall blonde head of Alex at the bar. We squeeze onto a bench both of us sipping elixir of apple. He, a tall glass of local cider and me, a nip of apple spirit that warms me to my toes – those dusty bottles behind the bar have such irresistible labels. Johanna and Frederick join us. Ex girlfriend and boyfriend, they have walked all the way from Austria together, most of the time.

The door swings open and in walks the girl who passed me in the rain. Brushing back the fringe of her soaked auburn hair Uta tells us this is only her second day of walking. We share three hearty serves of food between us before rolling out the door for one last lap of road. For the second time today I am torn to throw off my pack at the next village but don't. It's as if we are a river moving closer to the sea.

Across the Romanesque bridge, *Puente de Peregrinos*, Molinaseca's narrow main street is a joy hung with strings of flags and lined with immaculately maintained medieval homes. Alfredo's *refugio* on the other side of town is a chalet style converted church. Pitched around the perimeters of its large yard are a tattered collection of blue tents. Alex has already claimed one, preferring solitude for the night. I concur and he takes me on a tour but most have puddles inside from last night's rain and mattresses mottled with mildew. Inside I check out a claustrophobic attic choking with beds, the verandah lined with more bunks and exposed to the western wind and finally the main entrance doubling as a kitchen. Here there are only three mattresses each half hanging over a steep slate stair, probably once a choir pew. As long as I hug my body to the wall I shouldn't fall out of bed.

Alex has cooked his way across most of the Camino. We buy bread, spaghetti, chorizo, olives, a slab of sharp sheep cheese and a bottle of wine but there is not a fresh vegetable for sale in town. After several inquiries an old lady sunning herself on a plastic chair waves us across to a field. There are cabbages, lettuce, aubergines and onions and behind them spinach, tomatoes, peppers and basil. We walk along ploughed ridges of earth to an old man bent over weeding. He stretches up as far as his bowed back allows and with a nod and not a word takes our bag, filling it row by row until it looks as though we'll have enough for the whole *refugio*. '*Gracias*,' Alex says following behind, '*pero, ese es bastante, de que es abundancia.*' That's enough, that's plenty, but he doesn't stop until the bag is full, finishing for good measure with a long stem of fiery red chillis. No matter how hard we try he will not accept money.

'*Ruegue para mi en Santiago,*' he says in a loud voice with a smile that creases his face into a thousand wrinkles.

'*Si, Gracias, mucho gracias,*' we say in unison, shaking his leathery hands. We will pray for you there.

As we wander back I look over to the mountains we crossed today. Heavy storm clouds tumble down the ravines. I can't believe I walked all that way. My exhilaration suddenly gives way to head to toe exhaustion. I take one of the chillis, remembering how my grandfather used to entertain us as children eating them straight from the bush in his garden. I nibble the end, swallow a few seeds and a few moments later fire burns from my throat down to my belly. It's a fire that swallows my fatigue. It swallows the memories of today – Gaia's red flowers at Foncebadon, Red Tara dancing at the foot of the iron cross, the Lark that Ascended in Manjarin and the eyes of a knight who wore a red satin cross – until all I am left with is this moment, walking towards clouds now tipped with the vermilion of a setting sun. Walking behind a gentle friend who likes to cook spaghetti and play classical guitar.

19

Tathata

Molinaseca to Cacabelos

The precise moment between sleeping and waking eludes me.

On insight meditation retreats by day six or seven life has slowed to a snail's pace. I can almost catch that elusive slip back into consciousness. Almost. The split second transition between a dream and awake is slippery as a fish. But through the day, as awareness fine tunes, the relationship between the intentions of the mind and the actions that follow begin to be more accurately witnessed – the way a fisherman knows, as he flicks his rod, the hook will land where the fish are biting. Nothing is exempt from this arc of mindfulness. We walk, sit, see, hear, and eat with an internal microscope scanning out from our mind to our fingertips, our ears, nose, eyes and tongue. We begin to observe how relentless the bombardment of sensory information is and how the mind perpetually busies itself finding ways to relate. It is, at first, a disquieting realization.

Eventually, even the microscope drops away. After a day fraught with knee pain and restlessness, I would return to the hall for one last meditation before bed; slowly plump up my cushion, cross my legs and start over. Breathing in, noticing my abdomen rising, breathing out and noticing it fall. Breathing in, hearing the bell, silently noting *hearing* then back to the *rising* of my abdomen then breathing out noting *falling*. Cumulative hours of effort, of ease then frustration or boredom, sharp mind, dull and daydreaming mind – all are building blocks for what happens next.

I like to think of it as a rough idling motor car on an ice cold morning. Once you warm up the engine you pull out of the driveway. You travel through familiar and unfamiliar territory until eventually you come to a place where you can take your hand off the wheel, your foot off the accelerator. Momentum happens by itself. Effortless effort replaces effort. From this place of non-doing *tathata* arises. *Tathata,* another one of those Pali words difficult to translate. Things are as they are. A state of absolute presence or suchness, a relationship with life as light as the weight of a dragonfly on a willow leaf, encompassing as the sky.

Or think of the violent floundering of a drowning woman; if instead of struggling she lies on her back, opens her arms and breathes. She is held afloat by the very ocean that at first terrified her. Tenderness too is implicit in the experience of *tathata*. Having never given birth I can only imagine how a mother touches the skin of her child for the first time. Like this.

In the seventeenth century a monk called Brother Lawrence was assigned his first job in a monastery as cook for a hundred mouths. After fifteen years he was moved to the office of sandal repairs. Despite a crippling war injury and chronic pain he found a way to go about his work, much like the mindfulness practice of Vipassana. Keeping my mind in His holy presence, he writes, and recalling it as often as I found it wandered from Him. I made this my business every hour, every minute. In his letters, *The Practice of the Presence of God*, Brother Lawrence goes on to explain the outcome of such a life, one that in many ways parallels *tathata*. In my affectionate regard for God I find myself often attached with greater sweetness and delight than that of an infant at the mother's breast. If at any time, my thoughts wander from this state, from necessity or infirmity, I am presently recalled by inward emotions so charming and delicious that I cannot find words to describe them.

Brother Lawrence speaks of the grace of God and the Buddha speaks of *Dharmakaya*, that omnipresent and boundless state of truth. Are these really so very different? Jesus said to the Pharisees: Everyone who sins is a slave of sin. If you obey my teaching you will know the truth, and the truth shall set you free.

What are sins but actions propelled by the loop of

desire and hatred. The Buddha's antidote for this endless cycle of craving and aversion is a teaching called the Four Noble Truths.

The bell is softly struck ending the hour; you slowly open your eyes to one candle flame in a room filled with the shapes of other meditators. You uncross your pins and needles legs and wait for feeling to return before bowing and standing up, not needing to mentally note each intention and movement because there is only sensation and presence. Outside is a galaxy of stars and you are not separate from them. Then you see the Southern Cross; the mind jumps in and labels it: Southern Cross. The union of seer and seen is broken. So you return to your silent noting. Seeing ... thinking ... right foot ... left, all the way back to your room. The noting continues through each action, brushing teeth, toilet, climbing into bed, lying down... until the final task of the day comes, watching through that internal microscope each subtle sensation in the transition from waking to sleeping. Consciousness to unconsciousness.

I can only imagine what I dreamt last night. The wind howled and whistled under the eaves outside and the yard full of tents, straining at their ropes and pegs, billowed in and out like a collective blue lung. Half my mattress bobbed over the stairwell like a boat adrift in a black void and I remember nestling close to the wall for stability. Did I dream of sirens, I wonder, pulling me down to the ocean floor or a Templar knight throwing me a rope?

Waking up this morning was not an easy transition.

My awareness surfaced like a heavy weight well after my body. I did what I always do: dress, roll my sleeping bag into a tight ball and into my pack, splash my face with cold water, put on my boots, walk out to the road and turn west. In neither night nor day I follow an unforgiving concrete path parallel to a bitumen road, past a meat factory and through wasteland. On the horizon, where the sun should be, looms a nuclear station, its white funnel ominously shaped like a sandglass and flanked by chimney stacks spewing smoke. I yearn for the wilderness of yesterday.

Further along, in the small village of Campo I cup my hands and take a long drink from its ancient stone fountain. Cool water tasting of mineral. It is as if I needed to drink from the earth in order to quench my separation from it and I am comfortable again with the weight of my pack; happy to be walking into the dawn. The last lights of Ponferrada twinkle in the distance and I choose the longer route down a country lane.

Ponferrada's medieval castle is ideally placed for a fortress, flanked by cliffs and the River Sil. It is also a perfect keyhole into the plunderous history of Spain. The land on which it sits pre-dates the Romans. They came, they conquered and continued to use it for a citadel until defeated by the Visigoths who ruled for four hundred years until the last decade of the tenth century. By this time the Moors from North Africa ruled a predominantly Muslim Spain, with the exception of one Christian enclave in the North. Al-Mansur bi Ilah would have none of this and led a series of campaigns seizing not only Ponferrada but Santiago and Leon.

Two centuries later Spain was reclaimed in a victory that oozed opportunity for king and church. Enter the Templar knights and the great pilgrimage route to Santiago was set for a renaissance. Leon's King Alfonso IX granted them this piece of Ponferrada land and from the crumbling ashlar blocks and horseshoe arches of the Visigoths the knights resurrected a fortress. Within its walls they built a monastery, a palace and a plaza, stables, a chapter house and chapel, guest rooms and a dungeon, kitchens and servant quarters. Even a cemetery. It took them sixty years, but woe, in another twenty, the Templars fell from grace and were expelled. A succession of counts and feudal lords ruled for another six centuries until the 1800s when its walls and buildings were plundered like a quarry for Ponferrada's roads and municipal projects. A soccer field inside its fortress walls was proposed in the early twentieth century but a year later the site was declared a National Monument, just in the nick of time.

History has thick skin. The image of St James as Moor Slayer flashes across my mind – Santiago Matamoros raising his sword as he rides into battle on a rearing white horse. And a selective memory too, I think, as I remember the terrified infidel about to be crushed under his stallion. Is it divine providence or judicious joke that a castle built to defend a Christian city, and before that a pagan one, has now become a mecca for tourists? Did I say Mecca? Muslims lived and ruled here for two hundred years and, to put things in perspective, occupied the greater part of Spain for a total of seven centuries.

Under their reign Christians and Jews held the status of *dhimmi*. They were subject to Muslim law but, for a special tax, allowed to practice their religion, albeit discreetly. In this orchestrated atmosphere of secular tolerance Muslims and non-Muslims flocked to the libraries and universities established by the Moors. When the great monastery of Cluny boasted a five hundred book library, Cordoba offered close to ten thousand texts. Heavens! Even a shelf for Arabic translations of the bible. There were illuminated manuscripts on every subject imaginable: Greek philosophy, astronomy and astrology, mathematics, medicine, music and poetry. And if you wanted a copy to take home the library supplied you with paper and reed pens they called *qalams* or second tongues.

The only mention of the Moors I find in a tourist brochure is the fact that Ponferrada's Virgin de la Encina was hidden in an oak tree when the Muslim invaders were approaching. Some centuries later the Templar knights find her. Two hundred years glossed over in one sentence. Did the Moors leave any ruins here in Ponferrada? Nobody seems to know.

If St James were alive today I'd wager he'd be scratching his head. It was eight hundred years after his burial that the church canonized him. The Muslims had an advantage. Mohammed's arm was ensconced in the Great Mosque of Cordoba and it was to this holy relic their armies deferred before going to battle. What better way to unite a fractured Christian Spain than a magical relic of their own? The discovery of St James's body near Santiago was perfectly timed. Add a bit of window dressing and *voila*, St James becomes Santiago Matamoros. It was a win-win situation. His bones, bequeathed with the power of absolution, inspired an estimated half million to don pilgrim garb each year and set off for Santiago, thus reviving the power of the Church. Am I walking down the road of two fundamentalist movements?

Attempting to navigate my way out of the perplexing twists of history and the suburbs of Ponferrada I am suddenly overcome with the conviction that I simply cannot walk one more kilometre. Why not catch a bus? The temptation dissipates all my energy and I stop, completely stymied, in the middle of a roundabout. Two studious looking pilgrims walk past. They look vaguely familiar. I want to ask them if they know where a bus terminal is but I am too embarrassed and to make matters worse I sense they view my pinioned state here in the middle of the road as infectious, possibly lethal. They give me a perfunctory nod – two elderly bespectacled men, dressed in convertible trousers and safari vests, sensible shoes and floppy hats each with a pair of walking poles. I watch them disappear, a well oiled eight limbed machine, their quick short steps in rhythm with each deft click then flick of a walking pole. *Alice in Wonderland's* white rabbit comes to mind, 'I'm late, I'm late, for a very important date.' An amusing distraction, and for a moment I forget mine.

Two fashionable young mothers walk out from the gates of a childcare centre. High leather boots, perfectly combed black hair swept up into ponytails, lipstick and makeup eyes. My attempt at Spanish, exacerbated by my state of mind, is pitiful. 'Autobus? Autobus?' A pilgrim asking for a bus? They look at each other, arching their perfectly plucked brows. 'Sacrilegious,' did I hear one say to the other under her breath? But they smile and point left up a steep street.

Halfway up and I stymie again. Get a grip Helen! Looking back I see the ring of El Bierzo's mountains in the distance. Somehow this wide view dilutes my obsessive one. The noose I've been tightening around my neck loosens a notch, then another. So caught in desire, I've lost sense of who I am and where I am. And then of all things, a real live bus pulls out from the kerb at the top of the hill. Cacabelos, I read on its front window. That's my destination! I could hail it but I don't. Instead I wave to the driver as he passes. He waves back and toots the horn.

Several coal heaps and furnaces, a few more suburbs and a lot of bitumen later I reach Compostilla on the edge of the city, a lush leafy laned community of elegant two storey houses. Tudor homes covered in ivy, rose gardens, manicured hedges and expensive cars. An old lady sits at a table on the pavement outside her house with a bowl of roasted capsicums in her lap. I stop to watch as she slips each blistered skin away from the flesh, breathing in the perfume of roses, sweet pepper and charcoal. In the intimacy of our moment together I realize I am not estranged from her because I am not estranged from myself.

Columbrianos, Fuentes Nuevas, Camponaraya. I walk through vineyards from one medieval village to the next. The Camino in autumn is a perpetual grape harvest. By now Basque vines will be bare and pruned back ready for the winter but here I am surrounded by laughter, the rustle of leaves and a luscious thud each time a bucketful of grapes is tipped into the tarp lined barrow of a red tractor.

'*Hola! Peregrino,*' one farmer calls, inviting me to take a photo. With pilgrims passing every day this is one innovative way of ensuring his image will be carried all the way to Santiago. He holds up his arms, a sickle in one hand and a huge bunch of green grapes in the other, his round face beaming.

A man invites me over to a neat as a pin tin shed. Given my last encounter in that Navarette garage I should probably think first about this. But the day is balmy and he seems very polite. He helps me with my pack, as a gentleman might help a lady with her coat, and sits me down on a white vinyl lounge affording a view over his vines. He produces a chilled bottle of wine and proudly pours a long stemmed glass. 'Godello grapa,' he announces, giving me a genial pat on the knee. How appropriate I think taking liberties with translation, a glass from the grape of the Gods on a day like today. It is perfection, zinging with sunlight and the soft aromatics of apple peel and honey.

What on earth possessed you to want a bus? Look what you would have missed. I chatter away to myself as I wind through more vineyards and fields of corn and pumpkins turning butternut gold. I cross a small stream and enter an orchard that takes my breath away. Apples as far as I can see cover the ground. Hundreds of them, thousands, gold and green, in a dapple of sunlight. The air is syrupy as fresh fermented cider and I half-expect a fig-leaved Adam and Eve to appear. I lightly tug at a Golden Delicious hanging heavy on a branch and it drops into my hand.

Munching away I remember a conversation with an aboriginal elder. He said to me, 'Lovey, if we'd been in that Eden place there would be none of this sin business. Forget the apples, we'd a killed that old snake, put him on a fire and eaten him.'

All these apples at my feet spark another memory. I was an impressionable twelve or thirteen and besotted with the leader of a Christian youth camp. He was tall and handsome and I was a perfect candidate for conversion, ripe as the apple I now hold in my hand. One day on a bushwalk I came upon two branches fallen across the path in the shape of a cross. It was an apparition of biblical significance that stopped me in my tracks. I rushed back to camp to confide my discovery. Instead of taking me in his arms and chastely stroking my burning cheeks, his reply across the table was, 'Jesus is asking that you take him into your heart.' Like a good girl I took his advice, but underneath my desire for him smoldered into guilt. In my mind, instead of embracing Christianity, I had fallen from grace.

I take another bite and wander down the muddied grooves of an old dirt lane through farmhouses and market gardens and into Cacabelos. I cross a bridge, pass an old mill and a wooden olive press, and arrive at the *refugio*. Groups of pilgrims languish in the sun as others tend to feet and hang out washing. The room assigned to me is small, clean and, hallelujah, has only two beds. After many arrivals and unknown sleeping arrangements my expectations are curtailed. It's the best way to avoid disappointment and a daily lesson in non-attachment. So when a room like this comes my way it is better than Christmas.

A Burmese Sayadaw would probably observe this bounce for joy, and say in the driest of dry voices, 'Only *anicca*, note the arising of joy and come back to your belly.' Just another swing of the emotional pendulum, do not get too excited. One of the beds has been neatly spread with a sleeping bag and when I return from my shower I find Uta's smiling face at the door.

Heading into town I have trouble keeping up with her. Enough is enough my body drones, thigh and calf muscles one step away from paralysis. As for my ankles, they've swollen into elephant trunks. Nothing, I think, that an anti-inflammatory swallowed with a nip of pacharan won't fix. A small voice inside my head berates me for disregarding all things herbal and homeopathic. Such gentle natural remedies require an equal respect for the body, a pulling back from whatever it is that exacerbates the condition. And time. I can afford neither.

Tractors laden with grapes chug home from the fields. Workers come and go from the bars, the bakery and the general store in the old colonnaded plaza. Bernard from Switzerland joins us and can't keep his eyes off Uta. He began his pilgrimage from the front door of his house four months ago and is today, looking, I have to say, as spic and span as his object of desire. On hearing I am from Australia he tells me he will be meeting his wife there next month for a holiday. 'Your wife must miss you after all this time,' I say stirring the pot. 'No, not at all,' he says, squirming for a second in his chair. 'We both agreed this break would be good for us. This is my long service leave. Thirty years in a bank, same, same every day.' He turns toward Uta. 'And what do you do, dear?'

'I'm an editor for a television news network.' This sparks an animated conversation about war crimes, embezzlements and honest reporting as the sun drops down behind Nuestra Senora de la Plaza. I can just make out the outline of its thirteenth century Virgin in the niche above its main door. Cover your ears my lady, you do not want to hear what has become of the world.

In the Bar Casa Lazaro, at a table spread with white plastic lace, we eat local dishes of *tortilla berciana*, a red pepper omelette and *botillo*, a pie filled with chickpeas, potatoes, pancetta and El Bierzo's pride and joy, a cut of pork flavoured with oregano, paprika and garlic then cured over an oakwood fire. Our wine comes from the

Mencia grape, grown in the vineyards outside Cacabelos in the same alluvial earth that clings to my boots.

With Bernard happily ensconced between us, we return to the *refugio* for a night of luxury. No bunk beds and no symphonies. Outside a man paces back and forth in the dark talking into his mobile phone. Why do people shout when they use those things? His voice echoes across the compound. I wrap myself in a sarong and open the door. One glare is all he needs and he retreats around the corner. Uta and I collapse on our beds in a fit of giggles for a day lived well, a good meal to end it and just for the joy that giggling brings. 'Shhhh! *Vraiment, impossible,*' comes the irritated and insistent voice of a Frenchman over the partition wall.

20

The Donkey and the Laughing Man
Cacabelos to Ruitelan

A perfect world full of perfect people, now there's a thought. But it would probably be boring and who is to say my perfect is the same as yours? I rationalize this way and that as I set out into the dark. We were woken up by our neighbours on the other side of the wall and their incessant rustling of plastic bags. On and on they fidgeted like a couple of mice until Uta and I shhh'd them. Adding, '*Vraiment, impossible!*' just for good measure. I was able to drift off for a few precious minutes before the hinges of their door creaked open followed by an oddly familiar click-flick tap-tapping of their poles towards the gate. The two white rabbits from Ponferrada running late again. I wanted to laugh at the comedy of it but at such an hour all I could afford was a curse at the insensitivity of these early rising old men.

Red roses trail up the flaking whitewash of a sleeping mansion in the small village of Pieros. Parked at its front door is a tractor full of grapes, green and black, glistening under the cover of morning dew. The ancestral home of a viticulturist perhaps? I would give up a day of walking just to take off my boots, hitch up my trousers and climb aboard for a merry squelching of grapes into must. But this ritual has been replaced by the precision of hygienic machines. What once involved a whole village and was cause for lots of singing and dancing is now done with the turn of a switch.

A dirt path veers from the main road through orchards and vineyards, saving me from an overdose of cynicism. According to the *Codex Cailixtinus* I am nearing the tenth stage of the Camino: Villafranca del Bierzo, final port of call before Galicia. Pilgrims on their last legs, beset with consumption, a failing heart or any other malady that might prevent them from reaching St James, can receive the same plenary indulgences here as at Santiago de Compostela.

Confession and communion in Villafranca's Iglesia de Santia is all that is needed and if, after absolution, a pilgrim dies, why there is the convenience of a cemetery next door.

A couple I remember seeing in Rabanal's chapel rest on the church's steps. We bask together like three lizards in the sun, our backs against stone columns. On one of the capitals above is an intriguing frieze of the three wise men bundled up and horizontal, sharing a blanket and having a nap. A very long nap. Eight centuries have pockmarked their sleeping faces. On another capital, wearing turbans and long robes they ride their horses towards Bethlehem guided by a star.

Next door Jesus Jato and his family run the El Fenix *refugio* named for its rise from the ashes of a fire, not once but several times since their arrival in the 1980s. It looks to me as if it has been here forever. In a chaotic courtyard of trellised tomatoes, cucumbers and geraniums an animated conference is taking place. For three euros Jesus offers a daily service transporting packs to *refugios* further along the way. This, for a puritan is almost as sacrilegious as taking a bus. I've already failed that test and given I am contemplating the steeper of two paths out of Villafranca I take it as good as a green light. I sprout my own phoenix wings and practically skip out the gates, nine kilos of possessions lighter.

Villafranca's thousand year old history boasts eight monasteries and six pilgrim hostels. The fact that a plague decimated the population in 1589, numerous floods besieged its streets and a succession of French, English and Spanish squabbles laid much of the town to ruin, has done nothing to diminish its charm. Urns of rose bushes and garden benches line its plaza and I spy a café at the end.

I sip my coffee at an empty table near the front. 'Can I join you?' a girl says in an unmistakable accent. 'You're Australian,' I say pulling out a chair, wooed by the sound of home. Lina's fiancé, Bill, swings through the door carrying a roll of bandage and a tube of ointment. His voice is deep, dry and wonderfully drawled all the way from Wagga Wagga. I had forgotten how convivial Australian company can be. Our conversation inevitably turns to feet and Lina declares she is a podiatrist. She may as well have said I am an angel from heaven come to minister the crippled. Her feet are fine but Bill's are covered in weeping blisters.

'I am so used to them now, after fifteen minutes of walking I forget they are there.'

Lina shakes her head, 'The way you are going your feet will be scarred for life and I am the one who has to dress and bandage them every day. But hey what do I know?' She shrugs her shoulders, laughs, and turns to me. 'Let me take a look.' I roll up my trousers and show her the place where my ankles used to be.

'Mmm. Make sure you elevate them every night but don't expect the swelling to go until you have rested for at least a week. As for shin splints, by all means keep taking the anti-inflammatories but remember, at best, all they do is mask the pain. Half the Camino seems to be popping them and I haven't heard of any legs dropping off yet.' She pauses. 'The kindest thing you can do is take small steps and drink lots of water.'

We walk as far as the medieval footbridge on the edge of town before parting company. Lina and Bill take the highway and I scramble up a goat track. Halfway I stop to catch my breath and look back to Villafranca's bell towers and domes, palace walls and the terracotta roofs of stately homes built long and narrow to fit the thin slices of land between river and road. They glint like jewels on this extraordinarily clear summers day; a lost Atlantis that I don't want to leave. I've climbed so high if I cup my hands the whole town fits into them. An optical illusion, I know, much like desire. Wanting something impossible to have throws my mind away from the present, out to a fantastical world, and I miss the delicate wildflowers brushing my feet. I make a wish before continuing, with small shin-friendly steps, up to a plateau where hills of heath and wild grasses roll into a sky so vast it is as if all my wanting evaporates into it. Far, far below ant-like pilgrim figures string the edge of a motorway scarring its way west through the mountains.

I remember *Soledad* the third of the seven ingredients – solitude. Someone had penciled beside it, *Cumplendo su promesa*, a promise to God or the Virgin to walk alone. I've chosen the best path for this today, more strenuous and, as a consequence, less traveled. The only people I see are two young girls and the three of us interweave quietly, as if in a dream – the high altitude perhaps and the deep silence of a windless day broken occasionally by the distant sound of a tractor or the moo of a cow. It is easy to wax on about feelings of peace in a place like this. The Christian mystic, Thomas Merton wrote: True solitude is not an absence of men or of sound around you, it is an abyss opening up in the centre of your own soul.

And I recall the cautioning of one Vipassana teacher

towards the end of a retreat. 'The true test for a meditator is being able to take the mindfulness developed in these weeks of silence into the marketplace.'

Groves of Spanish chestnut trees replace the heath. Every now and then a chestnut falls with a thud to the ground. I am walking into the eve of another harvest and can almost hear the slow splitting of husks. The Galicians call them *Ourizos*, hedgehogs, for their prickly spines. Before the advent of potato and wheat, chestnuts were a poor man's staple, roasted and eaten whole or ground into a starchy flour for a simple bread. Add water, olive oil, salt, some rosemary or raisins and bake in the coals of a fire. Sweet to taste with a crumbly texture, spread with soft cheese or dipped into a thick broth, just the thing for a mid-winter meal.

In the distance is the hamlet of Pradelo, the first sign of life for miles. I fantasize about a tall glass of cider and a handful of warm roasted chestnuts. Yes, I think, but the road forks away and I haven't the energy to take a detour. My last El Bierzo apple will have to do. As abruptly as the chestnut trees stop the descent begins. I thought the climb out of Villafranca was steep but this hairpin track of scree verges on vertical and I slip-slide down making smaller hairpins on the hairpins in order to stay on my feet. An old man riding a scruffy grey donkey with the longest ears I have ever seen appears around a bend. He breaks out into a laugh at the sight of me. But it's music to my ears after a morning of silence. I note the donkey's tiny steps, he has no bridle and the man, no reins. Maybe he's not laughing at me at all. Maybe there is a symbiosis here the rest of the world has lost. There are no reins to let go.

Laughing man riding his unbridled donkey.

The tap-tapping of my poles echoes off the empty sidewalks of Trabadelo into the rustling of chestnut leaves and a buzz of bees returning to their hives, legs soaked with the nectar of wildflowers. I hear a faint hum that soon turns to a roar and look up to the incongruous sight of cars and trucks speeding along a four lane *autopista* in the sky. This massive highway supported by giant viaducts soars over the top of whole villages and for the next couple of hours the Camino quite literally falls in and out of its shadow. I'm not particularly bothered by it. It is as it is and I am where I am.

'*Hola,*' an old woman wrapped in a crocheted shawl motions me to sit beside her. She hands me a fava bean pod from the bowl in her lap. '*Venga, comer!*' Eat.

The plump beans inside are tender and sweet. She lets me help and I lose myself in the sensation of fingers running along the insides of each velvety pod; each popping of bright green beans into her bowl. I relax my back against the bench and my arm against her soft ample arm. My body decides that here, in the village of Vega de Valcarce, is where I will stay the night. No, it insists with every muscle, not one kilometre more. But my pack is in Ruitelan, an interminable two kilometres away. My feet drag like they've been balled and chained and my mind too until a singsong of babbling water drowns out my dirge. I catch glimpses of a river rushing through the gorge below and have an idea.

Down a rough track, over a rickety wooden gate, in a meadow of catmint and comfrey I face an audience of cows. Three return to their grazing and the fourth, the one with horns, follows me to the water's edge. He seems docile enough but all the same we keep a respectable distance. Hidden from the road, dappled by oaks, poplars and chestnuts is a perfect pool rippling over a bed of smooth river stones. I strip off. The poor cow gives a few disconcerting snorts and backs away a couple of steps. A naked woman in this neck of the woods? Perhaps the first seen since the days of the Druids. Ice cold water fizzes every cell of my body alive. I let out a wild shriek and the cow snorts again. Tingling head to toe I perch on a rock to thaw and in celebration of my rebirth, eat the last bar of chocolate.

Hugging Ruitelan's one and only street is Pequeno

Potala, a whitewashed house run by Luis from Catalonia and Carlos from Andalucia, vegetarian cook and shiatsu therapist, and *hospitaleros* extraordinaire. I feel my way into the dark cocoon of a loft, past beds and siesta bodies, to the familiar shape of my pack.

Two iron bells hang in the *espadana*, a thin square belltower, of the Church of San Juan Bautista across the road. Inside, in a space of soothing simplicity and honeyed light, a fair haired woman sketches the statue of a small angel in a niche. I watch from behind how each pencil stroke defines first an eye, then a cherubic smile, an upstretched arm and the shape of a wing. Life and art, present and past, rendered into one.

I laze in the *refugio* garden with Ursula from Finland who walks with Lisette, the artist, painting her way through every village church. A silver haired, white aproned Carlos appears, benignly raising his black bushy eyebrows. He leans against the door and lights the cigarette dangling from his mouth as he surveys us and the *feng shui* fountain gurgling in the middle of his garden. The calligraphy of Confucius, half hidden in the hallway behind him, hints at a philosopher's heart.

The dinner bell rings and we squeeze into a tiny candlelit room made even smaller by a map of the world covering one of its pink walls. Who should be sitting at the table alongside the two Finnish girls but Uta and oh la la the white rabbits. Claude pours the wine while Pierre introduces himself and suddenly I remember the day we met – it was not at the roundabout in Ponferrada but all the way back in Larrasoana – they were sitting at the same table as Daniel the retired policeman with his tortoise carved staff.

They remember Daniel too. 'Have you seen him?' I ask. But, '*Mais non.*' They confer for a few animated moments before telling me the last time was in Pamplona. I feel a twinge of sadness. When you meet a person who touches you, a part of them, more than memory, stays.

We raise our glasses to the day, to lost friends and new ones, then ladle into bowls a seriously garlic scented broth thick with fava beans and wilted greens. Ursula passes the bread and in a voice barely audible says, 'I can't imagine in a week I will be back in Finland, back to work cooking in the kitchen of an old people's home.' She says it not dolefully, but with affection for all the residents there; the wheelchairs and walking sticks, the depressed silent single residents, the still married after all these years ones and the two effervescent centenarians. Over a salad of soft white cheese dusted with paprika, layered between tomato, basil and endive Lisette explains how she will work many of her sketches into woodblocks for an exhibition. Claude and Pierre listen, enamored, as they polish off the cheese. Next comes a platter of spaghetti, a bowl of glistening pesto and another basket of bread. What a joy after days of meat to be eating vegetarian food, simply prepared and cooked with love.

I climb into bed and lie wide awake watching, through the attic's three tiny windows, a straggle of Milky Way stars streaming across the dark new moon sky.

Lisette lies in the bed opposite writing by torchlight. Uta is downstairs in the same room as Claude and Pierre – they had made a pact over dinner, no giggling in exchange for no pre-dawn plastic bag crunching. I hear the sound of a kiss from the bed next to mine; the couple sharing it making a perfect spoon to carry them into sleep.

21

Music

Ruitelan to Triacastela

'Ave Maria,' a maiden sings and I open my eyes. Through the small window of our loft there are still stars in the sky. *'Du laechelst, Rosenduefte wehen, Indieser dumpfen Felsenkluft.'* The mighty cavern's heavy air shall breathe of balm if thou hast smiled.

I let myself be cradled in the arms of Schubert's *Lady of the Lake,* breathing in the aroma of the oiled timber beams above and the coffee brewing downstairs. *'Der Jungfrau wolle hold dich neigen. Ave Maria.'* Hear for a maid a maiden's prayer.

Schubert's hymn to the Virgin, sung by a maiden hiding in a mountain cave, carries me into visions of medieval knights and carriages winding their way up to O Cebreiro, the mountain I will be climbing today. A pleasant dream until it finishes and I am blasted out of bed by the next track on Pequeno Potala's wake-up play list, the trumpeting trumpets of *2001: A Space Odyssey*.

Guidebooks have given O Cebreiro, with its steep ascent and unpredictable weather, a formidable reputation. Luis and Carlos's choice of music, humorous or symbolic or both, only add to the level of anticipation practically bouncing of the walls of the dining room as we elbow our way through breakfast. Outside in the hallway preparations are in earnest – the tensioning of backpack straps, windbreakers and raincoats made ready and water bottles checked. I squeeze out into a grey morning, happy to have the familiar weight of my pack again, a kind of teddy bear comfort.

I stop for a pee behind a deserted cow shed in Herrerias and twist my ankle in a gutter. 'A fine start,' I berate before coming to the realization that I am alone with no one to complain to, no sympathetic friend to soothe my misfortune. Better to relax, be tender with myself, walk carefully and watch where I am going. Soon though my muscles warm up, my ligaments adjust and the pain is gone.

A stone cobbled *corredoira* winds ever upward into a saturating mist and the shrouded path of vine entwined old trees cloaked in moss. A beam of sunlight breaks through them transforming a primeval world into an enchanted dewdropped web. Indra has a kindly disposition today, I think, as swirls of blue sky appear through the trees. I feel exalted to be strung limb by limb and head to heart in the net this Buddhist deity weaves. Each dewdrop is reflected in every other drop of dew that clings to the threads of his mythological web, a world where, whether we realize or not, everything is connected. The way that metaphorical butterfly flapping her wings on the other side of the planet effects the thinning of the mists above me. And maybe, if I look carefully into one dewy drop, David's face will emerge, but all I see is my reflection. I miss him suddenly and long to muse and to chatter about this and that, laugh at one of his dry jokes, give his hand an affectionate tug.

I brush my hands along mossy banks as if this might quench my craving. The soft sponged body of earth, dense with the odour of fallen leaves and crumbling bark, will have to do as my lover for today.

Trees give way to hills marked into neat rectangles by hedges and low stone walls. A symphony of late summer colour flanks the trail heralding the beginning of Galicia. Bright yellow gorse and broom, delicate sprays of pink and purple blossoms. I inhale the cleansing scent of tiny white rosemary flowers. I close my eyes and listen. To the wind singing into the spaces between each spined leaf, to the jubilant rattle of seeds in a pea pod. An imagined witch joins in with a rhythmic swish of a scythe as she gathers broom for a tea to bring on the birth of a young village wife or to slow the palpitating heart of La Faba's blacksmith.

Not so long ago, for the benefit of O Cebreiro's cows, Bach's *Magnificat* echoed down the valley from loudspeakers installed in the church's tower by Father Elias

Valina Sampedro. *Magnificat anima mea.* Was this for the benefit of a cow's soul I wonder, or to make her milk sweeter? Was Father Sampedro a lover of cheese? The music stopped in 1990 when he died.

Today it is the Celtic lilt of bagpipes and flutes trilling down from the summit. Its origins though leave me flat. Past the *polloza* museum, two shops vie for attention with music and displays of tacky trinkets. I am drawn in despite myself. Having to carry everything is a definite disincentive to consume. Even the weight of a postcard requires deliberation. But, after days of feeling a part of the environment as opposed to skimming the surface on a ten day tour in search of the perfect piece of memorabilia, I confess to being curious. I walk from one end to the other out of place and unseduced.

I return to the *polloza* and crouch down to enter its two rooms, one for the family and the other for their cows. There are no windows in its round stone walls and no chimney through the low thatched roof. A claustrophobic darkness engulfs the ghostly shapes of old wooden chairs, a straw bed and a smoke-stained *lareira*, the heart and hearth of Galician homes. A huge iron cooking pot hangs over its pit and I imagine the strings of sausages and legs of *jamon* that would have hung here five hundred years ago, curing in the smoke swirling up from the *lareira* and out through the *polloza*'s roof.

'You've come from Ruitelan? That's only seven kilometres,' the girl at the *refugio* mutters as she examines my passport. 'Hardly justifies you taking one of our beds.' I am taken aback by her cavalier attitude but stand my ground without attempting an excuse. She points me up the stairs of a soulless modern building with the acoustics of a basketball court. It's a rude awakening after the simple domestic comforts of Ruitelan and the intimate room in Cacabelos.

The girl at the desk has worked her way under my skin and by the time I have unpacked, navigated soap, towel and clothes in a cupboard of a shower with no hooks or shelf, I've plunged into loneliness. The boisterous group of Spanish bike riders banging on my shower's paper thin door only add to the feeling. All I can do is curl up on my top bunk, turn to face the wall and hope for sleep. Am I homesick? Or is it that from O Cebreiro it is less than a week to Santiago, and from there a nine hundred kilometre per hour flight back to Australia. I'm almost done but am I ready?

An Australian voice wakes me – Collette. And she is talking to *California Dreaming* Asterix who I haven't seen since Burgos. Collette stands at half Asterix's height and is half his age. Despite being a world apart, with her Catholic faith and defense corps career and his world still suspended in the lyrics of Arlo Guthrie and Jimi Hendrix, they have become best of friends. The three of us make a natural trio, given we have all chosen to walk alone, and as we venture out into the clear blue of a late afternoon I leave the *poor me* behind.

The ancient Celts were the world's earliest pilgrims, setting out to sea in small boats with no oars or sails and no destination other than the god in their hearts. It was all about the journey – tossed from wave to crashing wave, lashed by wind and burned by the sun, then washing up on an unknown shore. I take a bold leap from here to the other shore in Buddhist teachings. Any destination other than a calm-abiding heart only results in suffering. Here I am a simple vehicle of flesh, bone and blood, complicated with forty nine years of habit and memory. And my journey? Whether bailing out my boat or installing a motor, dropping anchor or setting sail for another shore, there is nothing as profound as an open heart.

Only one carved stone remains from the Celtic temple where the church of Santa Maria la Real now stands. Collette has timed our visit for mass and I sit on a side pew watching a hundred red candles flicker at the feet of O Cebreiro's Romanesque Virgen del Milagro. Behind her is the Holy Grail, or one of them, a reminder of the miracle on an awful winter's day seven centuries ago when a lonely priest set about preparing communion for his meager parish. Just as he is consecrating the bread and wine the door opens and in from the howling wind, followed by a flurry of snowflakes, came one freezing peasant. The priest is unamused and berates him for his tardiness and lack of faith, accusing him of climbing the mountain only to fill his belly. In an instant the white wafer of bread in his hands turned to meat as if just cut from a live body and the wine he had poured began to thicken and smell of blood. We are told that these now lie in two very ornate silver reliquaries donated by Queen Isabel herself, en route to Santiago in the fifteenth century.

An old woman in black brushes past me to light a candle and offer a coin to the Virgin. Holy Grails and reliquaries seem empty vessels compared to this Madonna who, it is said, inclined her head to contemplate the miracle. The church has since embellished the tale by suggesting the boy Jesus on her lap opened his eyes at that same moment. This evening she is dressed in a lace-edged velvet cape, cerulean blue like an O Cebreiro summer sky. Those requesting favours and those with favours newly bestowed have threaded wedding rings on each of her fingers and the raised fingers of Jesus too. Gold bracelets and necklaces are draped over their wrists.

Pongo en tus manos cuanto soy y cuanto poseo, I put in your hands whatever I am and whatever I have, reads a prayer on the back of the card we were given when we entered. A prayer of surrender I think, as I look to the Virgin of Miracles, much the same as the prayer I chant to White Tara. All objects of attachment, aversion and ignorance – friends, enemies and strangers, body, wealth and pleasure – are offered up to her without any sense of loss. 'Please accept them with pleasure and inspire me and others to be free.' A prayer to one is a prayer to the other. In the giving up of who I am, if it is wholehearted and unconditional, all ideas dissolve, even the goddess. 'To Tara, dustless and space pervading, I bow with formless body, without limbs and without frame, observing no homage or object of homage.'

I light a candle and add it to the halo of the others flickering around the hem of the Virgin's cloak. In the shadows dancing on the wall behind her I swear there are the shrouded shapes of Galician gypsies and a few wandering Celts kicking up their heels at each new gift proffered to their Queen, knowing well we are all, in the end, just a play of light.

The Milky Way has spread herself across the sky and from our mountaintop home her stars seem brighter, milkier. Enticed by the muffled strains of a *gaita*, the bagpipes I now know are as Spanish as castanets, we enter a bar. To Celtic rhythms and Gallego voices we slurp steaming mouthfuls of *Caldo* Gallega, a turnip top, potato and chorizo broth.

Galicia is the most forgotten enclave of seven Celtic nations. She remains true to her roots through music and a multitude of festivals. Annual celebrations placate the ghosts of witches and evil spirits, revel in the harvests of a Summer Solstice and, woven into these ancient rites, religious processions for each parish Madonna. *O felix culpa*! O happy guilt, villagers sing to pipes and drums as they dance and carry her on a palanquin of flowers from the church into their streets; for without sin God would not have considered giving his son through the vessel of Mary.

Gallego, Galicia's language, sounds more Portuguese than Spanish. It was an offshoot of Latin in the Middle Ages and the language of choice for poets in the later courts of Leon. Alfonso X's *Cantigas* to the Virgin are still sung today. As we order a second course another bagpipe nasals its way in and the voices take on a ribald tone, unbefitting tales of Madonnas and miracles. But perhaps not. Consider one of Alfonso's *Cantigas* where a priest sews himself a pair of underpants from an altar cloth and as punishment the Virgin makes his legs grow the wrong way around.

Three dessert plates of fresh Tetilla cheese, named for its nipple shape, come quivering in pools of light golden honey. The Spanish pilgrims next to us have ordered the same, it being an O Cebreiro speciality. 'Is like tits. You know the story?' one of them says and proceeds to tell us how, when Santiago's cathedral was being built, a sculptor of the Portico de Gloria endowed Queen Esther with enormous breasts. He matched this with a delighted leer on the young face of the prophet Daniel who looks across at her. An order was given to cut the breasts off.

Manuela, the senorita of the house who is generously bestowed herself under a full length apron, interrupts our conversation. 'Ask any Galician and they will tell you this can be verified by the difference in the texture of stone on her chest,' Paulo translates. 'The people of Santiago were so horrified by this *mastectomia* that they moulded a cheese into the shape of a breast as a protest.' She puts her hands on her hips. 'And that is why Galicians are passionate about their Tetilla!' Flattered by our applause Manuela shouts us all a nip of the local firewater.

Hardly two steps out the door I trip and, to avoid a

full facial bitumen encounter, take my weight with one knee and a hand. I am quick to blame the pitch black night and a fallen branch and not, as I limp back to the *refugio* on Asterix's arm, that last glass of orujo. A glance in the bathroom mirror, my first in days, reveals a red blotchy rash covering my neck, spreading up to my face and full blown across my arms and chest. As I curl up in bed nursing a sprained wrist and swollen fingers, feeling my knee swell by the minute and fearing that I might be stricken with an incurable skin disease there is, finally, no hope for poor, falling apart at the seams me. How inconsequential thoughts are I think as I lick my wounds. Wasn't it just yesterday I swore I could keep walking forever?

The scene is set. Thirty six soundly sleeping, snoring bodies, stacked two by two in three rows. A sliver of moon has traveled halfway across the sky and there are at least another two hours until dawn. The fluorescent tubes down the centre of our room hum to a blinding start. Two pilgrims have decided to leave early and are apparently under the impression none of us will mind. They rustle their plastic bags, zip and unzip zips, clomp back and forth to the bathroom in their boots and, god bless them, whisper to each other in case anything louder might disturb. I simply can't believe it. Dear sweet sensible Asterix is the one who finally says something. 'Hey guys, there are people trying to sleep. Turn the god damn lights off.' He pauses. 'Please.' They do.

Did they learn anything from this I wonder or will they do it again tomorrow? I'm curious to see their faces so I can shoot daggers if I ever pass them on the road but in their final hustle and bustle before heading out the door all I see in the beams of torchlight bouncing mercilessly and merry across the room are two furtive shadows. I fall into a fitful sleep, grateful for Asterix and, strangely, grateful for the whole experience. I have learned something. It is okay to speak up. Asterix, for all his new age espousing, stands firm and at home within himself and from there, seeing right from wrong, responds. Simple as that.

The moon has disappeared and a black ribbon of road lies ahead. My knee has turned dark blue and if I take anything but the tenderest of steps it threatens mutiny. Screams it. Alone and self-absorbed in this predicament I suddenly feel the spirit of the limping woman outside Burgos beside me. I remember her threadbare sneakers and the way I winced at every step she took but on her face there was not an ounce of tension, only serene conviction.

Brother Lawrence suggests: You should leave off human remedies and resign yourself entirely to God. He sometimes permits bodily diseases to cure distempers of the soul. I did not pray for any relief, he wrote, but for strength to suffer with courage, humility and love.

It is the same in Vipassana practice. Not to seek distance or escape from any pain but rather hold it in the arms of a gentle, non-invasive awareness. Some people with terminal illness choose meditation as their last medicine. What could be more motivating to a committed practitioner than the imminence of death? Whether the result is a conscious transition from life or, in some cases, a complete cure, both are a radical transformation. What imprint of our lives do we wish to leave behind and what imprint do we carry when we go? On a retreat in Burma I remember one woman suffering from cancer. After two weeks she began to experience tremendous body pain but the Sayadaw, with dispassionate affection, encouraged her to keep practicing. It was an opportunity to dive into the deepest layering of mind and body and, as long as her awareness remained firm, no harm would come. Even in death, no harm would come. The Sayadaw's faith in the practice was that absolute.

A steel statue of Santiago appears like a dawn raider leaning into the western wind. *Ultreya*, go forward with courage. Further on down the cowpat splattered main street of Hospital da Condesa, Carmen, with her cropped silver hair and flour-dusted dress, offers every pilgrim who passes fuel for the journey. I take a thin, warm pancake rolled in sugar. How kind that she gets up early each morning to cook for us. I thank her and prepare to limp on, 'Hey, *peregrino, euro. Uno euro*,' she calls to me with her hand out. One euro! For a paper thin pancake? I pay begrudgingly and, stonefaced, she takes my coin. Two

Spanish boys laughingly berate her for such extortion as they hand over their money. The three other locals I pass in the village have stooped backs and weathered faces like walnut shells. They look old enough to have witnessed three maybe four generations of pilgrims making their way to Santiago. Hospital da Condesa has existed as long as the Camino. Who am I to curse an elderly lady eking a living from the constant traffic traipsing past her door?

Wild roses and blackberry brambles line the path to the pass of Alto do Poio, higher than the clouds. Collette and two French women, Marie and Catherine, catch up to me. I feel like company but am moving slower than a tortoise. Collette is struggling with a bandaged knee injured days ago but she ploughs on regardless. My knee on the other hand is still a new and uninvited guest and the sensations are intensifying. If my awareness shifts too far from the task of gently placing my foot down, an iron clamp locks around every muscle, tendon and ligament and when it lets go waves of dull throbbing follow. To make matters worse, my wrist on the same side is turning a lurid crimson and is sensitive to the slightest pressure so I cannot use my walking pole for support. I descend into self pity watching the three of them nimbly disappear. If I was Catholic would this pain make more sense?

A phrase from Sunday School days long, long ago works its way around and around my head: Suffer the little children to come unto me. Eventually, instead of smothering my mind and knee with resistance, I begin to soften into the pain. Each step becomes interesting, and by the time I reach Triacastela I feel as if I've made friends with the entire cast, crew and audience interacting inside my body. My prima donna monologue changes into a conversation and a relationship ensues. Mr Pressure turns to Mrs Burning and she in turn moves across the set to Miss Pin Pricks. Their director gives them permission to improvise and they do, with gusto. So intrigued is the audience that they forget who they are.

The world my cast of characters moves through comes to life. In a crush of gravel underfoot, a stone dislodges and rolls down the embankment scattering a trail of ants. A leaf drops from an oak tree and twirls sinuously down missing my cheek by an inch. I look up into the branches shading the path and blink into a shaft of sunlight pouring through, then come back to the sensations rippling under my skin. Breathing in for three steps and breathing out for five. Light then shadow, a ruffle of a breeze shakes more leaves free, breathing in breathing out, a tension in my ankle and a tingling in the ball of my foot, a pounding knee. An ancient lane of dappled oak shadows; the breeze drops and there is my small shadow moving among the leaves.

As I reach the door of Lucita's private refuge Collette rushes out. 'Can't stop, Marie's been stung by a bee. Got to get to a chemist.' Marie sits trembling on the edge of her bed, unrecognizable. Her lips have swollen into huge lumps of flesh and her cheeks are puffing so fast her eyes have closed into tiny slits. Catherine dashes from one room to the other in a state of panic. '*Mere sainte de Dieu,*

Lucita, docteur, rapidement, docteur,' she cries out. Lucita returns to the room with wet towels and ice, takes one look, gasps and rushes for the phone. '*No hay doctor acqui. Llamare la ambulancia.*'

'*Mere sainte de Dieu,*' is all Catherine can say wringing her hands, holy mother of God. I sit beside Marie, willing Collette back with medicine, and trying to stay calm to keep Marie calm. The more she panics the faster her body reacts. This is an allergic reaction gone too far for lavender oil or a plantain poultice. In five minutes an ambulance arrives, beating Collette by a few seconds. Marie and Catherine are bundled into the back and they disappear in a cloud of dust. We collapse on our beds too wired to speak, the ambulance siren still ringing in our ears.

In an hour they return, Marie's face miraculously taking shape by the minute as it turns from beetroot to pink against her blonde hair. Catherine wastes no time inviting us to dinner. We argue that no, they should rest and we will cook but Marie has her heart set on Soupe a la Provencale. '*Non, non notre plaisir,*' Catherine smiles holding up two bags of vegetables and fresh baguettes. They had charmed their ambulance driver into stopping at Sarria's local market on the way back. He'd been invited too but that must have stretched his line of duty.

Lucita's house fills with the sounds of laughter, laundry and chopping knives; perfect half-moon carrot slices, julienned sweet potatoes, lemon zest and the sizzle of red onions and garlic. A Spanish group cook a giant paella,

Collette and I bring a bottle of wine and a Brazilian couple make a salad. We eat at a long table under a painting of the Last Supper and afterwards take turns massaging each others feet, calf muscles and knees, trading theories on the best treatments for blisters and tendonitis, bee stings and swollen ankles. I close my eyes when it comes my turn for a knee massage. How wonderful to be touched and to be a part of this community, united in injury. We are an Ark, I think, two by two from far corners of the world moving closer and closer to the spires of Santiago. I am so tired I lose all sense of where my knee ends and my friend's hands begin.

22

Angels and Bridges, Lanterns and Brooms
Triacastela to Portomarin

Lucita is nowhere to be found and I need to call a taxi. My knee has turned a vivid shade of blue and feels like one of those swollen blowfish covered in poisonous spines. The slightest pressure erupts like lava into every cell and all the spaces in between. I cannot walk another kilometre. I know I have said these words before but this time it's for real. Not a pilgrim is left in town – I seem to have slept through this morning's exodus. I limp back and forth from the front door to the gate hoping to catch the eye of a passing stranger but Triacastela is deserted. Someone, anyone, please. I wait. I limp. Wait. The truth dawns. A Galician *meiga* has been meddling with the affairs of the living while we were sleeping. This wicked sorceress has bewitched the town, turned everyone to stone, let the air out of its one and only taxi's tyres. The Celtic underworlds have conspired. There is nothing for it and no logic left. I am swept up by the tide of the Milky Way, a piece of flotsam among so many stars, and thrust out the door.

For an hour I hobble along an empty highway beside a mellifluous river. We weave mist into the mist, lazy trails of steam rise from the water in the gorge below and from my lungs a billowing of drenched breath. Into the song of the river I go as we both travel towards the sea. She takes the path of least resistance, over and around a tumbling of river stones and I feel her current move loose and easy into the rhythm of my feet, swirling warm and anesthetizing up to my knees, sing a path to my heart then pour out of my eyes until the world looks different. I have slipped into it – am not separate from it. *Tathata*.

Only eleven kilometres to Samos, no need to hurry. Dark green, white veined vines of ivy curl over moss covered fallen branches and the round trunks of ancient oak and chestnuts flanking the path. A mushroom, or is it the spirit of a fairy sprung from the night before, peeps up from a crevice of leaf litter, her stem luminescent white with a ruffle of pink and orange for a bonnet. Slabs of stone planted vertically in the earth fence in the occasional meadow. It's an enchanted world, a green orb that whirls through my lungs every time I take a breath.

Teresa of Avila writes about a place deeper than the heart: The centre of the soul that fills from a heavenly spring. This soul perceives a fragrance, an experience more delicate and expansive than any physical sensation.

Spiritual delight, she calls it, but cautions her sisters: Only God holds the favour of this water. These and many other favours that we don't know how to desire, she describes in the fourth dwelling place of *The Interior Castle*. I stop in my tracks remembering how Beatrice and I had talked about just this on the day we left Burgos, of hearts and chakras, the compassion of a Tibetan Geshe and the fearlessness of St Teresa. Midpoint in our bodies, between heaven and earth, is the fourth of seven chakras. When uncontaminated by worldly desire the emerald energy of the heart chakra radiates out through the meridians of our arms infusing what we do.

One should let the intellect go, St Teresa says. Surrender oneself into the arms of love, for His Majesty will teach the soul what it must do.

My fingertips tingle and my heart pounds with the realization of how universal truth is. Waves of heat rush up and down my body. I want to burst but at the same time contain the sensations spinning inside me. What am I supposed to be doing? Walking! So I walk. Beside the course of a river chanting again to the goddess whose silver body against mine feels as familiar as the skin she rests on. And today she is Green.

When Avalokiteshvara, the Buddha of compassion, looked down from heaven, one story goes, he wept seeing the countless number of suffering beings. Two Taras were born from his tears. A peaceful white lady, mature full breasted and wise and a youthful girl with skin the colour of emeralds, ever ready to leap into action. 'Don't be frightened,' she cries, 'I shall swiftly save you.'

'Let him do whatever he likes with us,' Saint Teresa says.

And for the rest of the way, instead of wincing each time pressure inflames the tissue around my knee, I let go into it. Again and again. My body a vehicle and my mind simply a conduit for each sensation. 'Samsaric beings!' Green Tara calls out from behind every tree. 'Cling not to worldly pleasures. Enter the great city of liberation.'

I cross and recross the river until one final ascent brings me to a view of the monastery of Samos in the valley below, a sprawl of massive stone walls large enough for a city of monks.

Bells for mass ring out from the church's Baroque façade. Three monks begin a Gregorian chant casting the occasional disapproving glare at a bus group, more intent on flashing this way and that with their cameras. The little light that penetrates the church is all but swallowed by its massive brick walls. Not so, the lacklustre voices of the monks. A huge dome turns their off-key chanting into an interminable echo. If not for the golden angel about to blow her trumpet and a gathering of white cherubs cavorting mid-flight above the altar I might have left.

We are hustled through a door near the sacristy for a tour of the monastery, an hour long navigation through a labyrinth of hallways lined with modern murals depicting the life of San Benito. I feel like I am trapped inside the pages of a comic book commissioned by Franco. Finally we are released into a cloister filled with sunlight, manicured hedges and apricot and pink rosebushes. A keystone near the entrance is carved with the words, *Que miras, bobo?* What are you looking at, stupid? And I contemplate the waste of an hour.

As I take my place in the queue beside the petrol pump next door to the monastery's *refugio* all my thoughts dissolve into one – a bed and a hot shower. A clerkish looking man stamps my *credencial* then assigns me number thirty two. Halfway down the concrete cellar of a room a hulk of a man sits on my bed oblivious to my presence, unlacing his shoes, his pack on the bunk above, bed thirty three. I wait patiently as he slowly, painfully, peels out of his socks. They are soaked with sweat and blood from clusters of evil looking blisters between his toes and covering his heels. He puts his socks on my bed and begins a close examination. I look at those socks on the bed and wait another few minutes before summoning up the courage to return to the desk and ask, like some kind of Oliver Twist, 'Please sir, can I have another bed?' He gives me a look then replies with a definitive and irritated, 'No.' I return to number thirty two and the man is still there. The socks are still there. I can't stay, that's the truth of it, shoulder my pack and walk out the door.

Retracing my steps to the road, chin trembling and on the verge of tears, a voice inside my head clamours, 'What do you think you are doing? Sarria is another sixteen kilometres.' I look back across a patch of yellow sunflowers to the monastery, five storeys high, hundreds of dark windows framed in white stone. A bird in a cage sits on a window and behind, illuminated by the afternoon light, is the silhouette of a Benedictine monk smoking a cigarette. Does he wait for her to sing? A bird singing inside its cage is all very well but how much finer is the song when she realizes the cage door is open. The part of me daunted by distance is outsung by the thrill of freedom. Freedom to make a choice and to have the courage to follow through.

I have the river again as my companion. A primitive stone angel stands in a niche by a bridge and above her is the inscription: Those who cross entrust themselves to the souls of purgatory. I ponder this but in the end have no idea, or inclination to know, what she means. In a hamlet of farmhouses I peer through the window of a tiny white stucco chapel. Behind the altar between pots of plastic roses are two Madonnas, one in white and the other in a robe of royal blue. Inside the narrow doors ajar either side of them are two lanterns on long beams propped up against the wall. In one cupboard is a broom and in the other a spade. These are the images I take onto the last leg of road.

The Madonna, the lantern and the spade.

Step by step up the penitential stairs of Sarria's Rua

Maior my lanterns and broom carry me toward a pink blushed sky and the happy faces of Alex, Lina and Bill, sitting outside the church of San Salvador. The main *refugio* is full and has overflowed into the gymnasium next door but there is, they tell me, a private one up the street.

At a café advertising *Platos Tipicos*, we are served by a man old enough to be my great grandfather. The wife presides behind the louver doors of the kitchen. His attempts to placate her pressure cooker voice, as plates crash about in the sink and saucepans bang back and forth on the stove, are to no avail. Eventually though, he appears with a platter of *Conejo con Castanas*, rabbit and chestnut stew, fragrant with bay leaf, sweet paprika, garlic and saffron. Refills of house wine woo my bones into submission and wash down one of the most resplendent meals in recent history.

In a blur of surfeit and exhaustion I open the door to my room to find a mess of three Spanish men, two in their underwear playing cards and the third, on the bunk above mine, horizontal with a girl astride massaging his back. This is the point where the Camino shifts gears. To be given a Compostela, earning you the rights to plenary indulgence, you must walk an uninterrupted minimum of one hundred kilometres into Santiago and that means, for those in a hurry, starting at Sarria. No matter how debauched or drunken your path to the spires, all will be forgiven at the end. I take a deep breath, introduce myself and stumble over boots, packs, beer bottles and an empty pizza box, to my bed.

An invitation is extended for a game of *El Tresillo* but I am hopeless at cards at the best of times let alone one where the rules will be explained in Spanish to a woman who drank one too many glasses of wine after walking twenty seven kilometres on a day she swore she could not walk one. My decline is accepted graciously and we share a nightcap of takeaway steaming *chocolat caliente* instead. Between bone cracks and moans from above and the slap of cards on the floor below I drift into sleep.

Like a small boat bobbing toward the sea I am swept out into the dawn along with a fleet of others. Even though pilgrim numbers have surged, as everyone settles into their own rhythm there is space between us. I pass a cemetery, cross a medieval footbridge, traverse a forest of chestnut trees and walk through hamlets of stone houses. The lanes are rutted by the long ago passage of oxen pulling wooden carts and now the daily traffic of cows, tractors and pilgrims. What must the locals feel having this constant stream of itinerants tramping through their front and backyards? There are certainly no one euro pancakes for sale here. If the village dogs are any indication we have become invisible. A pilgrim it seems is not worth a sniff, let alone a wagging tail.

As for the pilgrims in this hundred kilometre homestretch to Santiago, gone are the *'Buen Caminos.'* Groups of young Spanish kids in sneakers and Doc Martens, hip baggy jeans and jackets striped in soccer team colours, forge ahead with a vigour I have long forgotten. As I watch yet another pack overtake me and disappear around the bend, accompanied by the beat of a rap band from a cassette recorder, all I can think is will I get a bed tonight?

After a slow, steady morning and half the afternoon I reach the high bridge over River Mino and the submerged city of old Portomarin, drowned half a century ago by the dam upstream. I lean over in the vain hope of seeing a hospice roof, a fortress wall or the remnants of a medieval bridge, the one that was rebuilt after a spat between Queen Urraca of Galicia and her estranged husband Alfonso. He was, she accused, impotent and physically abusive. Bridges come and go in hot blooded Spain but the waters of the Mino, according to the *Codex Calixtinus*, are sweet and healthy to drink.

As tired as I am the river way below, made fat and lazy by the dam, draws circles around my mind, as if my search of its surface is a pebble thrown into it and what ripples out are images and thoughts gleaned from these last few days of walking. Footsteps and the staffs of more pilgrims tap towards me then fade away. Ours is a river of bodies – some propelled by the bones of a saint, others by interior dreams or simply a release from the four square walls of home and habit. I feel my heart slow now I have stopped. How it beats hard when I climb a hill, races in the face of fear or beauty and gently pulses at its own time as I sleep. A strange and mysterious organ this heart of mine – the way it can open and close like a clam shell.

The image of those lanterns in the Madonna's cupboard returns – two bright lights. The spade from the other cupboard digs beneath the surface of who I think I am. What do I want? To be at ease, to be happy, to stay open. What is it that separates me from this? And I realize I am standing on the reason and the solution – the ruins of a bridge below me and the one built in its place. A bridge is like a hand held across the water, an offering of safe passage. I am at once back in Burma at the end of a long day reciting the last line of *Metta Bavana*, a prayer for Loving Kindness. Under the whir of ceiling fans we would chant '*Sabbe satta sukhi hontu,*' may all beings be happy and free, and as we walked back to our huts through monsoon air thick with mosquitos I would look across to the twinkling lights of Mandalay reflected in the ripples of the Irrawaddy making its steady passage to the sea.

Wisdom is a fire that burns ignorance to ash. But without the compassion of *metta* we remain disconnected – from ourselves and others. In the foothills of the Himalayas the Buddha recited to his monks the *Karaniya Metta Sutta*, a Hymn of Universal Love: Just as with her own life a mother shields from hurt her only child, Let all-embracing thoughts for all beings be yours.

That man on bed thirty two peeling out of his blood-soaked socks. Both of us had been so intent on our own wellbeing no bridge existed between us.

As I walk to the end of Portomarin's bridge I visualize his face and chant under my breath the simple phrases beginning each *metta* meditation. 'Just as I want to be happy, so do you want to be happy. May you be happy. Just as I want to be free from suffering, so do you want to be free from suffering. May you be free from suffering.'

There are no beds left in the *refugio*. 'May I be happy.' And after knocking on a dozen doors – pensions, hotels, hostels – I realize with a sinking stomach there is not a bed left in town. 'May I have ease of wellbeing.' I wander up and down an arcade of shops and cafes full of showered pilgrims relaxing after their day's walk. One of the card playing boys from Sarria calls out to me and after hearing my plight says he had reserved a bed for his brother thinking he walked behind but miracle of miracles he had arrived in front. He takes my pack and shows me through the back door into a maze of rooms, past dubious looking showers without doors and rows of bunks hung end to end with washing, to a bed as fine as any I have ever seen. Under a luxurious trickle of cold water I look down to find that the top strap of my pack has pressed a scallop shell imprint onto my skin – a half circle of ribs splayed out like the hand of a friend.

I walk back to the bridge and meet Alex along the way. 'Spaghetti *con tomate* tonight? The *refugio* has a state of the art kitchen ... relatively speaking,' he says with a smile. Before heading back we watch a play of colour from sky to water and back as the sun sets. We talk of inconsequential things then fall into intervals of silence nourishing as a *metta* prayer.

'Do you know the word *mudita,* Alex?'

He shakes his head.

'Sympathetic joy. It's the only word I can think of to describe how happy I am to be here and to have met you.'

'Heart speaks to heart,' he says with another of his gentle smiles, 'if I may reply in the words of Saint Augustine.'

23

Room at the Inn
Portomarin to A Rua

Ascending Monte de San Antonio in the dark we look like a file of lights zigzagging up the holy mountain of Meru. Two figures run past, their packs jiggling from side to side, confirming indeed that something sacred is within reach. But when the path levels onto a mist swathed plateau of low spiked heather there are only the ghosts of whores to greet pilgrims. I imagine them in their open air brothel accosting solitary travelers with a bit of leg or cleavage. These women should have their noses cut off, Pope Calixtus admonished in a twelfth century sermon.

The Camino today, for all its legends and miracles is, I think, a thoroughly sanitized version of the medieval one. I pick a sprig of yellow gorse and continue my naïve way through the mist turning the pages back from lusty ghosts to the bright pristine morning when Adam found Eve. I imagine them falling in love in a serpent-free paradise, living on apples for breakfast, figs for lunch and mead for supper, until the unexpected sight of a tall eucalyptus tree catapults me out of fantasy back to the bush between our house and the sea, into the arms of David. Am I ready to return? What will it be like? I feel excited at the thought of being with him, then nervous remembering Eileen's words back in Rabanal. 'The real Camino begins at home.'

I am determined to not fall back into habitual reactions if ever David and I disagree. Holding to my convictions while accepting the truth of his seemed like drawing a line in the sand, only to be washed away by the pounding waves of life's vicissitudes. My jellyfish recoil was a far cry from the selfless surrendering of a perfect Buddhist practitioner. Sometimes, in my bewildered attempt at understanding our dynamics I excused it as just a play of polar opposites, male and female. It was an uncomfortable view, one to send shivers down a feminist's spine, and I shudder now at the idea.

At home our duels repeated, the arguments would be different but the dynamics the same. David the logician and me, the antithesis, drowning in a sea of self-made emotion; while outside our four walls friends would say I seemed self assured, exuding calm. What then was my real face? A voice inside quips back, 'What was your face before you were born?' But I am caught in a tangle of memory and in no mood for Zen koans. It does, though, leave me wondering if I am trying to explain away something that is essentially mysterious. 'Keep digging,' the Madonna's spade says, 'don't lose yourself in platitudes.'

Gravel crunches and scatters under my feet as I go this way and that in my head. Could the simple truth be that I crave equality with him? But is that what relationships are about – a set of checks and balances? Is that what life is about? What prevents me from a free expression of who I am? I cannot, in honesty, blame David or anyone else. And me? Am I really so spineless or is it more a case of being thoroughly consumed and oddly comforted by the habitual grooves I have worn into forty nine years.

Maybe the *I* is the problem – the twisting turning *I* faced each time I sit on a meditation cushion, courting disaster as I hold fast to the conglomeration of *my* body and *my* mind. Haven't teachers expounded the dangers of this over and over? It is a thought that hits me like a red light. Haven't I experienced time and again, on retreat and each day of walking – nothing stays the same? Do I feel this most basic of Buddhist principles in my bones or am I just some *faux* woman nodding her head? As the mist clears I walk out onto a ridge bathed in morning sun. I watch the way my breathing falls like a pulse between each footstep and each thought too, allowing my mind to settle, give up its arguments and admonishments. What a relief to be present. Resting in this rhythmic, uncomplicated movement gives me space to see below the flurry of my thoughts into the source of my conflict. I can name it – I just want to be loved. My mind, though, is still not satisfied and keeps unwrapping. The strings, the paper, the padding.

I come face to face with the fear of not being loved. Any time I disagree I risk its loss. Whether in an issue with David or a conversation with someone on the street, better to swallow than hazard confrontation or worse, utter abandonment. Each acquiescence like a lie. Knots begin to loosen inside me and I slow down to absorb this realization. Equality metamorphoses into one shining word – acceptance – and the core of who I am reveals itself, fluid and unnameable.

My mind hovers like a hijacker, wanting to contain the experience, make sense of it. But its attempts at analysis are thwarted as three syllables resonate inside my head. *Anicca*, impermanence. I feel as if the last layer of ideas, carried like extra bricks in my backpack for a lifetime and one Camino, peels away. The tourniquet I've so cleverly tied round my heart loosens and I take a deep breath of air soaked with the scent of wild things.

A stone cross appears with a moss-stained skull carved on its base, scarred and worn from centuries of wind and rain. Deep black pits of eyes stare through me. What foolishness it is holding on to anything, they seem to say, as if warning me to let go, even of this. Above, where the cross meets, is a carving of not Christ but the Virgin, a primitive almost abstract rendition of Mary with a face more natural than holy, more innocent than worldly.

I leave the woman on the cross behind not knowing

what will happen when I am home. How it will be living together. 'Expect nothing,' my Zen teacher used to say. 'Nothing is best. Not even good luck. All we really need is to return to our original simplicity.'

I feel Mary's eyes following me as I enter the village of Eirexe. There is nothing to fear.

At one o clock Dona, the *refugio* caretaker, arrives with key and register but she is out of sorts and suspects everyone in the queue. A pilgrim berates her for the surly attitude and she unleashes an indignant tirade. Yesterday two women hustled their way in for the last two beds leaving the pilgrims behind them no choice but to walk to the next village. It was later discovered they had a driver who, every day, drops them off a hundred metres short of a *refugio*. Despairing that her beloved Camino is degenerating into a free-for-all she spent the morning calling other *hospitaleros* in the hope these unscrupulous villains will be caught, tarred and lynched. I give her hand an affectionate squeeze and coax a smile as she hands me back my *credencial*. For every action there is an equal and opposite reaction. If not in this lifetime then in the next. Maybe those two women will reach Santiago and all their sins will be forgiven. Maybe not.

Dona's mother is keeper of the key to Eirexe's small thirteenth century Church. At the entrance to her old granite home is a slate paved courtyard with an open air oven and stable full of tools, bales of hay, a tractor and a mound of potatoes. A large black dog languishing in a pool of sunlight near the front door aims a lame bark in my direction. Dona senior appears then disappears. She returns carrying an antique key in two hands.

'*Vamos*,' she says with a smile that wrinkles the wrinkles of her face and I hadn't even mentioned the church. I offer to carry the key and am astonished by its weight as I follow her through a field of dark green nettles. The path is narrow and by the time we reach the church my ankles are a mass of stinging welts. Dona escapes the same fate, her bandy legs shielded by high muddy boots and stockings thick as bandages.

Last week there was a fiesta and each gravestone has a jar of lilies or dahlias propped up beside framed photos of the dead. Their sepia eyes burrow into mine while Dona's, magnified to the size of an owl's behind her thick rimmed glasses, coax me from my burning body to the church door. She puts both hands out for the key. The stone front step is polished to a shine and worn into the shape of a bowl. More than seven hundred years of prayer breathe life into this simple village church. Fresh flowers and new candles sit on an altar covered with a fine white cloth crocheted by Dona herself. The unequivocal eyes of a Romanesque Madonna meet me in the in between places of who I think I am; reminding me of this morning's encounters. The skull, a virgin and me. 'Come,' she says, 'the nettles have extinguished all but the barest thoughts of who you are. This is as it should be. Come.'

Half an hour out of Eirexe, from curiosity more than needing to know, I stop to consult my map and realize with horror my reading glasses are missing, left behind last night in the bar. I peer back through the predawn shadows of the road, Eirexe's lights disappeared. What use are glasses at this stage of the journey? Just another crutch to carry. If I don't know the way, I wait. Simple.

The scent of cow, hay and fermenting apple rises into the air as the earth warms. Corn silks whisper in the breeze and a stand of blue gums reminds me again, home is close. It's a strange sensation to be suddenly enveloped in an environment heavy with memory. Strips of brittle rust coloured bark peel away from huge grey trunks and long dark green leaves waver above with a familiar song and scent. For the next kilometre I walk as if waking from a dream in the shadow of these feral giants all the way from Tasmania disoriented and unsure of where I am and how I fit.

I breathe a sigh of relief as I enter a grove of centenarian oak trees near the hamlet of Casanova. I am in Spain again among red tiled roofs, medieval churches and *horreos,* and only two days away from Santiago. As if to assuage any doubt, in the village of Leboreiro, a bus called Gaia pulls up. Sixty seven elderly pilgrims alight, with staffs and matching bandannas bright as gorse flowers tied around their necks. They congregate in the old town square, a religious *carnivale* of yellow, their chattering pitched with excitement as they stamp their feet and adjust their daypacks ready for a salvation march. I have a choice, move quickly and overtake them or let this sea of bodies roll ahead.

I let them go. Under my feet are paving stones as old as the Camino and across the square is the simple thirteenth century church of Santa Maria, its grey stone bricks stained burnt orange and white from Galician lichen. On the tympanum is a white carving of the Virgin and Child with angels swinging censers either side. The fragrance these stone angels spread alludes to the Madonna ensconced inside and another legend. In the early days of their church villagers noticed a heavenly perfume and light emanating from a nearby fountain each evening. They dug beneath it and discovered a smiling Virgin statue. She was bathed and placed on their altar but each night while they slept she returned to the fountain. This continued until the same carving was chiseled over the front door as appeasement. Until half a century ago the more superstitious of Leboreiro's parishioners continued insisting their Madonna could still be found combing her long hair each night beside their fountain.

As I catch up to Gaia's troop another legend from another continent comes to mind. High in the Himalayas a Tibetan *dakini* washed her long black hair at a spring. She put the strands that came loose into the crack of a rock and from them an oak tree grew. The veins on each of its leaves spelled out the syllables of Tara's mantra. *Om Tara tutare ture soha.*

With beaming faces and jovial shouts of '*Ultreya*,

make way, make way,' Gaia's pilgrims let me pass. Their verve is infectious on this brightest of days. I am in the arms of the Camino again – two eyes, ten fingers and two functioning knees. Across a medieval four arched bridge is the village of Furelos and before I know it a priest has herded me together with a group of Spanish teenagers into his church for a tour. Christ hangs by only one blood stained hand to a crucifix. He looks towards the palm of his right hand also bearing the mark of a nail and held down to us. Except for the urgent clicking of cameras there is a hushed silence. It is a moving and unusual image and the priest, standing to the side, appears satisfied with its effect.

A queue of pilgrims winds around three walls of Melide's *refugio*. There are one hundred and thirty beds and I estimate the line is close to that. I loathe queues but waiting one hour outweighs walking another eleven kilometres to the next village. We file in, get *credencialed,* then make a race for the best placed pine bunk. I score with a window and a wall then brace myself for a cold co-ed shower in the bunker bathroom on the floor below. Every bed has been taken and every inch of floor in the town's youth club next door is now covered with sleeping mats, packs and bodies. For a town that used to have more inns than houses, four hospices for pilgrims and the poor, complete with straw pillows and beds large enough for two, Melide may well have to reinvent itself if the Camino continues its boom.

Crowds, snores, blocked showers and overpowering

toilets. I am suddenly overcome by the fatigue of my body and a mind dulled to the idiosyncrasies of each hostel. A surprising thought surfaces – one more day of walking is enough! Yes, I am ready to go home. And as I weave my way back to Melide's main *Calle* I daydream of a clean shower and privacy; waking up and having nowhere to go. When I eventually come back to the present – right step, left step – it dawns on me that my mind is ricocheting more than usual from content to discontent, from happiness to unease then back again. With the end of my journey close I feel as if I am being cornered; my mind insisting that I make a stance. But what? There is nothing I can do. 'Here-Now,' my Zen teacher would say and no matter what the question, this was his answer. 'Minds wander, that's what they do,' he had added one time when Here-Now seemed just too simple to be true. *Nostalgia de eternidad, realidad de lo transitorio; Svaha! Ahora- Esto!* The nostalgia of eternity, the reality of the transitory; Svaha! Now-This!

Behind the front counter of Pulperia Ezequial an old lady in a checked apron pulls out an octopus from a copper vat of simmering red wine, eight plump tentacles swinging. I watch, mesmerized, as she snips the tentacles into bite-sized pieces each marinated to a deep burgundy but tender white on the inside. Generous portions are slapped onto wooden platters, doused with virgin olive oil then liberally sprinkled with hot paprika. This is it, the *pulperia* of all *pulperias* and nothing else matters. '*Uno plato, senorita, por favor.*'

I take a seat beside Maria, a plump, auburn haired and rosy cheeked three day old pilgrim, free from two teenagers, a husband and a part-time nursing job in Madrid. The owner, who seems to have taken a shine to her, fills a clay jug full of white Ribeiro wine from an oak barrel and pours it into five terracotta bowls. Two are for his regular customers seated at the end of our table, retired gentlemen in open necked shirts and trousers held loose and high by braces. '*Salud*!' We make a toast with Ezequial's obligatory accompaniment to melt in the mouth octopus. Made from Albarino grapes, Ribeiro is crisp, light and dry. I think of riverbank orchards, peach and apricot. '*Amor y*!' Maria adds, and to love. We devour Melide's pride and joy with our fingers. Tables empty then fill again with locals and pilgrims. As soon as one octopus is pulled out from the vat another is plunged in. A waiter rolls out a second barrel of wine and our host, with *pulperial* authority, produces an unlabeled bottle and splashes a few rough calculated nips of *bagazo* into our bowls.

Maria whose cheeks have now flushed a bright red warns me how dangerous this fire-water is and I remember my last encounter with *orujo* in O Cebreiro. My first sip burns a spirited way down to my fingers and toes. The sting of yesterday's nettles pales in comparison. '*Para*, don't worry,' Maria slurs, translating something about the good fairy Anjana. According to our host his homemade *bagazo* carries her blessings. Wherever Anjana goes she leaves a trail of flowers instead of footprints. A vial of magical and miracle inducing *orujo* never leaves her hands.

It's late afternoon in the *refugio* and I am barely conscious when the bunk bed next to me collapses with a thud that rocks the whole room. The man on the top fell to the floor with, luckily, his mattress as a buffer. The bottom bunk now speared by two of the top bed's splintered legs is empty. Anjana be praised.

Setting off into another eucalypt forest I chant, for a change, '*Bodhi svaha*,' the mantra of my Japanese Zen teacher. He was a nimble sixty year old then, supple as a child, and could run for miles chanting these two words. Awake Hooray! is one inadequate but to the point English translation, of which there are many. Four syllables, four steps. Inhale for three, exhale on the fourth.

Bodhi svaha comes at the end of the last line of the Heart Sutra: *Gate gate paragate parasamgate. Bodhi svaha.* Let's go! Let's go! Go to the Other Shore! With a mere fifty kilometres to Santiago what better prayer to chant. 'No!' The voice of my Zen teacher cuts in, as if he is walking right beside me. 'There is no other shore.'

'Here-Now, Here-Now, Already Here-Now. Altogether Already Here-Now. Awakening Fulfilled!'

Up dales and down, across medieval bridges, through meadows of fat cud-chewing cows, oak forests and more eucalypt forests and the hamlets of Tabernavalla, Calzada, Boavista. '*Ultreya*,' I whisper to the pilgrims passing me, as if I do not exist – commuters on the Penitent Express. Then there are the pilgrims who have walked the soles of their shoes thin. Some have sped up as if caught in the slipstream of a Milky Way that will, in a few days, disappear over the edge of the world, and others have slowed to a snail's pace, squeezing every last ounce of pleasure from a journey they don't want to end.

The tall Spanish couple I sat behind in the church of Rabanal and then met again on the steps of the Peurta del Perdon in Villafranca stride past me, their footsteps and staffs in a quiet, intimate rhythm. We greet each other with an almost shy, '*Buen Camino*,' and I watch them thread their way through the shadows of blue gums. I match my footsteps to theirs, '*Bo-dhi-sva...*' breathing out for three, '*ha*,' breathing in. They disappear and I fall silent until I come to a large rectangular stone chiseled into a mortar at the side of the path. Between fallen leaves floating on rainwater, in a bowl where apples were once crushed for *sidra*, I catch the unruly reflection of someone who looks like me.

Three men on horses saunter past, then I meet up with them for a coffee and a greasy *tortilla* at a littered roadside *taberna*. Further along a pair of bronze boots mark the spot where a sixty nine year old pilgrim, Guillermo, died eleven years ago – one day short of Santiago. Would his passage to heaven be toll free? Not so for the four English men and women I meet decked out in state of the art trekking gear. After thirty kilometres Santa Irene's small *refugio* sits pretty as a picture on the other side of a highway but, as I join them to cross, one turns and says, 'Sorry, but there won't be any beds left here. Our group has reserved the whole place.' They booked a *refugio*? Isn't that against the code? I blush at their snub then degenerate into muttered retaliations as I retrace my steps. Tonight, I think with a vengeance, I will stay in a room with a single bed, white linen, plump pillows and a floral quilt; primp myself into semi-respectability for the finale tomorrow. The village of Rua lies less than an hour away.

One word, 'Hallelujah,' wings its way through the ether, slicing through my vitriolic stamp of feet. I play with it till it takes on the rhythm of my steps. 'Hall-el-uj,' three celebratory syllables on an out-breath and, 'ah' on the in-breath, lifts me up and carries me the last two kilometres to the tall conifer trees, whitewashed walls and oak paneled door of Hotel O Pino.

The man at the bar appraises me first before taking a leisurely moment to survey the register. '*Si, una cama*, one room is left,' he says, giving me a key and pointing to stairs leading down to the basement, a wing reserved for the overflow. Overjoyed at such luck I lean across and kiss him on both cheeks – not customary behavior but for a road-dazed pilgrim he responds with a smile. Four rooms lead off a narrow corridor and share one small but immaculate bathroom. I turn the key, open the door and there it is, a double bed covered with a frilly eiderdown of pink roses.

24

Silver Bells and Cockle Shells
Santiago de Compostela

With skin smelling of apricots, buffed by a full-size fluffy towel and clean hair fragrant from apple shampoo I leave the hotel without bothering to convert the euro bill into dollars. It was worth it.

An unearthly quiet blankets Arca's streets, quiet as the bones of pilgrims buried in the shadows of eucalypts long before the sounds of twenty first century boots. The circus-sized tent tacked onto the side of the *refugio* is a sea of deserted blue mats. I pass a couple at a crossroads consulting their map by torchlight but this morning arrows and maps seem as inconsequential as buoys adrift in an ocean. There is a soft glow to the sky ahead and a rumour of warmth from the sun rising at my back. These are the things I have come to know. I breathe in the colours of dawn and they saturate my heart, the barriers between me and the world I walk disappeared.

In this neither here nor there osmosis my mind has nowhere to go and nothing to cling to; my senses are content resting in the sway of the pack on my back and the sound of my shoes, the lemony scent of blue gum leaves. But not for long. A bitumen path takes a circuitous route around an airport runway; its hard surface soon jarring into the tendons of both legs. Heaven has ditched me again. I am a pilgrim ghost walking through no man's land, a wanderer outside the gates of the Bardo. I'm suddenly lonely but crave no one in particular. As if in response a distant mooing of cows serenades me up one more hill and out from the pages of a Zen story tumbles the image of a small roly poly boy. He walks beside me leading a docile ox on a rope.

In twelfth century Japan the Zen master Kaku-an ink-brushed ten pictures of a boy and an ox, accompanying each with a verse. What is the meaning of the journey in the Ten Ox-herding Pictures? The story begins with *shohosshin*, the first stirring of the heart, when the boy realizes something is missing and begins a search for his original self. I think back to the day I first read about the Camino. A stirring of the heart began then too. It was one desire that refused to be compromised.

The boy finds traces of an ox by riverbanks and under fragrant grasses. The ox is a metaphor for his mind. The animal's hoof prints hint of a way out from the tug-a-war games an ego plays. Then he sees the ox. The path to liberation from suffering is possible. He catches it but:

How wild his will and how ungovernable his power! And how well I remember those first few meditation retreats when my cornered mind kicked and shouted for a way out. The boy persists and eventually the ox grows pure and docile. The mind settles down.

My imaginary friend looks up, winks, then takes a flute out from his satchel. He climbs on to the ox's back and begins to play as they set off for home. This is the sixth picture. They disappear over the hilltop as one silhouette. The morning sun has already risen three bamboo lengths, the whip, the halter and worldly attachments abandoned.

Now they have gone I am left with nothing but the chitter of birds. This is my last day as a pilgrim. In a few hours my uncomplicated days of waking up and walking finish. Am I the same or different? My body feels light and the effort it takes for one more climb is effortless effort – slow short steps up into the eighth picture, an empty circle.

How may a snowflake exist in a raging fire? Kaku-an asks.

Of course I am different, with every step, every breath, the person I think I am disappears. Am I not a pilgrim for life?

Inside Lavacolla's parish church I find an angel draped in a pink shawl with a vase of plastic roses at her feet. In her left hand is a golden palm leaf, a symbol of heaven's rewards, and on her right balances a lighthouse – a strange sight in a church three days walk from the ocean. It plunges me into another of Kaku-an's koans. How can darkness exist when there is light? A priest walks in, clears his throat and motions me outside as if I am a trespasser. There are pilgrims who walk the Camino without ever visiting a church. What is it that compels me in? Is it the stained light that bathes me whenever I enter these silent places, the cherubs and saints, the messiah and his virgin mother? I have no personal investment in them, no faith. And yet I cannot deny they are part of me, of my childhood, of my mother and my father's father. Just as I walk from Roncesvalles to Santiago, a different woman now to the one I was when I began, I traveled from one religion to another – from Our Father who art in heaven to *Gate gate paragate, parasamgate bodhi svaha*. It was not a matter of turning my back on a Christ for a Buddha, I simply chose a different path. Perhaps the reason I visit every church and cathedral is to better understand the language of each – the verbs of their prayers – what it means to be engaged, and the signposts lit by them along the way. The quality of light may be different but it is the same self-made darkness that is illuminated. The doors of Lavacolla's church swing shut behind me and I am left blinking into the glare of the sun.

Loosely translated Lavacolla means, place to lather up your scrotum. With Saint James less than two miles away the *Codex Calixtinus* encouraged pilgrims to: wash not merely their virile member but, having taken off their clothes, wash off the dirt from their entire body. Church sentries were posted to ensure no filthy lice-infested man or woman passed this point. What a sight it must have been, this ritual ablution, and what colour the water, as pilgrims washed for the first time in months. A derelict picnic ground beside a tiny creek now marks the spot. Several pilgrims overtake me oblivious to the fact we should all be stripping off here in the middle of suburbia. A faint whiff of apricot still lingers on my skin. *Bodhi svaha.* Let's go, let's go.

A tree in blossom at a river's edge fills the circle of the ninth Oxherding picture. There is neither boy nor ox, only water that flows of itself, and flowers that are naturally red, Kaku-an writes. This is *Sambhogakaya*, a state of being where things are as they are and there is nothing to do. The times I have glimpsed this pristine place are few. The mere thought of holding on to it is like trying to grasp a reflection in water.

I once despaired to a teacher that for every step forward I take in my practice it seems I take ten steps back. He shook his head. When I questioned whether such a word as progress exists in meditation practice he said, 'What you experience remains in you. You may think you lose it but it is there. It is all compost. Just keep practicing and the fruits will come.'

When I reach the Mount of Joy, named for its vision of Santiago's three spires, the cathedral's towers are nowhere to be seen. What once brought pilgrims to tears, and to the ground to kiss it a thousand times, is now hidden behind a bank of modern apartment blocks. Instead, to inspire awe in the pilgrim, is a monument that would make a Moscow square proud; a monstrous glob of cement etched on all sides with pictures commemorating the visit of a pope. I cringe and turn to face the wind raging in from the west.

The tenth picture Kaku-an paints is of the boy in the company of a *bodhisattva*, each carrying a staff and gourd. Barechested and barefoot, he arrives at the market place; daubed with mud and ashes, smiling. He has returned into the world.

A rush of streets cling to the old city of Santiago and I walk the last hour as if in a dream. My limbs sway backwards and forwards by themselves, the sound of cars and trucks are no more than a faint whir inside my head. I am here but nothing has changed. There is nothing to do but walk.

A familiar figure walks towards me. Alex! I snap back into a world of words and the warmth of touch. We hug as best we can with packs on our backs. 'I arrived over an hour ago,' he says with uncharacteristic urgency, 'but got completely lost looking for a *refugio* and now it's late and I don't want to miss mass.'

'Mass?' I repeat. 'At the cathedral?' He nods and looks at me askance, as if to say, did I lose my head between here and Sarria? And suddenly I realize this really is it. The place I have been walking to for thirty days is under my feet. 'Okay, don't worry, we'll make it.' I laugh away my tears then switch to pragmatic mother figure with map. 'There should be a private one a couple of blocks away. Can you see it?' And there is, with beds to spare.

There is no need for the miraculous powers of the Gods, Kaku-an goes on to say.

'There is a bus that will take you to the old city, otherwise you have to walk half an hour,' the *hospitalero* says. We both hesitate before looking at each other. 'Let's take our chance,' ventures Alex. 'Catching a bus at this point seems a bit ridiculous don't you think?' Free of our packs, with sweat-streaming faces, we dash up a long cobbled street to Rua San Pedro then through the Porta De Camino – a door in name only, one of seven original entrances through the old city walls that vanished a long time ago.

'Hey, Alex it's the gateless gate!' I laugh out loud but he's in no mood for a koan spar; there are confessions to be made and an apostle who is waiting. Mumon, a twelfth century Chinese Zen master and probably the most prolific of all koan creators, attempted to confound his monks out of their minds. He challenged them with forty eight koans beginning with: The great way is gateless, approached in a thousand ways, once past this checkpoint, you stride through the universe. How appropriate, I think, as I struggle to keep Alex in sight.

To a peal of cathedral bells we weave our way down Casas Reais, the Rua das Animas and into Rua da Azabacheria. It's as if we are picked up and carried, such is the wake of centuries of pilgrims, wave upon wave of weary bodies and hearts on fire. And then, before I have a chance to absorb Churriguera's baroque take on the Gates of Paradise, we are inside standing shoulder to shoulder with a thousand others.

The sweet voice of a nun echoes over the sea of bodies. Security men, batons at their waists, direct us through to the back. Move over Burgos and Leon; Santiago's cathedral is a kingdom unto itself. Eighty seven metres long, sixty five metres wide in the transept and a cupola thirty two metres high. Even this was not big enough to accommodate the flood of pilgrims one Holy Year. In 1207 the fight to be closest to the high altar was so impassioned the floors needed to be cleansed of blood and the church reconsecrated.

An old woman ignores the guards and elbows her way past me, through a flock of Japanese tourists, a convention of name-tagged Italians, camera touting Germans, Spanish families, and hobbling pilgrims, many still lugging backpacks. But aren't we all pilgrims? Whether we have walked eight hundred kilometres or stepped off a plane? I look at the faces around me, a mix of bewilderment, joy and curiosity. And faith most of all. Kneeling and standing, steeped in prayer for the living or dead; for themselves or perhaps an enemy. This is a Holy Year and plenary indulgence can be granted to all. But it is not automatic, first you need to recite a particular prayer, then receive the sacrament of confession in one of the dark paneled booths lining the cathedral walls. Each is posted with the languages that the priest inside speaks.

St James reigns supreme on a prancing white stallion high above the main altar, a shimmering, glorious affair flanked by giant angels dripping gold. From where we stand he is the size of a matchbox. As for the poor souls about to be trampled under his horse or decapitated by his sword – I can only imagine the terror engraved on their faces. Centred in the altar niche below is a second more forgiving St James, Romanesque and regal, on a silver throne. This is the statue every pilgrim hopes to hug and if I look closely I can make out a slowly moving line of ant-size bodies in the *camarin* behind him, each in turn embracing his broad cloaked shoulders.

There is, finally, a third unseen layer, the foundation upon which all this spectacle lies. In an underground crypt, we are told, are his mortal remains. Saint James, son of Zebedee, brother of John and disciple of Jesus, and martyred by Herod in Jerusalem. His body was laid in a rudderless boat and pushed out into the Mediterranean Sea. His corpse made shore at Galicia, the land James had preached in after the death of Jesus. The miraculous discovery of this same body in a field of stars eight hundred years later set off flurries of activity. Here, where Santiago de Compostela's cathedral now stands, on a site where pagans once worshiped Jupiter, a succession of churches have venerated James. His body, the *Codex Calixtinus* proclaims: Is here in its entirety, divinely lit by paradisiacal carbuncles, incessantly honored with immaculate and soft perfumes and diligently worshiped by attentive angels.

Santiago's riches tempted first the Normans, and then the Moors who destroyed the cathedral and took off with its bells for their Cordoba mosque. A string of Spanish kings and plunderers craved the holy relics and a cat and mouse game ensued until, eventually, no one remembered where the bones of Saint James were hidden. But their loss did not deter a constant flood of pilgrims hungry for miracles and willing to give to the church coffers whatever it took to expedite them – a mutually satisfying relationship. No matter what the urn on the cathedral's altar contained, the simple faith of a medieval Christian took as crowning achievement one touch of what was purported to be a remnant of the divine. Then, in 1878, the bones were officially found again! Lots of bones, and all of them aligned east to west beside a church dating back to the fifth century. I attempt to count out a logical timeline with my ten fingers but it's complex for the likes of me, not a mathematical bone in my body. 'Slippery history,' is what my history teacher used to quip, out of earshot for fear of persecution. 'Many lacunae, convenient or otherwise, many Chinese whispers.'

Into fourth century Galicia, a yeasty mix of Celts, Romans and Christians, enters a man called Priscillian. Born near Santiago he took to heart St Paul's words: Know ye not that ye are the temple of God? Priscillian blended St Paul's teachings with a mystical asceticism encompassing the sun, moon and the equality of women. His appointment as Bishop of Avila outraged the orthodox church. In their fight against *Priscillianism* women became their main target. Forthwith no woman could be deemed a true virgin until the age of forty and they were forbidden to pray in the same room as men.

Allegations were made of sorcery, astrology and strangest of all, given Priscillian's strict views on celibacy, sexual orgies. In the end Priscillian's main claim to fame is that he was the first *heretic* to be executed by the church. Galicians hailed him as a martyr and his body was returned to Santiago for burial.

Are the bones beneath this cathedral in fact a melange of two holy men? *Qué horror*, could this even be a case of an emperor's new clothes? Or is it, I wonder, looking down at my dusty worn boots, simply a case of ashes to ashes?

Oversized umbrellas held high over the heads of three priests bob their way down the main aisle. An intense hum of voices, and an urgent fusion of elbows, shoulders and outstretched arms closes in. It is the Eucharist of all Eucharists and I join them for a piece of wafer thin bread. I'll not be entering a confession booth, nor converting to Catholicism but crave all the same to be part of this ritual, to taste something sacred on my tongue. A young Japanese girl takes the bread placed in her hand and puts it in her pocket. The attendant holding the priest's umbrella nails her with a scathing look until she takes it out and puts it in her mouth.

As the umbrellas retreat eight red robed *tiraboleiros* gather in front of the main altar and, to the majestic chords of the cathedral's organ, the *botafumeiro* is lit. The same nun rises again to the microphone to sing one of David's psalms, 'Receive my prayer as incense,' while the men form a circle. Together they haul down the ropes hanging from a four hundred year old pulley in the dome of the church. Collective 'Oohs,' and 'aahs,' and the frenetic flash of cameras accompanies each swing of the censor north to south. Clouds of frankincense are released, enough to mask the stink of a thousand pilgrims. Up and down the *tiraboleiros* go in a medieval dance, pulling and releasing their ropes until the *botumafeiro* self-propels like a reckless smoking silver bullet that will, at any moment surely crash through the windows and we'll all be showered in translucent shards of stained glass. But no, in a few short minutes its swing slows, until one *tiraboleiro* hurls himself at it, catches a hold and for a second he too has lifted off the floor in a spinning of smoke. The congregation breaks into joyful applause.

The believers and the curious disperse through the cathedral's four doors. I turn to leave and realize I have been standing all this time next to the grand Portico de la Gloria, long associated as the main entrance for pilgrims. Does this then mean I came in through the back door? Have I committed some kind of medieval misdemeanor? But all around me, in flesh and in stone, are radiant faces. The living have been liberated and the dead immortalized by the great sculptor, Maestro Mateo, their expressions as alive and real as ours despite being carved over eight centuries ago. I follow the tide to the *parteluz,* the main column supporting the Portico's central arch. My hand goes where a million hands have gone before, into five holes worn deep and marble-smooth amongst the vines and leaves of Jesse's tree.

St James sits in the branches above watching the multitudes, one by one, take part in this ancient ritual. Were it not for a telling halo of jewels his countenance could be that of a farmer at the end of a pleasing day toiling his fields. And we? Are we the seeds gathered from mountains and *mesetas*; fields of fallen apples and waysides of weeds? His large feet are firmly planted against the tree trunk and in generous sized hands he holds a staff and an unfurled scroll. *Misit me Dominus*, it reads, The Lord sent me. I want to add the last line of Mumon's poem: For he who touches, lo! The dead trees are in full bloom! I imagine Mumon-san, crazy Zen monk, his robe hitched to the knees, weaving his way around the columns in a happy jig. The music of the twenty four Apocalyptic elders crowning the arch above accompanies him – a cacophony of canticle voices, fourteen zithers, four psalteries, two lutes, two harps and one hurdy gurdy.

Words and laughter silently spill from the granite lips of this twelfth century biblical pantheon. To the right and left of Jesse's tree, apostles carry on animated conversation. Beside Isaiah I spy the beguiled face of young Daniel and across from him the beautiful albeit breast-less Queen Esther. There is Adam and Eve and Moses along with Christ and St James who metamorphose again and again among angels, the redeemed and the condemned. A fat man devours an empanada while a ghoulish figure prevents him from swallowing, a drunkard attempts to drink the last drops from his wineskin while hanging upside down and a poor man is being strangled by his octopus dinner. Pure theatre as enthralling and entertaining now in its patina of stone as it must have been for a newly arrived medieval pilgrim. Not knowing how to read she would have wandered these sculpted worlds, made all the more tantalizing by dazzling coats of polychrome, like the pages of a book. Citizens of Santiago sat as models for each of the Portico's figures and, in the inspired hands and eyes of the artist, they themselves became mediums for transformation.

El Romanico – the language of Romanesque stones. I begin to understand. Beside this seventh and last ingredient for a pilgrim, the nuns of Leon had written, *lo limpiamos mucho le quitamos los rezos y las angustias de la gente que ha rezado y que ha llorado entre esas piedras*. If we clean it too much we take from it the prayers and the anguish of all the people who have cried between the stones.

Perhaps that is what I felt when I placed my fingers inside Jesse's tree, an imprint of all the prayers, thanks and resolutions left by a streaming of pilgrims. We too can surrender into this marketplace, of the human and the divine, where there is no boundary between flesh and stone; past, present and future. Letting go of time and space, all that remains is the breath of a God that does not distinguish.

Are my thoughts misguided I wonder, am I a wolf dressed in scallop shells and Christian cape? Two tiny figures deep in conversation carved into the *parteluz* below St James catch my eye. The veiled woman on the right unencumbered by tendrils or vines is Mary. Her words seem whispered in comparison to the joviality of all the men. I move close to her gaze and all thoughts of sacrilege disappear. I have walked more kilometres than my bones care to remember. The weight of questions and procrastinations I carried through church doors has disappeared. In place of what I did not understand there is beauty. And mystery. And if I am to know anything let it be this, this, this and only this present moment.

For the seventh and final dwelling place of the *Interior Castle* St Teresa begins by saying: When a little stream enters the sea; there is no means of separating the two.

Two centuries later Jean Pierre De Caussade, a French Jesuit priest, wrote in *The Sacrament of the Present Moment* that: The will of God is present in each moment, an immense ocean which only the heart fathoms insofar as it overflows with faith, trust and love.

It doesn't matter how God is visualized. What matters is how God is experienced. 'In your kitchen, at your work, wherever you are, you have arrived at your final goal,' my Zen teacher would say. On black cushions facing the wall, every morning after zazen meditation, we chanted the Heart Sutra on long out breaths, each Japanese phrase whole unto itself. From the beginning: Shiki soku ze ku ku soku ze shiki, form is emptiness, emptiness is form, until the end, *Gate gate, paragate, parasamgate, bodhi svaha!* And again we chanted it, and again after that. Three times, until our hearts and minds and the room we shared vibrated with the clear sharp syllables of this ancient alive sutra.

Chants, meditation, prayer, contemplation – these are the many coloured boats moored to our shore, vessels to carry us into and across the deep. All we need do is climb in, haul up the anchor of who we think we are and set sail.

Cathedral of Saint James at Santiago – end of the journey.

Ten more steps and I am hurtled five centuries into a flamboyant baroque world built as a protective façade for the Portico. A few more steps into a blinding sunlight and I am standing in the cathedral's vast Obradoiro Square. I find Alex lying down with his head towards the spires. From this dizzying angle the towers seem to swim in the sky. I stretch out beside him and close my eyes. As dirty and tattered about the edges as I feel, I suspect that here is as close to the end of a rainbow as I will get. At least for today. My body sinks content into the stones and my mind flashes to random moments and pieces of the road I walked to arrive here. I am alone in most of the images, filled with joy. For this I am overwhelmingly grateful.

We peel ourselves off the sunwarmed granite, circle the cathedral then slowly unwind through Santiago's old streets. I find myself looking for familiar faces – Beatrice and the baritone, Stefan, Fiona, Ivano, Carmen, Consuela, Daniel. And then, all the faces for which I have no names. I had no idea when starting out on my lone pilgrimage how many dear friends I would make. In a corner of the Praza de Cervantes a hungry queue waits at the doors of Casa Manolo and I catapult back to that first night in Roncesvalles when I sat beside one brave, weathered *Quexana*.

I take out my notebook just to run my fingers across his exuberant handwriting, and there it is, Casa Manolo, scrawled across the top of the first page. Where is he now? Fast asleep, snoring like a champion under an old oak, his copy of *Don Quixote* opened at Montesino's cave? In his dreams is he also being seduced by a venerable old man in a cloak of purple serge ... a rosary in his hands of beads larger than fair-sized walnuts, every tenth one the size of an ostrich egg. 'It is many centuries, valorous knight, Don Quixote, that we who dwell in these enchanted solitudes have been waiting to see you, so that you may inform the world of what is contained here.'

'*Salud*!' Alex and I raise wine to invisible friends. We made it to Santiago and are therefore entitled to eat our fill from scallop shells. *Coquilles St Jacques* comes on a platter, two to a shell and drenched in a cream sauce. I send praises to my *Quexana* for being there at the beginning and somehow here in spirit at the end. His Casa Manolo has filled to bursting. Bill and Lina swing in through its doors and we begin '*Saluds*' all over again.

Light headed and somewhat disembodied knowing there is nowhere to go tomorrow – no need to fill water pouches, squeeze sleeping bags into stuff packs, smear feet with paw paw ointment or bandage up blisters – arm in arm we make our wobbly way back to the *refugio*. I wanted to walk the Camino alone and I did but I had not anticipated the laughter and the tenderness of friends. Each meeting unexpected, each face an open book giving me the chance to be an open book too. It is as though the quiet solace of the road exists in simpatico with community. If a pilgrimage, that is at heart a personal journey, also offers this then why should I settle for any less at home? Is it so difficult to step out from the safe net of habits and four walls into the full catastrophe of every unpredictable moment?

Each time I re-enter the world after a meditation retreat I feel as if I have shed a skin. Colours are luminous, silence and music both as sweet and the sensuality of skin touching skin akin to a miracle. I am filled with hope – one chasmic step from expectation – and no hurdle in a relationship is too big. In the euphoria of a spring-cleaned mind I forget that for every challenge faced sitting on a meditation cushion and every insight gained, life offers up extra doses of grit. What was different for the Oxherding boy in that tenth picture? He had come full circle; returned to a world where everything and nothing had changed.

As I fold my *credencial* one last time a copy of a prayer from Triacastela falls onto my lap. It had been left behind by a pilgrim on the night we shared first a feast and then our wounds. To believe through love, and not from fear, I read. If you sense love, you will sense all that is around you.

My hand goes to Tara and the silver scallop shell lying against my chest. The answers to all my questions are here in this prayer and in these two symbols that feel as much a part of me as my own fresh showered skin. Tara's left hand held in a *mudra* uniting compassion with wisdom and in her right a white lotus flowering free from the mud of ignorance. And my little shell souvenir bought on that wild cold day in Manjarin, holding within its ribs a pagan and Christian past with meanings as varied as the pilgrims who, with a shell tied to their pack or around their neck, walk all the way to Santiago.

The first time I held a seashell to my ear and listened to the sound of an ocean – did I glean the vastness of it? And what am I left with now as I sit on the edge of my bed, on this last *refugio* night? I look at the women and men around me, awake and asleep, dressed and undressed, old and young, exhausted and exhilarated, drunk with wine or satiated by prayer or both and I think of how the ribs of the shell look like the back of an outstretched hand. A hand held out one to the other.

Love reconciles all contradiction and love knows, even when we forget, no matter how high or rough the waves, we are never separate from the ocean.

Tomorrow, for my last night, I will recline in an enchanted solitude. Maria Jesus had stationed herself outside the doors of Casa Manolo hoping for some pilgrim business. With her mother and grandmother, all born and raised in Santiago, Maria runs a *hospedaje* one street from the cathedral. For a song I will have a room with a balcony, a double bed, linen sheets and a wardrobe with a full length mirror. It was too tempting and would I am sure have lured *Quexana* himself. I wanted to give her a deposit but she shook her head and in a voice sweet as an angel's said, '*Tranquilo, tranquilo.*'

With those words still lilting in my head I lie awake in the shadows of underwear hung bunk to bunk. There's a hint of a snorer opposite and the street light outside is just a blur through windows misted over by the breath of fifty pilgrims. Our final Camino *refugio* is called *Acuario* – the Aquarium. Little fish, I think with a smile, all tucked into bed for one last night before being set loose into the ocean. I call into my dreams the mermaid from Ciraqui still combing her long stone hair.

'Make ready a scalloped shell boat for my journey.'

Credencial del Peregrino

Thank you for walking with me on my pilgrimage.

To read more about Helen's writing life visit her website at: www.authorhelenburns.com

Select Bibliography

Bernard of Clairveaux (1090 – 1153), *Selected Writings*, Emilie Griffin (edit.) Harper Collins 2006

Brother Giles (1190 – 12620), *The Little Flowers of St Francis*, Doubleday 1971

Brother Lawrence (1614 – 1691), *The Practice of the Presence of God*, Martino Fine Books 2016

Cervantes, Miguel (1547 – 1616), Don Quixote, Penguin 2003

Codex Calixtinus: *Pilgrim's Guide to Santiago de Compostela*, Melczer, W. (trans.) Italica Press 2009

De Caussade, Jean Pierre (1675-1751), *The Sacrament of the Present Moment*, Harper One 1989

Huineng (638 – 713), *The Platform Sutra*, Red Pine (trans.), Counterpoint Press 2008

Merton, Thomas (1915 – 1968), *New Seeds of Contemplation*, New Directions 2007

Mumon (1183 – 1260), *The Gateless Gate*, Boomer Books 2008

Nagarjuna (c.150 – c.250), *Precious Garland*, Jeffrey Hopkins (trans) Snow Lion 2013

Saint Anselm, 11th century, *Monologian*, Open Court Publishing 1903

Saint John of the Cross (1542 – 1591), *Dark Night of the Soul*, Tan Books 2010

Salzberg, Sharon, *Lovingkindness: The Revolutionary Art of Happiness*, Shambhala 2018

Shantideva 8th century, *Guide to the Bodhisattva's Way of Life*, Geshe Kelsang Gyatso (trans), Tharpa 2003

Shien, Kakuan 12th century, *Riding the Ox Home*, John Daido Loori (comm.), Shambhala 2002

Teresa of Avila (1515 – 1582), *The Interior Castle*, Tan Books 2011

The Heart Sutra 1st century, Tanahashi, Kazuaki (trans.), *Shambhala 2016*

Yamahata, Hogen, *On the Open Way*, Jiko Oasis Books 1991

About the Author

Helen Burns devoted three years to Asian Studies with a major in Hindi at The Australian National University, until the call to venture deeper overtook the need for a degree. Her first silent meditation retreat was in 1982 under the guidance of S.N. Goenka. She has since practiced in the Satipatthana tradition of Theravada Buddhism with Western teachers as well as the late Sayadaws U Pandita, U Lakhana and U Kundala, in both Myanmar and Australia. Her interest in all facets of Buddhism led her to the teachings of Tibetan Rinpoches and Geshes in Australia and India until the late nineties when she met Zen Master Hogen Yamahata and was his student and assistant for ten years.

After returning from the Camino Helen was awarded a Byron Bay Writers Festival residency for the development of an early draft of *The Way is a River of Stars*. The manuscript was later awarded a LongLines residency at Varuna, Australia's National Writers' House, and then shortlisted for the Varuna Harper Collins award.

To her work, she brings the perspective of a lifelong interest in cultural exchange, the arts and comparative religion. She has since published *Andal's Garland*, a novel exploring the myths, poetry and temple culture of South India. Helen lives with her partner dividing time between Byron Bay, Far North Queensland, and India. She is currently working on a third manuscript.

Lightning Source UK Ltd.
Milton Keynes UK
UKHW021144110722
405683UK00011B/2750